THE INNER MAN

BY FRANK HAMRICK

WITH

SPIRITUAL LEADERSHIP

BY J. OSWALD SANDERS

Positive Action
FOR CHRIST

The Inner Man

First edition published 1980
Second edition published 2002
Second Printing 2003

Printed in the United States of America
ISBN 1-929784-91-0

Edited by Dennis Peterson and Kraig Keck
Layout and Design by Shannon Brown
Artwork by Chris Ellison

Published by

PositiveAction
BIBLE CURRICULUM

Contents

Preface

The purpose of this study, *The Inner Man*, is to develop character and maturity in "the inner man." These lessons are written both to impart knowledge and to challenge you to right action. They are more concerned with what one *is* than with what one *knows* or *does*.

What one knows and what one does are important, of course, but God's greatest concern is what one *is*. As one of our lessons states, "We must *know* in order to *be* in order to *do*." Thus, we seek to teach you necessary biblical facts to change your inner being that your actions might be godly. Too often, Christian leaders emphasize what a student should *know* and what he or she should *do* without mentioning what they should *be*. Consequently, we develop "hollow students." They know and perhaps do right, but they are little more than automatons doing what they are programmed or coerced to do. Instead, we want to let the Lord perform a work in your hearts that you might be "strengthened with might by His spirit in the inner man" (Eph. 3:16) so that your actions are the result of inward purity and strong Christian character rather than mere conformity or outward compulsion.

How To Use This Book

This student textbook includes a number of unique features to help you make the most of your Bible studies this year, including the following.

Introductory Reading Assignments

Every chapter begins with a brief introductory reading assignment that will be a stepping stone into and an overview of the lesson. These readings should prepare you for and be supplemental to the teacher's lecture and the accompanying notes that you should take during that time. Chapters 19–30 include readings from a Christian classic, J. Oswald Sanders' book, *Spiritual Leadership,* the full text of which is included at the end of the textbook.

Student Work

Most of the lessons include work that you should do at home. Normally, you will want to do this work before your teacher begins teaching the lesson. That way you will already have a pretty good understanding of the subject matter, which should make the class time more productive.

Notes From The Teacher's Lesson

Every chapter also includes charts and diagrams that your teacher will use in the class lectures. These charts provide the "tools" that will help you focus on the key points of the lesson. You should fill in the appropriate blanks as your teacher presents the lesson and study them for the quiz that follows the completion of each lesson. (The quizzes include material from both your textbook readings and the teacher's lesson.)

Application Activities

At the end of each chapter is a list of topics, projects, and/or activities under the heading "Stepping Toward Effective Leadership" that will help you make practical applications of the lessons you've learned. These activities are designed to be used at your teacher's discretion to help you develop, think about, learn more about, and apply the principles learned from the introductory reading assignment, the teacher's lecture, and your homework. They might be practical projects, reading assignments, discussion or debate topics, review activities, or writing assignments. Your teacher may use all or only a few of these items as appropriate for your particular class and to fit the time available for your class. Bibliographic information for books included as suggested reading assignments is given in the "Recommended Reading List."

A Word About Quizzes And Tests

Your teacher will evaluate your work using a variety of tools, including chapter quizzes, Scripture memorization, various activities, and/or writing assignments, and possibly major tests covering several chapters or units. The questions for the quizzes cover the material in both the student readings and the teacher's lecture notes. The quizzes are made up of a variety of types of questions, including matching, short answer, true–false, multiple choice, and essays. The unit tests cover from three to nine lessons, with the average number of lessons being about six. The same types of items will be used on the tests as are on the quizzes. The individual classroom teacher will determine various point values and grading scales.

Unit One

The Foundations Of Leadership

1

The Purpose Of Our Christian School

Moses. Julius Caesar. Napoleon Bonaparte. George Washington. Thomas "Stonewall" Jackson. Robert E. Lee. Charles Spurgeon. Dwight L. Moody. Theodore Roosevelt. Winston Churchill. Douglas MacArthur. Ronald Reagan.

What did all of these men have in common? They were all famous and effective leaders. Some of them excelled in warfare. Others were great statesmen. And some of them were effective religious leaders and educators. But they all knew how to lead men, and they had that knowledge because they knew how to lead themselves.

Earl Nightingale, in an article titled "The Most Effective Leaders," wrote, "Every organization, from the smallest to the largest, is a reflection of its leadership."

That fact can have either good or bad results, depending on what kind of leader is in charge. For a negative example, consider Nazi Germany with Adolf Hitler at the helm. He at first seemed to be a very effective leader, accomplishing great feats in rebuilding Germany and raising her from the ruins of World War I and the Great Depression. But he had the wrong philosophy, goals, and methods, and his perverseness was reflected downward through the chain of command to the individual members of the Nazi *Schutzstaffel* (the SS, Hitler's bodyguard, intelligence, central security, and exterminators of "undesirables"), which carried out his desire to liquidate the Jews and anyone who dared oppose his plans for the Third Reich. Hitler and his dream of a master race ended with his suicide in an austere bunker under the bombed–out ruins of Berlin. Few, if anyone, mourned his departure from this life.

On the other hand, consider the positive example of "Stonewall" Jackson. He loved God, refused to dishonor the Lord's Day, demanded great things of both himself and his men, and achieved military objectives that still amaze military strategists around the world today. Any serious student of the War Between the States must stand in awe of the man's military genius and ability to achieve victory in seemingly impossible circumstances and against overwhelming numerical superiority. And although he demanded much from his soldiers, they loved him and mourned deeply his death at the Battle of Chancellorsville. His commander, Robert E. Lee, said upon learning of Jackson's death, "I have lost my right arm."

Not everyone can be a leader in the sense of the men listed at the beginning of this chapter. After all, leaders must have someone to follow them. And it's no disgrace to be a follower. In fact, every effective leader learns first the importance of being a loyal and obedient follower. As Gaines S. Dobbins wrote in *Learning to Lead*, "Effective Christian leadership is consecrated and dedicated discipleship. Before a leader can attract and maintain a following, he must himself have learned how to follow."

However, as Napoleon Hill pointed out, "it is no credit to *remain* a follower." Every follower should aspire to improve himself steadily and regularly, thereby preparing himself to assume, in God's perfect timing, his own leadership role.

As students in a Christian school, you have a great honor and privilege. You have the opportunity to receive an above–average education, a *Christian* education, which should help prepare you for being much more than a mere follower. Evangelist and Bible teacher Oliver B. Greene wrote that "the greater the honor bestowed, the weightier the responsibility." And Christ Himself stated, "Unto whomsoever much is given, of him shall be much required" (Luke 12:48).

To help prepare you for this requirement, our Bible studies this year focus on the principles of godly leadership. You will develop an understanding of the foundations of spiritual leadership in the first unit, of which this chapter is only an introduction. You will also examine the attitudes that must be present in the effective leader. Using J. Oswald Sanders' classic, *Spiritual Leadership*, you will study the standards and qualities of godly leaders and face the realities of the price that one must pay for such leadership. Finally, you will analyze two case studies of effective spiritual leadership: Nehemiah and Joshua.

As you progress through each lesson, you will realize that if you are to be a leader who lifts others out of their sinful conditions, shows them the Savior, and helps them grow in His grace, you must be growing yourself. Ralph Waldo Emerson wrote, "If you would lift me, you must be on higher ground."

The principles of effective *spiritual* leadership are also applicable to other areas of life, including various vocations and careers. And this fact should not be surprising because for the Christian *every* area of life is sacred. For the Christian, there is no division between the sacred and the secular; all ground is holy ground, and every bush is a burning bush.

As you learn about leadership this year, your responsibility is to "do your duty," that is, to obey God's leading and instruction. As Robert E. Lee so often said, "Do your duty in all things. You cannot do more. You should never do less."

Notes From The Teacher's Lesson

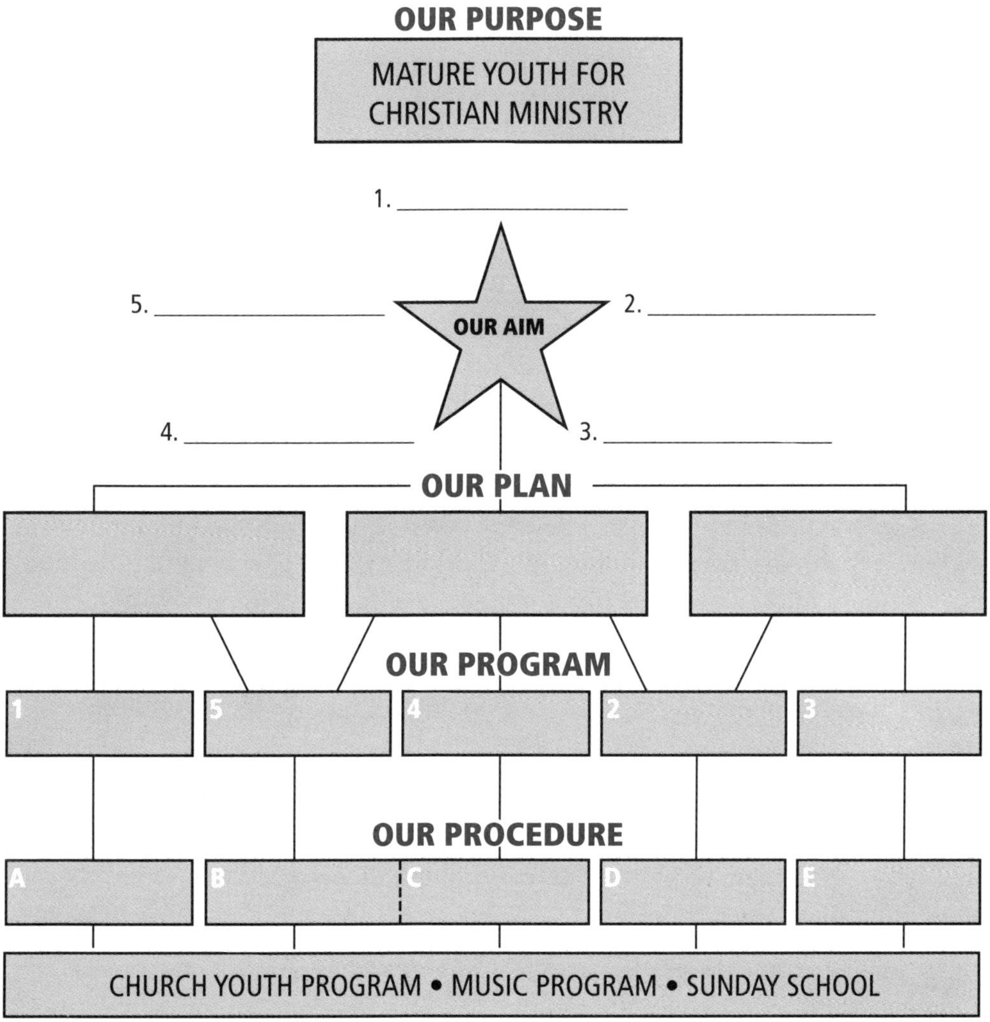

Stepping Toward Effective Leadership

- Read a biography of a great leader from the Recommended Reading List (or any other biography that your teacher approves). As you read, list the qualities of the person that made him or her an effective leader.

- Explain the following statement as it relates to Christian leadership: "Only those who live under authority are fit to wield authority" (Larry Christenson, *The Christian Family*). How does this statement relate to the family? The Christian school? The church? One's ministry? One's vocation (occupation)?

- In light of the teacher's lesson for this chapter, what steps do you need to take to ensure that you are helping your school achieve its goal of preparing spiritually mature young people for Christian service?

- Using the ideals presented in the teacher's lesson, assess your schools' effectiveness in achieving the goal of preparing spiritually mature Christian servants in each of the following areas: chapel, Bible classes, Scripture memory requirements, sports/extracurricular activities, and academic demands and expectations. Specifically, identify any weaknesses, but for every weakness you identify list steps that can be taken for improvement. Be prepared to defend both every aspect of your assessment and your suggestions for improvement!

2

God's Plan For My Life

What is God's plan for your life?

"For *my* life?" you ask. "Well, I guess I'll go to college after I finish high school. Then, when I finish college—if I don't sign a professional basketball contract—I'll probably get a high–paying executive position with some Fortune 500 company and make a lot of money. I'll buy a big house and a Porsche—or maybe I'll get a Lamborghini! When I can afford it, I might even marry some beautiful thing and have a couple of kids. I'll retire when I'm fifty and just sort of enjoy myself the rest of my life. I plan to live the good life!"

Oh, you will, will you? but this sounds more like *your* plan than *God's* plan. Where does God fit into that plan of yours?

"God? Oh, well…I'll go to church most of the time. And I'll read my Bible, and…."

Does this sound like you? Most people have little, if any, room for God in their plans; He's crowded out by their concerns about material wealth, professional advancement, and other selfish interests. God does sometimes enable some Christians to obtain fabulous wealth, but more often He calls His people to lives of sacrifice. God sometimes allows some Christians to attain high levels of professional success and renown, but He calls more of them to lives of relative obscurity and less–than–opulent circumstances. Sometimes He gives some Christians wealth and success only to take it from them, much as Job lost everything he had.

When things don't turn out the way we planned, when we lose a lot of what we've obtained, or when things "go against us," we're tempted to grumble and complain. Instead, we should have the attitude of Job and Paul. We should be more concerned about God's plan for our lives than with our own plans for ourselves.

During the early days of the War Between the States, especially after Thomas J. Jackson earned the nickname "Stonewall" at the First Battle of Manassas, his wife, Anna, was impatient for her husband to be promoted and publicly recognized for his critical contribution to that Southern victory. Sensing her impatience, Jackson wrote to her from his encampment, "…I am thankful to an ever kind Heavenly Father that He makes me content to await His own good time & pleasure for commendation, knowing that 'all things work together for good.' Never distrust our God, who doeth all things well. In due time, He will make manifest all His pleasure, which is all His people should ever desire."

Jackson's advice to his wife is still good advice for each of us today! With it in mind, let's consider God's plan for our lives.

Student Work

Let's focus on God's plan for the individual. Notice that our purpose as a school is to produce mature Christian youth. Our study this year emphasizes the following two major themes:

1. spiritual maturity and
2. leadership qualities.

This lesson begins our studying of the first of these two topics, spiritual maturity. Included in our plan and purpose for this study is an ennobling view of

- God,
- Jesus Christ, and
- the Holy Spirit.

Various lessons, beginning with this one, focus on each of these Persons of the Trinity. Our prayer is that by studying these lessons you will have a fresh appreciation of what God can and will do with your life.

To bridge the gap between the previous lesson and this lesson, state what Ephesians 4:12 says Christians are to be:

"perfect," or ______________________________ to be able to do the ______________________________

Thus, God's plan for you includes making you mature, complete, and qualified to serve Him.

The Plan

According to Romans 8:28, what is God's plan for every Christian? ____
____
____

According to this verse, what two things must be true before all things can work together for our good?

1. ______________________________
2. ______________________________
____

Thus, Paul qualifies his statement so that it is equally true that things do *not* work together for *anybody* or *everybody* but only for those who meet these two qualifications.

According to this verse, can tragedy be good? ______________
Illness? ______________ Financial loss? ______________
Losing a ball game? ______________.

So *everything* that happens in the life of one who loves God and who is in His will is for his "perfecting," that is, it serves to make him what God wants him to be.

The Analysis

An examination of this verse shows us the following four things about God's plan for man.

God's Plan Is Beneficent (Kind And Good)

All things work together *for good.* What does that mean—money, popularity, and success or spiritual good? ______________________

Job teaches us the proper meaning of this phrase. God allowed Satan to take all of Job's physical comforts. What was Job's response to this loss in Job 1:21? ______________________

____

Paul explains in Romans 8:29 what he means by *good.* What is it? _____

____

So anything that makes us more like Christ is good, regardless of its effect on our comfort, health, wealth, or fame. Thus, a broken leg can be for our good. A disappointing loss in sports might be God's power seeking to mature us.

God's Plan Is Active

All things *work.*

God is always busy. Just because we don't see great things happening, we shouldn't suppose that God is asleep. The daily happenings of our schoolwork, conflicts, unjust criticism, ridicule, praise, tests, sickness, and deadlines are the threads with which God weaves our maturity.

Read 2 Corinthians 5:17. The words *passed away* and *become new* in this verse indicate continuous action. They are more literally translated "are passing" and "are becoming new." So, what is God doing every day in your life if you meet the two qualifications of Romans 8:28? ______________________

____

____

____

____

Because God is working through all of our circumstances, *complaining* is unthinkable! Griping is evidence of *immaturity* and the *inability to comprehend the good hand of God in everything.* It is *sin!*

In the apostle Paul's day, people reacted to adverse circumstances according to one of the following four philosophies, and we see many of the same reactions today:

- Epicureans—"Let us eat, drink, and be merry, for tomorrow we die." This is the attitude of *indifference.*
- Cynics—"I dare you to hurt me, Fate. Nobody can beat me; no circumstance will cause me to curse you or bow my head in defeat." This is the attitude of *defiance.*
- Stoics—"I can't avoid it, so why fight it? I'll just grit my teeth and force myself to accept it." This is the attitude of *resigned acceptance.*
- Christians—"I will rejoice and happily embrace bad circumstances or sorrow because God is using it to work out my good and His glory." This is the attitude of *joy in all things.*

Which attitude do *you* have?

God's Plan Is Inclusive

All things work together.

According to this verse, is there such a thing as chance or luck? _______
Why? ____

____

Read the story of Shadrach, Meshach, and Abednego in Daniel 1:3–21; 3:1–30. How did their ordeal in the fiery furnace work for God's glory?

____

____

____

____

How did it work for their good? ______________________________

____

____

God's Plan Is Harmonious

All things work *together* for good.

All of the events of life are interrelated. Like a formula, they combine and intermingle for our good. Taken separately, the individual experiences of life might seem anything but good, but, blended together, the result is always good.

Joseph is a good example of how numerous tragedies work together for good. Note the tragedies in each of the following passages:

Genesis 37:4— ______________________________

____

Genesis 37:18–28— ______________________________

____

Genesis 39:1— ______________________________

____

Genesis 39:7–15— ______________________________

____

Genesis 39:20— ______________________________

____

It must have been hard for Joseph to see how all of these experiences could be for his good. Yet, years later, Joseph faced his brothers and maturely summarized all of the events.

Read Genesis 50:20. What had his brothers meant to accomplish? _____

____

____

Instead, what had God worked through all of their evil? ______________

According to Genesis 50:20, what good came from all of these circumstances? ____

____

Who were these "many souls?" ______________________________

From what had they all been saved? __________________________

The Conclusion

What is the mature reaction to brothers or sisters who seek to torment you? ____

____

Why should you not gripe when a teacher gives you a heavy homework assignment? ____

____

What is wrong with fussing and fretting and griping about school rules?

____

____

____

____

How does 1 Thessalonians 5:18 apply to us in this regard? ____________

____

____

Thus, everything is working according to God's __________________ in Christ Jesus (1 Thess. 5:18).

Notes From The Teacher's Lesson

God's Plan For My Life

God Brings ______________ From Every Circumstance

Examples:

- William Carey
- Joseph
  - His Brothers ______________________________ Him.
  - They Sold Him To The ______________________________
  - They Sold Him As A ______________________________.
  - Potiphar's Wife ______________________________ Him.
  - He Was Cast Into ______________________________.
- The Israelites
- David

Complaining And ____________ Are Not Christian ______________

Stepping Toward Effective Leadership

- Write a two–page paper describing a first–hand experience that at first seemed tragic but that later proved that God was working even that incident together for good in your own or your family's life.
- Explain how Paul's own life experiences demonstrated the truth of his statement that "all things work together for good."
- Explain the role that the character trait of patience plays in our practical realization that "all things work together for good."

- If you're a football fan, read Dennis Byrd's book *Rise & Walk.* Explain briefly what happened to him and how his experience illustrates the truth of the lesson in this chapter.
- If you're a baseball fan, read Dave Dravecky's books *Comeback* and *When You Can't Come Back.* Explain briefly what happened to him and how his experience illustrates the truth of the lesson in this chapter.

3

The God I Serve

Unbelievers and shallow Christians have a distorted, perverted idea of who God is. Common "popular" references to God as "the Big Guy," "the Man upstairs," and "my Heavenly Buddy" certainly are not derived from Scripture. A study of every Bible character who saw God gives a much different impression.

The ancient Jews had such a reverential awe of God and His Word that after they wrote His name as they copied the Scriptures they were not allowed to continue using that quill; they had to get a new quill. (Imagine their writing verses that contained multiple uses of God's name; they kept quill manufacturers busy supplying writing utensils!)

For God to use a man or a woman, especially in a leadership role, He first causes that person to see Him for who—and what—He really is. And this revelation revolutionizes the person's service. An effective Christian leader who experiences such a revelation of God will not be proud or self–seeking; he will seek only to please God. He will be less likely to fall into sin because he knows and recognizes the holiness of God and his personal responsibility to Him.

Yet, neither will he be helpless and inactive. Rather, he will serve the Lord with power, enthusiasm, animation, and confidence regardless of what obstacles or problems might come his way—because he knows that he serves the Almighty God. He knows that he is on the winning side!

As we continue our study of the foundational principles of spiritual leadership, let's look at the God whom we serve, see how some major Bible characters reacted to God's revelation of Himself, and glean from their experiences lessons that will help us become effective leaders for Christ.

Student Work

The great leaders of the Bible had one thing in common—they had experienced a soul–stirring vision of an infinite, awesome God. And they were never the same again.

The purpose of this lesson and the following four lessons is to give you just such a vision of God. Nothing is so important to one's attitude and service as his or her view of God.

But beware! Instead of an exalting, exhilarating, ecstatic experience, such a view of God might thrust your face and soul to the ground with feelings of insignificance and unworthiness!

According to Zechariah 3:3, how did the clothes of Joshua (not Joshua the General but Joshua the High Priest) appear when he stood before a holy God? ____________________

The dazzling white of God's holiness made everything else appear faded and yellow. Joshua, dressed in this fashion, would be totally unworthy to serve as the high priest. Therefore, a view of God might cause one to see how sinful and unworthy he or she really is before the holy God.

Job

How did Job see himself before he saw God (see Job 33:9)? ____________________

____

____

According to Job 1:8, how did God see Job? ____________________

____

____

Few men have ever been so highly praised by God. Yet, when he got a correct view of God, what was Job's reaction (see Job 42:5–6)? ___________

____

____

Jacob

Jacob saw God at Peniel. According to Genesis 32:24, 30, of what was he surprised? ___________

____

Jacob's view of God forced him to face his own character and admit what he wanted to hide—that he was a deceiver (as the meaning of his name indicates). What did the Lord ask him in Genesis 32:27? ___________

____

____

The name *Jacob* means "deceiver, supplanter, cheat, or swindler." According to Genesis 27:1–12, how had Jacob cheated and swindled his brother Esau? ___________

____

____

Jacob did not want to admit that he was what his name said he was. But God would not use him or bless him until he faced his true character and admitted his secret sin. (Note that after Jacob wrestled with God, God *changed* his name from Jacob to *Israel!*)

Moses

Moses grew up in the Egyptian palace and faced kings and queens regularly as the virtual son of pharaoh's daughter. They apparently did not scare him! But in Exodus 3:2, 6, he faced God. What was his reaction?

____

____

Elijah

Elijah was undoubtedly one of the greatest and most unusual characters in history. He had such power that he could stop the rain, kill thousands of prophets of Baal, call down fire from heaven, defy a wicked king time after time, and go up to meet God in a chariot of fire. But how did God appear to him in 1 Kings 19:11–13? ______________________________

____

What was brave Elijah's reaction? ______________________________

____

____

This fiery man was subdued by a tiny voice.

Isaiah

Isaiah was not afraid to thunder forth God's warnings, woes, and judgments on king and people alike. What word did he use repeatedly as he warned the nation of Israel (see Isaiah 3:9, 11; 5:8, 11, 20)? __________

But when he was face to face with God in Isaiah 6:1–8, on whom did he pronounce woe? ______________________________

How did his lips seem to him when he was in the presence of a holy God?

____

What was he immediately ready to do? ______________________________

____

____

Ezekiel

According to Ezekiel 1:1, what did Ezekiel see? ______________________________

____

Describe the scene as Ezekiel tells us that he saw it in Ezekiel 1:26–28:

- Above the firmament— ____
  ____
- The throne itself— ____
  ____
- The color surrounding the throne— ______________________________
- The glory of the Lord as it appeared in v. 28— ______________________
  ____
- How Ezekiel reacted to all this— ______________________________
  ____

Daniel

- Daniel seemed to be a faultless man. Even his enemies could find no wrong in him (except perhaps that he prayed too much!). An angel was sent to tell him how much God loved him. But what happened to Daniel when he caught a glimpse of God in Daniel 10:7–9? ______________
  ____
  ____
  ____

Paul

- According to Acts 9:3–8, what did Paul (called Saul at the time) do when he heard God and saw His glory? ______________________________
  ____
  ____

John

No one seemed as close to Jesus as John the Apostle. He leaned on His breast at supper and followed Him every day of His ministry. And of all the disciples, only he followed Him to the Cross. Years later, as an old man in exile on the Isle of Patmos, John received a supreme view of Christ in all of His glory.

Read Revelation 1:13–17 and describe John's vision.

- His head— ______________________________
- His eyes— ______________________________
- His voice— ______________________________
- His face— ______________________________
- His feet— ______________________________
- John's reaction to seeing his Lord in His glorified state— __________
____

The Purpose Of The Vision

God's purpose in revealing Himself to these men was not to humiliate them but to prepare them for greater usefulness. Humiliation merely prepared the way for blessing and service. For example,

- Job received double what he had lost;
- Jacob's character was changed;
- Moses lost his *self*–confidence but gained *God*–confidence;
- Elijah was reminded of the source of his real power;
- Isaiah's lips were prepared for prophesying for God, and he remained humble;
- Daniel was prepared to receive a great prophecy;
- Paul was chosen and called to preach the gospel to the Mediterranean world, and that gospel spread eventually to the Western world, of which we are a part; and
- John was prepared to write the book of Revelation.

Conclusion

God has a job for *you!* But before you can begin to perform that job, you must have a vision of God through the Word of God. (He's not going to reveal Himself to you through a dream or miraculous appearance!) Do you *want* to see Him? Are you prepared for the consequences? When God grants such a view of Himself, it will shake your soul and sober your mind. You will never be the same again. The pattern in these visions of God was always the same:

- the vision,
- self–abhorrence (a hatred or despising of oneself),
- self–abasement (casting yourself down and humbling yourself),
- worship (deep, soul–stirring worship),
- surrender (a deep sense of obligation and a willingness to serve the mighty God),
- service (with no regard for one's own welfare but only that you might please God), and
- a changed life.

Are you ready for such a vision of God?

Notes From The Teacher's Lesson

The God I Serve

The __________________ For A Vision Of God

- We Must Know God's ____________________________________
- We Must Know God's ____________________________________
- We Must Know God's ____________________________________

The ________________ Of The Vision

In The Old Testament (Heb. 1:1)

- ____
- ____
- ____
- ____
- ____
- ____
- ____

In The New Testament Through ______________________________

In The Church Age Through His ______________________________

The ________________ Of The Vision

- Moses ____
- Isaiah Cried ____
- Joshua ____

The pattern was the same: vision, self–abhorrence self–abasement, worship, surrender, service, and a changed life.

The ____________________ Of The Vision

- Goodness And ________________ Of God
- ________________ Of God
- Authority And ________________ Of God

Stepping Toward Effective Leadership

- Why is humility before God so important in the life of a Christian leader? How does a clear picture of who God is contribute to a humble spirit and attitude?

- Explain the differences between true godly humility and the extremes of either lack of self–confidence (poor self–image) and proud egotism.

- Define a proper Christian self–image. Use Scripture proofs for your definition and the book, *The Biblical View Of Self–Esteem, Self–Love, & Self–Image.* (Check the Recommended Reading List for bibliographic details.)

- Explain how an accurate understanding of who God is can keep a Christian leader from sin and help him continue serving with the proper motives.

- Read "Knowing God," chapter 1 in *Spiritual Intimacy* by Richard Mayhue. As you read, list principles that help you develop the proper Christian view of both God and yourself.

Unit 2

The God Of Leadership

4

The Perseverance Of God

Radio personality Paul Harvey told the story of a man who seemed to fail at everything he attempted. He had always been impatient, expecting immediate results and often quitting when they did not come about.

When this man was only five, his father had died. When he was fourteen, he made the mistake of dropping out of school to get a job. He bounced from one odd job to another—from farming to operating a street car to serving in the Army—but he either didn't like any of the jobs he got or he ended up getting fired.

Finally, he became a fireman on a steam locomotive for the Southern Railway, and he actually liked that job. But then, shortly after he married, he was fired—on the same day that his wife told him they were expecting their first child.

His wife left him. The Great Depression hit, and he had an even harder time finding a job. He tried to study law by correspondence, but he soon dropped it. He tried one petty job after another—whatever he could find—but he lost each of them. He finally concluded that he was just a born loser.

Then he decided that he would kidnap his own daughter and hold her for ransom. But he failed at that, too. Later, he tried to run a little café, and it seemed to be working—until a new highway was built and traffic stopped coming past his café.

Before he knew it, he was an old man and got his first Social Security check—for a measly $105. He couldn't live on that. The realization of his age and his dire financial situation jolted him, and he decided to fight back with a vengeance. He refused to admit defeat and live the rest of his life off a paltry government check.

He took that first little check and started a new business venture. It became what you know today as KFC—Kentucky Fried Chicken. Colonel Harlan Sanders was the man who refused to accept failure as final.

Your attitude toward failure often determines the degree of your spiritual leadership. In the lesson that you're about to study, you will learn that no failure or setback needs to be final or permanent. By God's grace, you *can* overcome discouragement and temporary setbacks and be the leader God wants you to be.

Student Work

What does the word *persevere* mean according to the dictionary? ______

____

____

What does Philippians 1:6 say that demonstrates the perseverance of God?

____

____

____

So perseverance is a quality that doesn't allow a person

- to quit or
- to be discouraged—disappointed maybe, but never discouraged.

Stated negatively, a person who does *not* possess perseverance is *easily* discouraged and, therefore, seldom finishes what he begins.

To what degree do you possess perseverance? Let's study this quality of the effective spiritual leader and see how you can make it an integral part of your life.

What If God Were Not Persevering?

Israel

Because God was determined to mold His people into the nation He wanted them to be, He used many tools—both blessings and punishments—on them. Read Psalm 78 in its entirety. On a separate piece of paper, record briefly all of the things that God did for Israel in His determination to make of them a great nation that had character. List the blessings and the punishments separately (perhaps in two separate and appropriately headed columns).

Then record on a second sheet of paper the *six* different ways that Israel sinned during the same forty–year period, as though they were determined not to learn from God's training program. (Refer to verses 9–11; 17–19; 32; 36–37; 40–42; 56–58.) What if God had not persevered? What probably would have happened to Israel? ______________________

____

____

____

Jonah

Read Jonah 1–4. Then state how you see God's perseverance demonstrated in Jonah's life. ______________________

____

____

What would have happened if God had given up on Jonah? __________

____

____

How was Jonah's experience in a fish's belly for his own good? ________

____

____

Christ

What did Christ cry in John 19:30 that shows the perseverance of God the Father in relation to His Son? ________________________________

How does this show God's perseverance? ______________________________

____

What would have happened if God had become discouraged when the people rejected Christ's message of salvation? ______________________

____

____

Thank God that He is merciful and longsuffering and doesn't let man's failures discourage Him! His perseverance with us should make us persevering in His service.

But Because God Is Persevering…

His Plans Will Ultimately Be Accomplished

Read each of the following passages. State the plans that God will accomplish because He is persevering.

Philippians 1:6 —____

____

Romans 11:26–27 —Eventually, ______________________________ will turn back to God and be ____________________________________.

____________________ shall turn away from *ungodliness* ______________, and God will take away their __________________________________.

Matthew 16:18— The _________________________________ can never be defeated by the ____________________________________ The church will conquer and win.

Luke 1:31–33— ____

____

____

1 Corinthians 15:23–28— Christ will destroy ______________
He will conquer and subdue ______________ things. Then, Christ will turn everything over to ______________________
who will reign for ever and ever.

He Ultimately Subdues All He Pursues

In Genesis 28–35, whom did God pursue until He totally conquered him?

____

In Exodus 1–4, whom did God chase from a palace, across a desert, and into a rugged mountain before subduing him? ______________

What prophet did God chase into the sea? ______________

If God wants you, it is foolish for you to run from Him! You only delay the inevitable and bring many sorrows and problems upon yourself.

No Failure In Your Life Need Be Final

Failures are only temporary delays in God's plan for your life. God refuses to accept your failures as an excuse to quit working through you. Someone has said, "No past defeat put future victory out of reach."

Some men's greatest victories closely followed their greatest defeats. For example, Joshua was badly defeated at Ai, but he ultimately came back to smash Ai in his second attack and conquered all of Palestine. And Elijah, totally discouraged by a threat from Jezebel and hiding in a cave in fear of his life, soon led Israel to victory over Syria.

Notes From The Teacher's Lesson

God's Choice Versus Man's Choice

Man Looks At

- Outward ________________ (1 Sam. 16:6–7)
- ________________ (Prov. 31:30)
- ________________ (1 Peter 3:3–5)
- Academic ________________ (Jer. 9:23–24)
- Material ________________ (Matt. 6:19–21)

But God Looks At

- Inward ________________ (________________ , 1 Sam 16:6–7)

Jacob

God's ________________ With Jacob

- At ________________ (Gen. 28:10–22)
- At ________________ (Gen. 32:1–30)
- At ________________ (Gen. 33:17–34:31)
- At ________________ (Gen. 35:1–15)

Lessons From Jacob's Life

- God Hasn't ________________ On You
- No Failure Need Be ________________

Stepping Toward Effective Leadership

- Study the life of Peter. Using his triple denial of Christ (and his other related weaknesses) as an example of personal failure, show how his life demonstrates that no failure need be final. What did he later accomplish for the Lord that demonstrates this truth?

- Using examples from the lives of great men (e.g., Thomas Edison's numerous failed experiments), show how failures can be turned to success and how one's attitude toward failure often determines what his life becomes.

- Study the Israelites' wanderings in the wilderness, briefly summarizing the instances in which God demonstrated His perseverance toward them.

- Contrast the world's emphasis on physical beauty as a key component of success with the truth of the importance of *inner* beauty as discussed in your teacher's notes. What constitutes "inner beauty"?

- Persevering is hard. Read and summarize what Knute Larson says about it in his book *Run Steady, Run Straight.*

- Read and summarize chapter eleven, "Difficulties Concerning Failures" of Hannah Whitall Smith's classic work *The Christian's Secret of a Happy Life.*

5

How And Why God Disciplines

Perhaps you've heard the saying "No pain, no gain."

Athletes in all sports and at all levels of play undergo strenuous training, exercise, and practice to ensure that they perform at their best in competition. Members of sports teams practice day after day, often in extreme heat or cold and even to the point of near exhaustion. They give up certain types of foods and eat other prescribed foods to ensure that their bodies are physically fit and well nourished. They place themselves under strict curfews to ensure that their bodies get the proper rest. And if they violate those rules, their trainers, managers, or team owners impose disciplinary measures, including benching or fines, to communicate that they mean business!

In short, athletes deny themselves some things, demand of themselves other things—including a degree of physical pain—and put themselves under possible punishments to ensure that they are in optimum shape and ready for their contests.

Christianity also insists on certain forms of discipline. In dealing with His children, God demands certain things of them, restricts them from other things, and, when necessary, even imposes sometimes painful forms of discipline—all to teach them what is right and to ensure that they grow and develop properly into the men and women He wants them to be.

Sometimes athletes' coaches, managers, or owners discipline members of their teams in anger or frustration or perhaps because of extreme public pressure. But God's discipline of His children is always imposed in love. It is not always pleasant, but we know that it is always for our ultimate good and His glory.

In this lesson, we examine God's discipline and how He designs it to make us better and more effective spiritual leaders.

Student Work

Review

Thus far in our study, we have seen how our Christian school is designed to produce mature youth (Lesson 1) and how God is working through events and circumstances to produce mature Christian youth (Lessons 2 through 4).

- According to Lesson 1, what three areas does our program emphasize to make youth mature?
  - ______________________________
  - ______________________________
  - ______________________________
- According to Lesson 2, what is God doing to make us mature? ________ ______________________________
- According to Lesson 3, what do we need to help mature us and increase our faith and reliance upon God? ______________________________ ______________________________
- According to Lesson 4, what do we learn about God that affects our spiritual maturity? ______________________________ ______________________________ ______________________________

Now in the current lesson we will consider God's most effective tool in maturing us—discipline!

Definition Of Discipline

A dictionary definition of *discipline* is "training that develops self–control, character, or efficiency." The word *discipline* is a derivative of *disciple* and thus includes the idea of being toughened to follow a leader through both good times and bad, through both persecution and blessing.

Discipline is—

- any rule or regulation that is designed to strengthen your character, will, emotions, or body;
- any circumstance that is designed to toughen your character or increase your self–control;
- any program that exercises your mind and places demands on your will power and determination; and
- any job that demands sacrifice and sweat.

Examples Of Types Of Discipline

Rules And Regulations

God gave more than six hundred rules and regulations for Israel to follow. In Exodus 19:5–6, God told Moses one of the reasons He gave these rules: keeping these laws would make Israel a peculiar ____________________, a kingdom of ____, and a ______________________________________ nation. Besides creating order and aiding their health, these rules were designed to produce character (holiness) in the Israelites.

School rules, church standards, and your parents' rules at home are all forms of discipline designed by God and deliberately placed upon you by an all–wise God who is making you into the person He wants you to be.

Circumstances

Job was placed in horrible circumstances. With what result? A flaw in Job's character was corrected!

Although Job was an outstanding man of character and godliness even before his testing, he had one glaring weakness that was magnified even more under the pressure of his troubles. Read Job 31. In that chapter, Job is justifying himself before his three friends, telling them how perfect he is.

List at least ten things of which Job boasts in this passage.

1. ______________________________
2. ______________________________
3. ______________________________
4. ______________________________
5. ______________________________
6. ______________________________
7. ______________________________
8. ______________________________
9. ______________________________
10. ______________________________

Job's one glaring weakness was *self–righteousness.* God took all of that away from him through his horrible trials. Note Job's final reaction in Job 42:6:

____

____

Thus, God places us in all sorts of circumstances and hard times for the purpose of molding our character and perfecting us to do the work that He has planned for us.

Programs

Your Sunday school and Christian school programs are two examples of programs that are designed to develop your character. We have already seen how the various disciplines of the programs will strengthen your character and self–control.

Jobs

What kind of labor and toil did God place upon both the Israelites and David to harden and solidify their character?

- Israel (Exod. 1)—430 years ______________________________

  ____

- David (Ps. 78:70–71)— ______________________________

  ____

  ____

If we are to be Christ's disciples, God must toughen us for the rigors of following Him. This toughening process is His discipline.

How God Disciplines

Read Isaiah 28:23–29. In these verses, Isaiah teaches Israel how the farmer gets a fruitful harvest—by plowing, planting, and threshing.

Plowing

- What do we learn about the plowing in verse 24? ____________

- Does the farmer treat all soil alike? ________ Why? ________

- How does this illustration apply to the way parents discipline their different children? ____________

Planting

- How does God plant the relish (i.e., dill or fitches and cummin)? ____________

- Why? ____________

- How does God plant the wheat, barley, and rye (spelt)? ____________

- What does that fact teach us about what we allow to be planted in our minds? ____________

- How does 2 Corinthians 10:4–5 also apply to this point? ____________

Threshing

Why is the dill harvested with a rod or staff and not with a threshing instrument (tribulum or drag)? ______________________________

____

____

Yet, the wheat is bruised, or ground. This illustration teaches us that the severity of God's discipline in our lives depends on what God plans to do with us. God must discipline some of us more than He does others because He has a different work for each of us to perform in life.

Therefore, we must always thank God for His plowing and threshing because they are designed by a God who is, according to Isaiah 28:29,

____

____

What Doesn't Develop Character

We tend to praise the Lord for the material and physical blessings He sends our way, thinking that those things are the only ways He blesses His people. We think that a new car, new clothes, a job promotion or raise in salary, or a miraculous recovery from a major illness are ways God blesses us. Although God may very well bless us in these ways, His greatest blessings often come in reverse! That is, material blessings often lead us *away* from God whereas hardships and deep plowing and severe threshing often lead us *closer* to Him.

Let's look at some examples of this truth.

Jeshurun

Read Deuteronomy 32:13–15. How was God kind to Jeshurun (the code name for Israel)? ______________________________

____

____

____

What did that kindness of God do to Jeshurun? ____________________

____

____

The King Of Tyre

According to Ezekiel 28:12–15, how did God bless the king of Tyre (actually a reference to Satan, the real king of Tyre!) in the following categories?

Intelligence ____

Looks ____

Clothing ____

____

____

Talents (tabrets and pipes refer to musical instruments, that is timbrels and flutes) ____

____

Position ____

Privileges ____

____

Yet, what did all of these blessings do to him (Ezek. 28:17)? __________

____

____

Two Fathers

At least two fathers in the Bible are accused of not disciplining their sons when they knew that those sons were doing wrong. Read the following passages and state the sin of each father and the results.

David (1 Kings 1:5–9)—_______________________________________

____

____

Eli (1 Sam. 2:12–17, 22, 27–29, 33; 3:17–18)—________________

____

____

____

____

So you should thank God for parents who discipline and restrain you. They do so for your own good. They are God's instruments to mold your character and increase our usefulness for Him. From the preceding examples, we learn that softness and lack of rules and chores are not really blessings; they might well be curses!

The Harvest

When God plows, He has the harvest in mind. According to the following Scripture passages, what fruit does He plan to produce by His plowing?

Hebrews 12:11—________________________________

Romans 8:28–29— ______________________________

Do you welcome discipline, hard work, and stringent rules, or do you gripe and complain about them? Remember, it isn't the teachers or your parents who are doing the plowing in your life—it's God!

Notes From The Teacher's Lesson

Why Does God Plow?

God's ______________________ (Isa. 28:23–29)

His Plowing Is Never Any Longer Than ______________________

Our ______________________ To His Plowing Is Important

Different Soils Must Receive ______________________

God's ____________________

- He ______________ Important Seeds
  - Spiritual
  - Mental
  - Physical
  - Social

God's ____________________

- To Be ____________________ To His Image (Rom. 8:2)
- To Possess Balanced ____________________
- To Produce The ____________________ (Heb. 12:11)
- To Be Prepared For ____________________

Stepping Toward Effective Leadership

- Give at least one example from your own life that demonstrates that God's discipline was good for you. What specific evidence do you have of this truth?
- Explain the difference between mere punishment and godly discipline. Give examples of each. What are the results of each? Which produces the greatest long–term benefits? Why?
- Conduct a study of the life of Job. What does his life teach about God's discipline? Do you see yourself in Job's experiences? If so, how?
- If someone is doing wrong and seems to get away with it, what conclusions might Christians make? Use Scripture to support your conclusions.
- Explain the following statement in relation to believers in the context of this lesson: "Where there's sin, there's judgment."

- Explain what it means "to be conformed to the image" of Christ. Give examples to illustrate and support your answer.
- Read and summarize Mark R. Littleton's book *Delighted by Discipline.*

6

The Man God Uses

The story is told of a reputed atheist who repeatedly resisted attempts of local Christians to witness to him. He angrily ranted at them until people were afraid to approach him any more.

One morning, a local resident bucked up his courage and tried again to talk to the atheist about his spiritual need as the elderly gentleman chopped wood outside his home. But the man again flew into a raging tirade against Christianity. He shook his fist in the face of the man who had tried to witness to him and then turned both his fist and his face toward the heavens.

"If there really is a God, as you say," he screamed, "then why doesn't He prove it by striking this old atheist with a bolt of lightning?!" He shook his fist toward the sky for emphasis. "Go ahead, God! Strike me with a bolt of lightning! You do that and *then* I'll believe in you!"

The sad witness turned to leave (probably for fear that God *would* send a lightning bolt to strike the defiant man!). As he retreated, he heard the atheist laugh.

"I knew He wouldn't do it! There *is* no God!"

The atheist then resumed chopping his wood. Later that afternoon, he was stacking the wood that he had split earlier that morning. He reached down to pick up a length of wood, and a black widow spider that was hiding under it bit him. The wound got infected, and the man died a few days later.

God didn't need to waste a thirty million–volt lightning bolt on this defiant rebel; He used a tiny arachnid to do the job instead!

We serve a great God who does great and marvelous things. But He often uses small, unlikely, and seemingly insignificant things—or people—to accomplish His eternal purposes. No one can be too small for God to use. One can, however, sometimes be too big for God to use.

Often, we are surprised by who or what God uses. As we will see in this lesson, God often uses the *least* likely (to us) people to do His will. Let's examine closely, then, the man God uses.

Student Work

The story of Jacob and Esau is a perfect example of the particular lesson that we now consider: God's ways are not man's ways. Had *we* made the choice, we would have chosen Esau over Jacob.

Yet, God chose Jacob over Esau! We saw one reason for His choice in Lesson 4. Why, according to that lesson, did God choose Jacob? ______

______

______

Let's examine the heart and mind of God to understand better what He looks for in a leader.

What God Uses In Men

First Corinthians 1:25–2:5; 2 Corinthians 12:7–10; and Hebrews 11:25 outline *nine* lessons that define the qualities that God uses in men. Read those passages and record below the lessons they teach.

1. 1 Cor. 1:25—God's ways are not ______

   ______

   ______

2. 1 Cor. 1:26—God uses few ______________________________
____

3. 1 Cor. 1:17–28—God chooses ____________________things, ____________________things, ____________________things, things that are ______________________________, and things that are ______________________________

4. 1 Cor. 1:29—The reason God does this is ____________________
____

5. 1 Cor. 2:4—God's power does not rest in ____________________
____
____

6. 2 Cor. 12:7–9—If God uses a mighty man, He will first __________
____
____

7. 2 Cor. 12:10—A man is strongest when ____________________

8. 2 Cor. 12:9—God's ____________________ is made perfect (i.e., is able to work best) through a man's ____________________.

9. Heb. 11:34—God's heroes become strong through ______________

So, God is the God of the weak, the foolish, the despised, and the nobodies! Why? So that no human being can boast in the presence of God. Human weakness provides the best backdrop for the display of God's power. If a weak human accomplishes anything, it is a clear testimony to the power and working of God because the man is obviously too weak to do it in his own strength.

Examples Of This Principle

Many People Are Too Strong

Read the following Scripture passages and state who was too strong for God to use in each passage.

2 Chronicles 26:15–16— ______________________________

How did God use him when he was weak? ______________

____

____

What happened when he got strong? ______________

____

____

Imagine! A man who was *too strong* for God to use!

Ezekiel 28:12–17— ______________________________

In the preceding lesson, we learned the true identity of their king. His beauty, wisdom, and musical skill, rather than being an asset, became a liability. Why? ______________________________

____

____

Some of us let our skills, talents, appearance, wealth, and winsome personalities keep us from dedicating our lives to God. Talents, popularity, and physical appearance tempt us to use them where they will be most appreciated by other people. We must, however, allow our talents, popularity, and physical appearance to fall to the ground and die if we are to serve God. (That doesn't meant that we should go around looking or acting like uncultured slobs; we just surrender those things to God and don't make them the focus of our lives.)

Some Are Made Weak

God does not choose only the weak. He chose several mighty men, but for Him to use them, they had to renounce any dependence on their own strengths. Note some of the mighty men whom God used *after* they became weak.

Paul

Read Philippians 3:4–6, and list the seven outstanding strengths of Paul.

1. ______________________________

____

2. ______________________________
____

3. ______________________________
____

4. ______________________________
____

5. ______________________________
____

6. ______________________________
____

7. ______________________________
____

According to Philippians 3:7, what was Paul's attitude toward these strengths? ______________________________
____

In your own words, what does that mean? ______________________________
____
____

Paul was a highly educated man and an eloquent speaker who could rival the greatest intellectuals of his day. Yet, for God to use him, how did Paul approach the people of Corinth in 1 Corinthians 2:3? ______________
____
____

According to 1 Corinthians 2:1, 4, how did he speak and preach? Not with ______________________________
______________________________but rather in ______________________________
____

According to Judges 8:10, a total of how many soldiers (adding those slain and those who were left alive) gathered against Israel to overthrow it? ____________________. Gideon called an army of how many to fight them? ____________________ But God said in Judges 7:3, "The people that are with thee are ____

____."

Why? "Lest Israel ____

____."

God reduced the number in Gideon's army, first from 32,000 to________ (7:2) and then to a mere __________ (7:4–7). God just doesn't like men who rely on their own strength and power!

According to Judges 7:16, with what inadequate (humanly speaking) equipment did God arm Gideon's soldiers? ______________________

____

____

Imagine! Although they were outnumbered 450 to 1 and lacked both offensive and defensive weapons, they annihilated the Midianites! This is another example that *God's greatest weapons are fashioned from our weaknesses!*

Most Are Already Weak

According to Acts 4:13, what kind of men were Peter and John? ______ ____ According to Acts 3:6, what was their financial condition? ______________________

____

Yet, look how God used them!

David was only a youth with a slingshot when God used him to overpower Goliath. And, according to Judges 6:15, what sort of person was Gideon? ____

____

Remember, God does not use us *in spite of* our weaknesses but *because of* them!

Are you *weak* enough for God to use you?

Notes From The Teacher's Lesson

The Man God Uses

Characteristic	Jacob	Esau
Meaning of name		
Physical appearance		
Interests		
Rank in family		
View of "things"		
Character		
Possessions		

Had Man Made The Choice, Esau Would Have Headed The Nation Of Israel Rather Than Jacob!

Examples Of God's ______________________________

1. Jacob
2. Disciples
3. Unusual Instruments

Scriptural Reasons For God's ______________________________

That No Flesh Should ______________________ (1 Cor. 1:26–31)

That God's Power Might Be ______________________ (2 Cor. 12:7–9)

Practical Lessons

- Usefulness— ____

- Surrender—____

- Strength—____

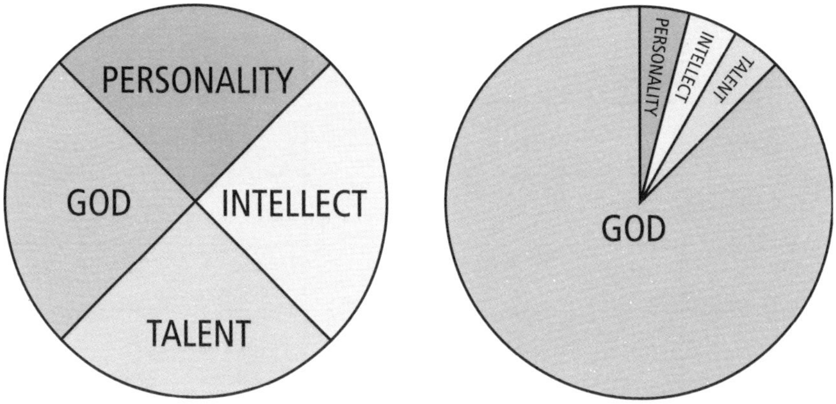

THE FULL MAN **THE EMPTY MAN**

Stepping Toward Effective Leadership

- Read about Bill Borden's statement "I take hands off" in chapter fourteen of Earl Palmer's book *The 24–Hour Christian*, pp. 137–141. Summarize the lesson you learn from that statement and list ways in which you can apply it to your own life.

- Lists of leadership qualifications usually include several predictable characteristics, including the ones listed here. For each characteristic or qualification, rate each on a scale of one to five (with one being "of little importance" and five being "of greatest importance") according to your estimation. Be prepared to defend your ratings before the class.

  ______ Physical health

  ______ Personal attractiveness, charm, and social graces

______ Intelligence

______ Educational background

______ Experience

______ Clearly defined goals

______ Enthusiasm

______ Perseverance in discouragement

______ Willingness to learn

______ Reputation (what others think you to be)

______ Character (what you really are)

______ Devotion to the task

______ Loyalty

- Read and summarize what Bob Welch says about self–centeredness versus self–sacrifice in chapter five of his book *More to Life than Having It All.*

- Study more about how God transformed the life of Jacob from a deceiver to one who was an instrument of God's blessing by reading chapters twelve through sixteen of *Changed into His Likeness* by Watchman Nee.

- Choose a respected leader in your church or school for analysis. What makes him a good leader? Rate him on each of the characteristics listed in activity two above. (Use the same scale of one to five that is described in that activity.) Then rate yourself using the same characteristics. What are your strengths? Your weaknesses? What steps must you take to improve on your weaknesses?

7

What God Hates

Howard Hendricks tells the following story in his book, *Don't Fake It…Say It With Love.*

> I was in a lovely Christian home while holding a week of church meetings, and I was somewhat taken back the first night when the hostess said, "What would you like for breakfast?"
>
> I said, "Ma'am, anything you serve will be fine for me."
>
> "Well, how would you like your eggs?" she asked.
>
> I said, "Anyway you serve them will be all right."
>
> "What time would you like to get up?" she continued.
>
> "You just tell me what time you have breakfast, and I'll be there."
>
> "Well, the children go to school and my husband works, so we have breakfast at 7, but we don't expect you to get up then."
>
> "That's all right; I'll be there at 7. I'd love to enjoy the fellowship of your family."
>
> This went on all week—"Would you like to have breakfast in your room…?" And I kept trying to be like one of the family. One evening after the meeting, we were talking about the spiritual life and this couple said,

> "You're the strangest person we've had in this house. We entertain Bible teachers, missionaries, and other Christian leaders, and each one of them has his own set of specifications. What is it with you?"
>
> That night I had a hard time getting to sleep. What in the world are we Christians coming to? Who's kidding whom? At best, we are unprofitable servants—but who could tell it from our actions? Not until we pour our lives out like libation offerings to people can God be exalted among us as He deserves.

Such humility is a scarce quality among would–be leaders today. The enemy of such an attitude is pride, and that is the topic of this lesson. As you study it, ask yourself if pride is preventing you from becoming the spiritual leader God wants you to be.

Student Work

In the preceding lesson, we saw what God wants in a leader—acknowledgment of weakness and surrender of all talents to God. In this lesson, we will see what God *doesn't* want in a leader.

Proverbs 6:16–19 mentions seven things that God hates. List them.

1. ______________________________

2. ______________________________

3. ______________________________

4. ______________________________

5. ______________________________

6. ______________________________

7. ______________________________

Of those seven things, the first and most prominent is ______________

If we are to be mature leaders, we must be able to identify and flee from pride. In this lesson, let's take a closer look at pride and learn how to recognize and deal with it in a godly way.

God's Opinion Of Pride

Read the following verses and state what God thinks about pride and/or proud people. (Use your own words, not the words of Scripture.)

- Psalm 101:5— ____________________
- Psalm 138:6— ____________________
- Proverbs 6:16–17— ____________________
- Proverbs 16:5— ____________________
- Proverbs 16:18— ____________________
- Proverbs 21:4— ____________________
- Isaiah 2:17— ____________________
- James 4:6— ____________________

The Bible's Definition Of Pride

Proud literally means "considering oneself above other people." We see pride most clearly in selfishness. Pride has at least four characteristics, each of which we will now examine closely.

Deification Of Self

This characteristic is best defined as seeking honor and praise that belongs to God alone. Two Bible examples of this are Satan and Herod.

Read the following passages and state how each reveals this aspect of pride (i.e., seeking honor for oneself that belongs only to God), and describe the consequences of that pride.

Satan (Isa. 14:12–14)— ____

____

____

Consequences (Isa. 14:15; Ezek. 28:16–19)— ____________________

____

____

Herod (Acts 12:22–23)— ____

____

____

____

Consequences— ____

____

Independence

Pride is self-sufficient. A proud person glories in being his "own man." This aspect of pride leads to such statements as "do your own thing," "I don't need anything," and "I don't do anything I don't want to do."

State how each of the following statements reveals an attitude of independence from God.

"Do your own thing."— ____

____

"I'm my own man."— ____

____

How did Saul act independently of God in 1 Samuel 13:1–14? ________

____

____

Note that for a king to do a priest's work by offering a sacrifice was a violation of God's law. What was the result of Saul's disobedience? ______

______

______

Contrast this attitude with that of Christ in John 5:30. What did the Son of God say? ______

______

He gloried in His dependence upon the Father. Pride, however, glories in its self–sufficiency and independence.

Contempt

Contempt is the most general concept of pride. It is looking down one's nose at others who might not dress as well as you do or who do not have the looks, personality, or ability that others might have.

According to Luke 18:11, who manifested this aspect of pride? ______

______

This aspect of pride uses people to build a great church or school rather than using the church to build a great people. It causes someone to pit two people against each other to make himself look better. It leads to gossip and criticism and causes friction between others while the contemptuous person stays out of the picture as much as possible so as to look innocent.

Competition

Too often, our desire to get good grades, win a ballgame, or achieve some other goal is based on pride. Although we hate to admit it, few of us do our best *for God's glory*; instead, we seek our *own* advancement!

C. S. Lewis, the author of the acclaimed *Narnia Chronicles* and other religious fiction, pointed out that no one is proud because he is rich or clever or good looking. He is proud because he is rich*er* or *more* clever or *better* looking than someone else.

Why do you study your Bible lesson? Why do you memorize Scripture? Why do you have your devotions? To outdo someone else or to honor God?

According to 3 John 9, how did Diotrephes reveal competitive pride? ___

____

____

Notes From The Teacher's Lesson

What God Hates

The ______________ Pride (Ezekiel 28:11–17)

- He Was The ______________ Created Being (28:12)
- He Was Perfect In ______________ (28:12)
- He Was God's ______________ (28:13)
- He Held The Highest Appointed ______________ (28:14)
- He Was ______________ Above All Others (28:14)
- His Glories ______________ Him (28:16–17)

The ______________ Of Pride

- Man's ______________
- Every Other ______________

The ______________ Of Pride

- The Test Of ______________
- The Test Of ______________
- The Test Of ______________
- The Test Of ______________
- The Test Of ______________

- Comparison/Contrast
- Perception (What We Really Are)
- Chastening
- Confession

Stepping Toward Effective Leadership

- Using reference sources such as *Bartlett's Familiar Quotations* and *A New Dictionary of Quotations*, make a list of spiritually instructive quotations on the topics of pride and humility. After each such quotation, summarize briefly the spiritual lesson that we can apply from it.

- Using an exhaustive concordance, write out the verses on pride that are found in the Bible. What percentage of those verses come from Proverbs? Why do you think Solomon said so much about this topic?

- Explain the following statement as it relates to leadership: "As the chest swells, the brain and the heart shrink."

- Explain the truth of the following statement: "Whenever you hear a siren, remember that it is a result of sin." List the different uses of sirens and illustrate how each, indeed, demonstrates a result of sin.

- Read the following chapters of Joseph M. Stowell's book *Perilous Pursuits*, and summarize what he says about pride:
  - Chapter 1, "Pleasure, Pride, and Passion";
  - Chapter 9, "The Fall of Pride"; and
  - Chapter 10, "Pride Revised."

8

Christ's Terms Of Discipleship

It was in the midst of the Cultural Revolution in Communist China. Radical young people in the Chinese Communist Party had begun a violent crusade against intellectuals, especially against anyone who seemed to believe or support anything imported from the Western world. They were especially incensed against religion, particularly biblical Christianity. Armed with this intense hatred and inspired by a little red book—*The Quotations of Chairman Mao Tse–tung,* the dictator of Red China—they carried terror and violence from village to village across the land. They burned, looted, tortured, and killed in the name of Communism.

One particular Chinese family lived in constant fear of their lives. The parents were both professors in a large university, intellectuals, so they were automatically targets of the Cultural Revolution. But they and their teenage daughter were also Christians, so they were doubly marked.

Then the day they had long dreaded came; the students of the Cultural Revolution came to their town and began to burn and destroy. The family could not escape. In the middle of the night, the students, tipped off to the presence of Christian intellectuals by a spiteful neighbor, battered down the door of their small apartment and dragged them into the street. The neighborhood was ablaze with bonfires fueled by the victims' furniture, personal possessions, and politically incorrect books.

Learning that the family members were Christians, the mob stripped the teenage girl of all clothing and forced her to stand in the midst of the screaming crowd in shame. Then they forced her to watch as they beat both of her parents to death. She tried to avoid watching the gruesome sight, but the students held her head so that she had to see their bloody deed. As her parents died, they called out to her, encouraging her to remain strong for the Lord.

She cried in vain for the tormentors to be merciful and humane. She watched helplessly as they burned her parents' professional books. But when a student started to throw the girl's Bible into the bonfire, she could no longer restrain herself. She lunged forward, grabbing the Bible from the flames. The students, however, tore it from her hands, and then one student brutally smashed the fingers of both of her hands with a large metal pipe.

"You will never hold a Bible again!" he screamed angrily in her face.

The news media do not cover such stories today, but such incidents nonetheless occur in many nations around the world. If the media do cover the violence, they avoid reporting its antireligious nature. Chinese Christians are still arrested and sentenced to "reeducation camps," where they are forced to do hard labor under appalling conditions or even are put to death. Christians in Indonesia and many other Southeast Asian and predominantly Moslem nations live in constant fear of their lives.

Consider, for example, the following items from the March 2001 *The Missions Banner*, which appeared under the headline "CHRISTIANS UNDER PERSECUTION."

"Sudan has been called 'a million square miles of suffering.' The Muslim government has waged war on the people in the southern part of Sudan, where many of the Christians in that nation live." It is "part of a religious war waged on the mostly Christian villages...."

"Egypt was the scene of one of the most hideous massacres...in modern times. [B]etween December 31 and January 2, 2000, twenty–one Christians were brutally murdered...by their Muslim neighbors."

In Nigeria, "being a Christian leaves one open to persecution."

In India, Hindu mobs "seek out Christians whom they kill without provocation and destroy their churches...." They are especially resentful of "the favorable publicity Christians have received for humanitarian efforts following the recent earthquakes in Orissa state."

In Turkmenistan, "Authorities continue a campaign to shut down Protestant churches. ...On February 17, authorities in the capital sealed off the only remaining Baptist church in the city."

Although the Lord so far has graciously spared the United States from such violence and overt persecution, even American Christians who are committed to following Christ will still have to pay a price for their commitment.

What *is* the price of discipleship? Are *you* willing to pay that price?

Student Work

The six previous lessons were designed to give a transforming view of God so that we might better understand what God has in mind for our lives. As we understand God's plan and mind concerning Christian leadership, we are better equipped to be leaders.

This lesson and the next ones conclude this unit by viewing the role that the Son of God plays in making us the mature Christians we should be. Unit 3 deals with the B–attitudes laid down by Christ and the role of the Holy Spirit in building our character.

Our current lesson deals with Christ's idea of discipleship. If one is to be a mature Christian leader, he must understand what Christ meant by discipleship. The word *disciple* brings to mind two things: discipline and following. A disciple is a person who has disciplined himself to follow another person. So all *good leaders are disciplined and faithful followers.* This lesson presents Christ's stringent demands on those who would be His leaders, further emphasizing that if one is to lead, he must be both a well–disciplined individual and an excellent follower.

But how can one lead and still follow? The two activities seem to be opposites. If I am following, how can I also be leading? The answer is simple: if we do not follow Christ, we will not lead others. A leader is doomed to failure if he forgets that *he is only as good a leader of men as he is a follower of Christ.*

Two Invitations

Read Luke 14:26–27, in which we find the invitation "come" offered twice, yet the two invitations are different.

- First, we must come ____________________(v. 26); this is *salvation.*
- Then, we must come ____________________(v. 27); this is *discipleship.*

Sad to say, not everyone who comes to Christ for salvation comes after Him in consecrated discipleship; therefore, the words *believer* and *disciple* are not synonymous.

- What, then, is a believer? It is a sinner who comes ______________ for ______________________________
- What is a disciple? It is a believer who comes ______________ for consecration.

Terms Of Discipleship

Being a believer is much easier than being a disciple! That is why Christ had many *believers* but few true disciples. (Even one of the Twelve was neither a disciple nor a true believer!) *Believing requires faith, but discipleship requires discipline.*

Christ laid down exacting and costly demands for discipleship. None of Christ's preaching was more unpopular than His messages on discipleship. He emphasized hardship, danger, persecution, and cross–bearing rather than a life of ease, safety, popularity, and fun. But such is the path of leadership. A leader must be willing and ready to meet the following demands of Christ. Four of these demands are negative and require denial and self–discipline. Three of them are positive and require outward actions.

Read each of the following verses and note the italicized phrase. Then record in the blank beside the reference whether the passage is a positive or a negative demand.

Matthew 16:24a: ______________________________

"Then said Jesus unto His disciples, If any man will come after me, let him *deny himself,* and take up his cross, and follow me."

Matthew 16:24b: ______________________________

"Then said Jesus unto His disciples, If any man will come after me, let him deny himself, and *take up his cross,* and follow me."

Matthew 16:24c: ______________________________

"Then said Jesus unto His disciples, If any man will come after me, let him deny himself, and take up his cross, and *follow me.*"

Luke 14:26: ______________________________

"If any man come to me, and *hate* not *his father,* and mother, and wife, and children, and brethren, and sisters, yea, and *his own life also,* he cannot be my disciple."

Luke 14:33: ______________________________

"So likewise, whosoever he be of you that *forsaketh* not *all that he hath* [possessions], he cannot be my disciple."

John 8:31: ______________________________

"Then said Jesus to those Jews which believed on him, if ye *continue in my word,* then are ye my disciples indeed."

John 13:35: ______________________________

"By this shall all men know that ye are my disciples, if ye *have love one to another.*"

Negative Demands

- The demand in Luke 14:26 is a demand on our *affections.* This demand requires us to love Christ so much that we are willing to sacrifice even our family ties and every other love in our life for Him if necessary.
- The demand in Matthew 16:24a is a demand on our *will.* It requires the destruction of *our* will and wishes in submission to *His* will.
- The demand in Matthew 16:24b is a demand on our *ego.* It calls us to choose a path of dishonor, reproach, and shame. It requires us to be willing to face persecution and loss of popularity for Him.
- The demand in Luke 14:33 is a demand on our *possessions.* It requires us to forget about being rich or having a lot of earthly goods and to focus instead on being Christ's disciple.

Positive Demands

- The demand in Matthew 16:24c is that we live only for *His* pleasure. That is, we will go wherever He leads. We will do whatever He bids. We follow Him—not our friends, the road of least resistance, wealth, or fame.
- The demand in John 8:31 is that we be consistent (i.e., always the same) in reading and studying and living the Word. This demand requires us to be faithful 365 days a year in our Bible study, devotions, witnessing, Scripture memory, and other spiritual duties.
- The demand in John 13:35 is to love those who are saved, that is, our fellow believers.

Requirements For Meeting Christ's Demands

Each of the seven demands also requires certain *inner* qualities if we are to fulfill the demand. Note each of the demands and the inner qualities necessary for their accomplishment.

Hatred Of Family And Self (Luke 14:26)

The Demand:

Obviously, Christ is not asking us to hate our families. Instead, He is saying that our love for Him should be so great that all other loves seem to be hatred by contrast.

The Requirement:

The discipline of our affections. A person must be strong enough to sacrifice the fellowship and closeness of his home situation and such amenities as TV, sports, dating, parties, etc.

Denial Of Self (Matt. 16:24a)

The Demand:

There is a difference between self–denial and denial of self. *Self–denial* means "denying yourself food, clothing, sleep, joys, etc." Christ is not talking about this. *Denial of self* means "to submit our will to His will." We are required to give up to Him all rights and authority that we might have. We thus emerge with *no* rights, and we can therefore never again say, "I will do what *I* want to do."

The Requirement:

The character of meekness. To meet this demand, a person must become meek.

Cross–Bearing (Matt. 16:24b)

The Demand:

To *take up the cross* means "to forget popularity and be strong to face persecution, mockery, shame, and teasing."

The Requirement:

The characteristic of being poor in spirit. We will never bear our cross as long as we are "stuck on" ourselves.

Following Christ (Matt. 16:24c)

The Demand:

This is a demand for us to focus our eyes on Christ with the intention of pleasing Him rather than seeking to please our own fleshly desires.

The Requirement:

A heart set on pleasing Christ above self.

Forsaking All Possessions (Luke 14:33)

The Demand:

To forget about being rich or having earthly goods and to focus instead on being His disciple.

The Requirement:

A proper set of values; having the right priorities in life. We put more value on godliness than on gold.

Notes From The Teacher's Lesson

Discipleship

The Demands Of Discipleship

Matthew 16:24a: ____

____

Matthew 16:24b: ____

____

Matthew 16:24c: ____

____

- Luke 14:26: ______________________________

____

- Luke 14:33: ______________________________

____

- John 8:31: ______________________________

____

- John 13:35: ______________________________

____

Christ And ______________________________

His Work Demands Only The Toughest; He Knew What The Disciples Would Face.

Christ's Terms Of ______________________________

- Christ Must Be ______________________________
- His Followers Must Be ______________________________
- His Followers Must Forsake ______________________________

The Reason For Such Absolute Demands

- Christ Is Building A ______________________________, And He Needs Only The ______________________________ (Luke 14:28–30)
- Christ Is Leading His Army In ______________________________, And He Needs Only The ______________________________ (Luke 14:31–32)
- Christ Knew What His Disciples Would Face In Their ______________.

Stepping Toward Effective Leadership

- List specific areas of your life in which Christ must be first. Give examples of things that you must be willing to give up if He is to be first in those areas.
- Contact such organizations as Voice of the Martyrs (Christian) and/or Amnesty International (secular) for information about religious persecution that is occurring around the world today. Make a world map. Color code each country to indicate where Christians are relatively free of persecution, where religious freedoms are limited, and where Christians are openly and/or officially persecuted. What steps can you as an individual and you as a class, school, or church take to help believers who are being persecuted?
- Read and summarize *Tortured for Christ* by Richard Wurmbrand, who spent fourteen years in a prison in Communist Romania for his commitment to Christ.
- Read selections from John Foxe's *Book of Martyrs.* List the prices that various martyrs paid for their commitment to be true disciples of Christ.
- Read and summarize the basic lessons of Jerry White's book *The Power of Commitment.*
- Although Christians in America have not yet been called to die for their faith, they nonetheless often suffer moderate (in contrast to the price paid by believers in other parts of the world) degrees of persecution in state colleges, on their jobs, etc. List and briefly describe examples of such persecution. What has led to such religious persecution in a land that has long prided itself in its "religious tolerance"? What steps can you take as both a Christian and a citizen to reduce such persecution?
- What did G. Campbell Morgan have to say about Christ's terms of discipleship and quality vs. quantity in a disciple's service of building for God in "Disciples for Building and Battle" (pp. 179–189) in *The Best of G. Campbell Morgan*?

- View the video "The Martyr's Cry" (by Voice of the Martyrs) and summarize the stories of persecution being suffered by Christians around the world. What effect does the video have on you?

they that mourn
the meek: for
which do hunger
shall be filled.
obtain mercy.
see God. Blessed
shall be called
persecuted
of heaven.
and persecute
you falsely, for
great is your
prophets which
in spirit: for theirs
mourn: for
for they
hunger and
they
filled. Bless
shall
ercy. Bless
shall see
Blessed ar
shall be called th
ich are persecuted
kingdom of heave
you, and persec
against you falsely,
for great is you
in spirit: for the
they that mour
the meek: for
which do hun
shall be filled.
mercy.
see God. Blessed are the
called the child
cuted for right
of heaven. Bless
you, and persecute you

9

Christ's Ideal Of Character

Shortly after Jesus heard that John had been arrested and was in prison, He left His hometown of Nazareth and moved to Capernaum to live. There, in the land of Galilee, He began to preach a message very similar to that which John had preached: "Repent; for the kingdom of heaven is at hand."

As He went about preaching, He chose twelve men whom He would teach to become the leaders of Christianity, "fishers of men." These men went with Him as He traveled about. They heard Him teaching in the Jewish synagogue. They listened as He preached the gospel. They watched as He healed "all manner of sickness and all manner of disease among the people." They witnessed His soaring fame, especially as He cast out demons and cured lunatics. And they were right there with Him as the huge crowds followed Him, eager to hear His words and experience His healing touch.

Then one day, they heard Jesus preach what became His most memorable public sermon. The crowds were prepared to listen to what Jesus said in this particular sermon because they had seen His miracles. They knew that God was with Him and that His message was from God. "He spoke as one having authority."

This sermon of Christ has become known as the "Sermon on the Mount" and is the longest continuous sermon of Christ ever recorded. More likely than not, even what we have preserved for us today is merely a summary of what Christ said, not the full sermon. And yet, what we do have of the sermon is packed with meaning and potential.

Christ preached this sermon on one of the mountains of Galilee. It wasn't one of the holy mountains of Zion and probably was not even the highest mountain in the area. It was just a common mountain that provided Christ a platform from which to speak to the people and from which they could all see and hear Him.

Famed Bible commentator Matthew Henry pointed out that God gave Moses the Law from a mountain (Sinai), but the similarities end there. Whereas when He gave the Ten Commandments God came down upon the mountain, spoke in thunderings and lightnings, and ordered the people to stand far back, when Jesus gave His Sermon on the Mount, He went up onto the mountain, spoke in a human voice, and encouraged the people to come close to Him.

And they did draw near. They listened eagerly because "they were willing to be taught," Henry stated. And the Twelve, Christ's primary audience (He merely let the crowd listen in on this lesson to the Twelve), knew that what He was teaching them He expected them to teach to others.

According to Henry, Christ taught this lesson "to guide and regulate our practice." It was a very practical sermon, not a deep, dark theological treatise. It is as applicable today as it was then and is beneficial for everyone, from the most spiritually immature to the older, more experienced Christian. His sermon reveals the duties of believers and prescribes rules by which we are to fulfill those duties. It shares with us, Henry said, "the character of those who are entitled to blessedness," but the principles are given in such a way as to seem like paradoxes, statements that on the surface seem to go against common sense. But as we read them, we must remind ourselves that God's ways of working are not the ways of man.

The Sermon on the Mount begins with a series of blessings that have become known as the Beatitudes. Henry stated that each of these statements of blessing has a two–fold purpose:

- to show whom we should honor and respect and
- to define what makes for true happiness.

In accomplishing these broad objectives, Christ's sermon refutes the world's false concept of happiness and offers quite a different concept. It also tends, Henry declared, to "remove the discouragements of the weak and poor who receive the gospel." It invites souls to come to Christ to find true happiness.

In the Beatitudes, Christ defines "eight characteristics of blessed [i.e., truly happy] people," "the principle graces of a Christian." Each beatitude includes both a blessing *now* and a promise of *future* blessing.

These beatitudes, or (as we will hereinafter refer to them) "B–attitudes," are the focus of this lesson and all of the lessons in Unit 3. This lesson gives you an overview of the B–attitudes, and each lesson of Unit 3 discusses an individual B–attitude. Read Matthew 5:3–12 in preparation for these lessons, and ask the Lord to open your spiritual eyes to wondrous practical truths that will help you become the spiritual leader He intends you to be.

An important objective of these lessons on the B–attitudes is that you will not only learn *about* this ideal person but also actually *become that person!* To do so, you must learn what each of the eight attitudes is, how you get them, etc., and that requires the learning of facts. However, learning only the facts will not make you this ideal person. So please, *don't just learn the facts; become the person!*

Student Work

Description Of Each Virtue

As we begin this part of our study, let's examine each of the virtues listed in Christ's Sermon on the Mount and get a description of each.

Poor In Spirit

This virtue means "emptied of self." Such a man considers himself to be insignificant. He is aware of his own weaknesses and his total need for God's power.

Mourner

This virtue is revealed by spiritual compassion for souls and/or sorrow for sin. A serious attitude about spiritual things, it is the opposite of indifference.

Meek

Meekness is "an attitude of mind that does not insist on its own rights and is always ready to waive its privileges in the interest of others." It doesn't seek prestige, high office, or being first in line.

Hunger And Thirst After Righteousness

The man who longs for spiritual things far more than material things exhibits this virtue. He spends most of his time, thoughts, money, and energy in a quest for spiritual growth or service.

Merciful

Mercy is the withholding of wrath from those who deserve it. It is being merciful to those who have been unmerciful.

Pure In Heart

This virtue is purity in thought, motive, and action.

Peacemaker

A peacemaker is one who steps in and restores peace where turmoil and strife exist.

Persecuted And Reviled

The man who exhibits this virtue is persecuted not because he is obnoxious but because he is kind, righteous, and loyal to Christ, and he does not fight back or retaliate when he is wronged or mistreated.

How Christ Exhibited These Eight Qualities

These eight virtues—or what we've called the "B–attitudes"—are actually a description of Christ, the Perfect One, Himself. Read the following verses and state what happened and which B–attitude it shows in Christ.

John 8:1–11

What happened: ______________________________

____

____

The B–attitude that Christ manifested: ______________

John 8:29, 46

What happened: ______________________________

____

____

The B–attitude that Christ manifested: ______________

1 Peter 2:21–23

What happened: ______________________________

____

____

The B–attitude that Christ manifested: ______________

John 5:19, 30

What happened: ______________________________

____

____

The B–attitude that Christ manifested: ______________

Colossians 1:20, 21

What happened: ______________________________

____

The B–attitude that Christ manifested: ______________

John 13:2–14

What happened: ______________________________

____

____

The B–attitude that Christ manifested: ______________

John 4:32, 34

What happened: ______________________________

____

____

The B–attitude that Christ manifested: ______________

Luke 13:34

What happened: ______________________________

____

The B–attitude that Christ manifested: ______________

Examples Of A Lack Of These Virtues

Bill calls Sarah a liar because she accused him of cheating. Bill, knowing that he didn't cheat her, eggs Sarah's house that night. What virtue does Bill lack? ______________________________

In his Sunday sermon, the preacher preaches against viewing pornography. Richard and Alyse look at each other slyly and smile—half in mockery and half in guilt—because they are both guilty. Which virtue do they lack? ______________________________

____

Jim spends about thirty minutes a week studying his Bible—when his parents make him—but he spends twelve hours a week watching TV. Which virtue does he lack? ____

____

Dan is known as a "pusher" because he's always pushing to be first in line and will always grab the biggest slice of cake. What virtue does Dan lack?

____

John is always eager to display his beautiful voice. What virtue does he lack? ____

Mark, hearing that his two best friends are now mad at each other over a girl, sides with one friend against the other. What virtue does he lack? __

____

Kristi lives a separated life, but she is so pious and obnoxious about her holiness that the other students mock and ridicule her, and she fights back against her tormenters. What virtue does she lack? ________________

____

Notes From The Teacher's Lesson

What Is Happiness And Success?

Man's Concept Of Happiness

Wealth – ________________ + Gratification Of ________________ + __________ ____________ + ________________________= Success And Happiness.

Christ's Concept Of Success And Happiness

Poverty + ______________+ ______________ + ________________ = Success And Happiness.

Christ's Ideal Person

- Poor In Spirit
- A Mourner
- Meek
- Hungry And Thirsty
- Merciful
- Pure In Heart
- A Peacemaker
- Persecuted

Stepping Toward Effective Leadership

- As a preparation for not only this lesson but also Unit 3, memorize the Beatitudes portion of the Sermon on the Mount (i.e., Matt. 5:3–12).

- How does A. W. Tozer define *meekness* in chapter nine of *The Pursuit of God?* How does he contrast the burden and the rest of which Christ speaks in Matthew 11:28–30?

- Read the *Autobiography of George Müller*. How did his life exemplify the B–attitudes?

- Read Exodus 19:1–20:21, which describes the giving of the Law to the children of Israel. Make a chart comparing and contrasting the details of that event with the details of Christ's delivery of the Sermon on the Mount.

- Read Stuart Briscoe's *The Sermon on the Mount: Daring to Be Different.* Then, as you study each lesson in Unit 3, note the truths about each that you glean from Briscoe's book. Share those lessons learned during the class discussion of each chapter in Unit 3.

- As the introduction of this chapter points out, the primary audience for the Sermon on the Mount was Christ's twelve disciples, not the general public. In light of that fact, what are the practical implications of the following quotation? Can—or should—we “legislate morality?” Debate the various views on this issue.

“One problem we have is that we try to get a fallen society to behave as if it were made up of Christians, and that’s something we will never do. *Our big problem is not getting a fallen society to behave like Christians. The big problem is to get Christians to stop behaving like fallen society! If only we could get Christians to act like Christians*, we would discover that the principles enunciated here produce a totally different moral, ethical, and social standard, making Christian behavior distinctive and unlike that of the rest of the world.” (Stuart Briscoe, *The Sermon on the Mount: Daring to Be Different*, pp. 1–2 [emphasis added].)

- How can Christians make a difference in a *self–centered* world?
- List some of the things that effectively keep people from being blessed, happy, content, and fulfilled?
- What are some practical ways for keeping our ambitions focused on what is righteous?
- List areas around you that are examples of the need for peace—spiritually, socially, personally. What steps can you take to be a peacemaker in those situations?
- List obstacles to peacemaking. How can we overcome those obstacles?
- Someone once said, “The darker the place, the brighter the light that’s needed.” What did that person mean? Do you agree with the statement? Why or why not?
- What are some ways of ensuring that when people see our good works they will glorify the *Father* and not *us*?

Unit 3

The Attitudes Of Leadership

10

Blessed Are The Poor In Spirit

The first time people met the young college student, they were struck by his apparent poverty. He wore out–of–date clothing. Certainly no one could accuse him of being too stylish or fashionable! He seldom smiled, and his face was a picture of sadness and deep seriousness. He never talked to anyone unless the topic was some deep spiritual issue. He dismissed dating and other social activities as unspiritual distractions. He prayed long, spiritual–sounding prayers filled with theological jargon that was often unintelligible to other Christians. He fasted often—and let everyone know it by announcing that he wouldn't be able to make meals because he was praying.

As time went on, however, some people began to suspect that all of this was just a spiritual show for the young man. It wasn't that he was deeply spiritual; he was just working hard to make that impression. And it worked—for a while. Eventually, however, as people got to know him better, they saw through the façade to the real person, who was mostly sham.

Fortunately, the Lord instructed this man that true spirituality is a condition of the heart, not an outward show. He developed a sincere poverty of spirit, got married, and went on to serve the Lord in an international ministry and to be a mentor for many other servants of the Lord.

That young man's original attitude was like that of the Pharisees. Jesus described them in Matthew 6 as doing everything they did "to be seen of men," "that they may have glory of men," to "be heard for their much speaking," and "that they may appear unto men to fast" (vv. 1, 2, 5, 7, 16). He said repeatedly that "they have their reward," meaning that they got what they were after in each case—other people saw them. But nowhere in the passage did He say that God ever blessed them or their outward actions. They clearly had the wrong motives.

On the other hand, Christ said that we should behave in the opposite fashion. We should give secretly, pray secretly, and fast privately—and never try to let others know what we're doing. The result will be that God "himself shall reward thee openly" (v. 4). This is true poverty of spirit. Let's examine this character trait in detail in the following lesson materials.

Student Work

This lesson and the next seven lessons deal with the B–attitudes that Christ desires in His leaders. This particular lesson deals with the first of those B–attitudes:

"Blessed are the poor in spirit: for theirs is the kingdom of heaven" (Matt. 5:3).

The Attitude

Definition

Poor in spirit means "emptied of self." It describes a complete absence of pride, self–assurance, self–reliance, and self–confidence in the face of Almighty God.

Explanation

What It Does *NOT* Mean

Poor in spirit does *not* mean financial poverty. God nowhere glorifies poverty.

Poor in spirit does *not* mean spiritual poverty. Spiritual poverty is to be without Christ. A man without Christ is spiritually poor, but he is not poor in spirit. Of course, neither does it mean a Christian who is weak in the faith or who is not growing in the wisdom and knowledge of God.

Poor in spirit does *not* mean poor spirited. A poor–spirited person is one who lacks enthusiasm, personality, fire, and drive. The person who is poor in spirit might bubble over with all of these qualities. Personality has nothing to do with this attitude.

Poor in spirit does *not* mean voluntary humility. Note Colossians 2:18: "Let no man beguile [deceive] you of your reward in a __________ ______________________________ The Roman Catholics accept this view. They believe that to be poor in spirit means to deliberately renounce (give up) riches and take a vow of poverty, as did the monks in monasteries.

Poor in spirit does *not* mean sadness and solemnity. According to Matthew 6:16–18, what did the Pharisees do to make people think that they were poor in spirit? ______________________________

____

What It *DOES* Mean

Poor in spirit means having a conscious awareness that we are nothing in the presence of a holy God. Seeing no goodness in ourselves, we depend totally on His grace, power, and will to accomplish whatever He wants through us. This attitude removes desire for man's approval, self–promotion, and bitterness toward others who might outshine us in His service.

Position

Christ included this attitude first in His sermon because it is obviously the key to possessing all of the other attitudes. The B–attitudes have a definite order, and this one is the foundation stone upon which all of the others rest. God never does anything haphazardly or accidentally. As we will see as we continue our study, whereas this attitude implies an *emptying*, the other attitudes manifest *fulness*. But we cannot be filled until we are first emptied.

The Example

Let's see how Paul manifested poorness in spirit.

Read Philippians 3:4–6 and list the political, familial/racial, moral, and religious wealth of Paul.

Political— ____

____

Familial/racial— ____

____

Moral—____

Religious— ____

Read Acts 22:3–4; 22:28; 23:6; 26:10–11; 7:54–8:1; 8:3 and describe Paul in the following two areas:

His father's position—____

Paul's own citizenship— ____

The character of a Roman citizen superseded that of all other people in the known world of Paul's day and placed Paul amid the aristocracy of any town of the time.

Paul's teacher was ______________________________. This man was one of the most distinguished teachers in the history of Israel, so Paul, as one of his students, was highly educated in the Jewish law.

His treatment of the church— ____

____

____

His treatment of Stephen—____

____

The Jewish population of that day would have considered all of the preceding facts about Paul to be assets. Truly, Paul was a man of prominence and political power and, if he had not been saved, he might have gone down in history as one of the most important Jewish leaders of his day. But when Paul got saved, his attitude toward these "assets" changed.

Read the following verses and answer the questions about his attitude toward his personal achievements.

Philippians 3:7— ____

____

Philippians 3:8— ____

____

____

According to the following verses, how did Paul honestly feel about himself?

Romans 7:18— ____

____

____

Romans 7:24— ____

____

____

According to the following verses, how did Paul view his former life (i.e., before his salvation)?

1 Timothy 1:13— ____

____

____

1 Timothy 1:15— ____

____

Thus, we see a perfect example of one who was poor in spirit. Did this attitude cause Paul to be lazy, backward, timid, or deliberately poor materially?_______ Read 1 Thessalonians 2:1–9 and Acts 18:3 and state how

Paul, although he was poor in spirit, related to each of the following characteristics.

- Laziness/work— ______________________________

- Timidity/boldness— ______________________________

- Desire for poverty/wealth— ______________________________

Paul's occupation made him independent. What was his occupation? ______________________________

According to 1 Corinthians 9:18, he stated that when he preached he made "the gospel of Christ without charge." Thus, according to Philippians 4:11–12, he could say, "I have learned ______________________________

I know both how to be ______________; and I know how to ______________________: I am instructed both to be ____________ and to be ______________, both to abound and to ______________________.

The Practical Application

How should you apply this lesson and attitude to your own life in respect to the following matters?

- Your choice of a vocation and/or college— ______________________________

Your attitude concerning your abilities or talents—______________

____

____

____

____

Your attitude concerning "dirty work" (e.g., picking up trash, mopping, cleaning restrooms, doing the most humiliating job in the school or family)— ______________________________

____

____

____

The Promise

What does this B–attitude promise to those who are poor in spirit? ____

____

This means that all of the blessings and benefits of the kingdom of heaven will be awarded to this person *both in this life and in the life to come.*

The Attainment

How do you become poor in spirit? *Not* by lifting yourself up or looking to your great assets. *Not* by trying deliberately to put yourself down. *Not* by deliberately suffering hardships, as did the monks. You become poor in spirit by looking to God. Read His Word, look at the Lord Jesus Christ, and view Him as we see Him in the Gospels. Look at His awesomeness, His love, His power, His tenderness, His courage, and His unparalleled voluntary suffering for us. Keep looking at Him. then you will have nothing to do yourself; *it will be done.* You cannot look at Him without feeling your absolute poverty and emptiness.

Notes From The Teacher's Lesson

Poor In Spirit

What It Is Not

- It Is Not ______________________________
- It Is Not ______________________________
- It Is Not ______________________________
- It Is Not ______________________________
- It Is Not ______________________________

How It Is Not Obtained

- Renouncing ______________________, Giving Away Our ______________________, Or Taking A Vow Of Poverty
- Staying ______________________ Of Christ And His Word
- Being ______________________, Or Without Courage
- Boasting Of Our ______________________, Looking Pitiful, Or Becoming A Hermit
- Suppressing Our Natural ______________________

What It Is

- It Is The ______________________ Of The World's Way
- It Is Based On Total ______________________

How It Is Obtained (James 4:7–8)

- Submit Yourself To ______________________
- Resist The ______________________

Draw ____ To God

- Have Face–To–Face Meetings With God In The Word.
- Be Much In Prayer.

Cleanse Your ____

Purify Your ____

Stepping Toward Effective Leadership

- List specific practical ways in which you can practice the B–attitude of being poor in spirit.
- Using your Bible and a concordance, list Bible characters who exhibited this B–attitude. Beside each name, explain briefly how this B–attitude was evidenced in that person's life.
- Explain why the statement "Money is the root of all evil" is incorrect. What is the correct view of money?
- Explain the difference between a "natural" quality or character trait and a "supernatural" quality or character trait. Give examples of each.
- List ways by which someone who is naturally shy, timid, nervous, and/or low–key (i.e., "laid back" or lacking natural enthusiasm) can better serve the Lord in spite of those traits. How can people who are naturally enthusiastic, outgoing, and calm help (or hinder) such retiring individuals?
- The Scriptures seem to offer conflicting advice regarding our actions concerning the devil. For example, James 4:7 tells us to "resist the devil," but other passages tell us to "flee" him and his temptations. How can we know when it's time to flee and when it's a time to fight? List the equipment that Scripture tells us to "put on" if we are going to resist Satan successfully.
- One key to developing poorness of spirit is drawing near to God. Read *The Practice of the Presence of God* by Brother Lawrence, and summarize what that book says on that topic.

11

Blessed Are They That Mourn

Something had gone terribly wrong. After having won its first major military victory, the general had led his army confidently against their next military objective, which was far weaker than their first opponent had been, but they had been repulsed. No, not just repulsed—they had been routed! And now the army was totally demoralized. What was wrong?

Upon investigation, the general learned that one man had not followed orders about how they were to deal with captured property after that first great battle. Rather than destroying everything, that one man had saved a little bit of the wealth for himself, hiding it under his tent. *It's just a little bit; no one will know,* he reasoned.

But someone *did* know, and not only that one man but also the entire army suffered because of his disobedience. What should have been an easy victory became a crushing defeat.

Joshua 7:1 says, "But the children of Israel [as represented by the deed of the one man] committed a trespass in the accursed thing: for Achan…took of the accursed thing: and the anger of the Lord was kindled against the children of Israel."

One man sinned; an entire nation suffered. What might have been the result if the disobedience had been even more widespread?

But the general of the army, Joshua, fell on his face before the Lord and mourned for the sin of Israel that had brought upon them the Lord's anger and judgment (Josh. 7:6ff). When Achan was discovered as the source of the problem, he confessed his sin (7:20) and was punished (7:25–26). Then, because the nation had mourned for its sin, it again attacked the military objective, the city of Ai, and gained a great victory. And they learned a valuable lesson about mourning for sin.

Another example of a nation that mourned its sin and was spared by God was Nineveh. God used a reluctant Jonah to warn the city of its impending destruction as God's judgment against it.

"Yet forty days, and Nineveh shall be overthrown," Jonah preached to "that great city" (Jonah 3:2, 4). Immediately, the people then "believed God, and proclaimed a fast and put on sackcloth, from the greatest of them even to the least of them" in mourning for their sins (Jonah 3:5–9). And God spared them.

On the other hand, Sodom and Gomorrah also received God's warning and condemnation; yet, they refused to mourn for their sins. Rather, they continued ("wearied themselves") persistently and flagrantly in them (Gen. 19). And God "rained upon Sodom and upon Gomorrah brimstone and fire…." (Gen. 19:24).

Nowhere in Scripture do we find God's condemnation of a nation for its particular form of government or its economic system. We often find, however, His condemnation and judgment against nations for their immorality and idolatry. Breaking God's moral law and worshipping anything or anyone above Him (and those two evils go together) is a guarantee of God's judgment. The only way such a nation can escape God's judgment is for the people of that nation to be truly sorry and mournful for their sins. Only then will God turn away His wrath from them.

The United States today is courting disaster because we as a people do not mourn our sins; rather, like Sodom and Gomorrah, we relish our sin and immorality. We are daily compounding and multiplying our sins. As a nation, our hands are covered with the blood of millions of innocent children whom we've slain before they were born by the practice of abortion. We tolerate and even condone immoral behavior, including homosexuality, adultery, pedophilia, pornography, and other wickedness. We call evil good and good evil. We have forsaken the God of our forefathers and have embraced the gods of materialism, pleasure, sensuality, tolerance, and political correctness. In so doing, we are daring God to smite us in His wrath. And it *is* coming.

We have only one escape route—to mourn for our sins. Our responsibility as believers is to face our nation with its sins, to call sin exactly what God calls it (rather than excusing it as "mistakes" or "diseases"), and to warn the nation to "flee from the wrath to come." But we can't do that before we first mourn for our own sins as individuals.

God promised in 2 Chronicles 7:14, "If my people, which are called by my name, shall humble themselves, and pray, and seek my face, and turn from their wicked ways; then will I hear from heaven, and will forgive their sin, and will heal their land."

Although working to preserve political freedom and our representative republican form of government and to defend and protect our wonderful free enterprise economic system is commendable, the real root of our national problems is neither political nor economic. Rather, it is moral and spiritual. Only sincere mourning can solve that root problem. And we must first apply the cure individually before we can apply it nationally. The only way to receive the comfort and blessing of God is to mourn first.

Student Work

In this lesson, we consider the second B–attitude:

"Blessed are they that mourn: for they shall be comforted" (Matt. 5:4).

The Attitude

Derivation

The word *mourn* is a translation of the Greek word *penthos*, meaning "grief," or "a strong feeling of pain."

Explanation

Mourn does not mean to cry in a natural sense. Clearly, as it is used in Matthew 5:4, *mourn* has a spiritual meaning. The Lord did not have in mind the kind of mourning that one does when a loved one dies. Just as *poor in spirit* did not refer to financial poverty, so *mourn* in this verse has nothing to do with physical crying. All of the B–attitudes refer to a *spiritual attitude* rather than to a physical condition.

Definition

To mourn spiritually means

- to be sober and serious about the things of the Lord (as opposed to flippant and carefree),
- to be brokenhearted over one's sinfulness, and
- to be concerned about the spiritual condition of the world around us.
- What characterizes the man or woman who mourns in this sense? He or she is
- sorrowful but not morose (gloomy, sad looking),
- sorrowful but not miserable,
- serious but not solemn, and
- soberminded but not sullen (gloomy or resentfully silent).

The true Christian leader is never a man who has to fake either deep sadness or great joy. He is a sincere man who looks at life seriously; he contemplates it spiritually, seeing sin and its effects. He has a serious outlook on life, but because he sees the grace of God at work through all of the problems, he is at the same time full of "joy unspeakable and full of glory" (1 Peter 1:8).

Position

To mourn is the natural result of being poor in spirit. As we confront God (a step that is necessary to our being poor in spirit), we begin to see His holiness and, thus, our sinfulness and this sobering reality causes us to mourn. So mourning naturally follows from being poor in spirit.

The Example

Note the following three examples of mourning in spirit. We examine one example for each of the three facets of mourning.

Elisha—Sober And Serious About Living For Christ

Read 2 Kings 2:23–24. This account reveals an unusual event in the life of Elisha the prophet. The children's phrase *go up* referred to the fact that less than a week before Elijah the prophet (Elisha's teacher and mentor) had "gone up" to heaven in a chariot of fire. The children who spoke to Elisha obviously were making fun of that event.

What do we see in this story that shows us how serious Elisha was about the things of the Lord? ______________________________

____

Living for Christ is serious business and should never be spoken of lightly. It is the most serious business in the world, and we should treat it as such.

List four ways we can make light of the things of the Lord.

1. ____

____

2. ____

____

3. ____

____

4. ____

____

Isaiah And Paul—Brokenhearted Over One's Sinfulness

Read Isaiah 6:1–5. Isaiah had a vision of the Lord that not only made him holy in spirit but also made him mourn over his sinfulness.

What did he see in the Lord that made him realize his own sinfulness? ____________________

What one fact about himself gripped Isaiah's heart upon his seeing the Lord? ____________________

No fun and games exist at such a time! We must be brokenhearted over our sin rather than flippant about it.

Read Romans 7:15, 18, 24. How did Paul manifest a mourning spirit in these verses? ____________________

List five charges that Paul brought against himself in these verses.

1. ____________________

2. ____________________

3. ____________________

4. ____________________

5. ____________________

Jeremiah—Concerned About The Condition Of Society

Read Jeremiah 8:18–9:2. Jeremiah's people were in captivity and he could not sleep for hearing the "cry of the daughter of my people" as they cried, "Is not the Lord in Zion?" Jeremiah was griefstricken because of their condition.

What does he mean by verse 20? ______________________________

____

How do we see his mourning spirit in verse 21? ______________

____

How do we see his mourning spirit in 9:1? __________________

____

The Practical Application

No man will have a mourning spirit who does not first take the time to meditate on the Lord's holiness and greatness and then on his own personal sinfulness. A good practice for every man is to pause at the end of the day and meditate upon himself and his actions and attitudes throughout that day and then to ask himself, "What have I *done*, *said*, and *thought* during this day? How have I behaved?" If we engage in such self–evaluation regularly, we will become, like Paul, painfully aware of the principle of evil that lives within us. We will then discover that a war is raging in our being between the sinful flesh and the Holy Spirit and the new nature. Therefore, we will begin to hate the sin and mourn because of it.

Do you ever mourn over your own sinful condition? What most concerns you about your spiritual condition? ______________________

____

____

____

How serious are you about the things of the Lord? How serious are you about the spiritual condition of our world and of people in general? ___

____

____

What three things most concern you about our world?

1. ____
2. ____
3. ____

For how many people on your prayer list do you truly mourn? ________

How serious are you about living for the Lord? Are you serious enough…

- to have a prayer list of unsaved friends?
- to search your heart every night concerning your spiritual condition?
- to surrender all of your popularity, dating, and even marriage (if God required that of you)?
- to do whatever the Lord wants you to do, even going to the mission field if that's what he wants of you?
- to give your very best efforts in all of your school work and activities?
- to attend all of the church services regularly and faithfully?

According to this self–check, would you say that you have a mourning spirit? How would *the Lord* rate you on these issues?

The Promise

"Blessed [happy] are they that mourn…."

What a paradox! The world would say that this is impossible. "One can't be happy by mourning, but by *forgetting* those things that bring seriousness," says the world. "Let's eat, drink, and be merry! Don't dwell on those bad thoughts."

How can a mourner be happy? The man who truly mourns because of his sinful condition is going to repent; in fact, his mourning *is* repenting. As the person repents and confesses his sin, Christ removes the sin, and joy follows.

How do we see this truth in Romans 7:25? ______________________________

____

____

The man who mourns over the sinful condition of the world knows that Christ is coming back, and this realization brings him joy. As we mourn for lost souls, we will witness and experience a new kind of joy. What does Psalm 126:5 say about this truth? ______________________________

____

Do you know this kind of joy? If so, share it with someone who *doesn't* know it. If not, you'll find it only in Christ. Seek Him today!

Notes From The Teacher's Lesson

Mourning Is A Serious State Of Mind

A Seriousness About The Things ____________________

A Seriousness About One's ____________________

- Incomplete ____
  - Sorrow Over The Consequences Of Sin
  - Vain
  - Regret
  - Remorse
- Complete____________—Turning From Sin And ____________

A Seriousness About The ____________________ *Of The World*

A Happy State Of ____________________

How To Become A Mourner

Agree With God About ____________________

- Minimize The ________________ Of Sin.
- Magnify The ________________ Of Evil.
- Make No ________________ For The Flesh.

Identify The ________________________ Of Sin

Visualize The Spiritual ________________________ Of Sin

Stepping Toward Effective Leadership

- List specific practical ways in which you can practice the B–attitude of mourning.
- Using your Bible and a concordance, list Bible characters who exhibited this B–attitude. Beside each name, explain briefly how this B–attitude was evidenced in that person's life.
- List some common excuses that people give for being unfaithful to the Lord's house. Beside each excuse, tell whether it is legitimate. If it is not legitimate, what steps can one take to remove it as an excuse? Next, list your priorities in life. Where on that list does the church fit? Can you justify its position on your list?
- Explain how church attendance is a barometer of one's spiritual condition. How faithful are you to the services of the Lord's house? If everyone in the church had the same level of commitment to the church as you have, what would be the result?
- Explain the purpose and meaning of the Lord's Supper. What are the various elements of the service and what do they symbolize? What are the scriptural qualifications for participants in the Lord's supper? What is the warning for participating "unworthily"?
- Does your church practice "open" or "closed" communion? Why?
- Explain the purpose and meaning of baptism. What are the prerequisites for baptism? Have you been baptized? (If not, why not?)
- Make a list of *personal* sins for which you mourn. What are you doing to ensure that you are less likely to fall into each of those sins?

- Make a list of *national* sins for which you mourn. What can you as a Christian who is an American citizen do (a) to increase public awareness of and mourning for each of those sins, and (b) to ensure that the nation is no longer committing those sins?

12

Blessed Are The Meek

"Assert yourself!"

"Toot your own horn!"

"Stand up for your rights!"

"Don't get mad—get even!"

These statements and others like them represent the ways of the world. They appeal to the natural man in each of us. And under certain circumstances, they sound quite legitimate even for Christians. After all, if no one else will stick up for you or promote you, you have to do it yourself, right? You have to be able to give out as well as you take, right? If you don't, the world—even other Christians—will walk all over you, right?

As crazy as it might sound, no, these are *not* the ways to success. God's instructions for success in life send a totally contrary message.

> "[B]efore honor is humility" (Prov. 18:12).
>
> "Let another man praise thee, and not thine own mouth; a stranger, and not thine own lips" (Prov. 27:2).
>
> "[I]n lowliness of mind let each esteem other better than themselves" (Phil. 2:3).
>
> "Answer not a fool according to his folly, lest thou also be like unto him" (Prov. 26:4).

These are some of the paradoxes of Scripture. They represent the Scriptures' prescription for blessing—*be meek.*

Contrary to popular opinion and practice, meekness is *not* weakness. Rather, it is a good sign of great inner strength and godliness of character. And that is the topic of this lesson. Let's see just how we can gain God's blessing by cultivating this character trait.

Student Work

This lesson deals with the third B–attitude:

"Blessed are the meek: for they shall inherit the earth" (Matthew 5:5).

The Attitude

Derivation

Meekness comes from a Greek word meaning "gentle, kind, forgiving."

Definition

Meekness is an attitude toward oneself that reflects itself in a kind, generous, self–abasing attitude toward others.

Explanation

Meekness is a compound attitude; at least three attitudes combine to form meekness:

1. being poor in spirit;
2. having a mourning attitude; and
3. surrendering all rights, claims, privileges, and desires for the best interest of others.

A meek person sees himself as nothing and thinks of and treats others as being better than him. Perhaps the best definition of meekness is in Philippians 2:2–3: "Fulfill ye my joy, that ye be likeminded, having the same love, being of one accord, of one mind. Let nothing be done through strife or vainglory; but in lowliness of mind let each esteem other better than themselves."

Position

From what we've learned already, we can see clearly why this B–attitude is third. It is only logical that before one can be meek, he must be poor in spirit (i.e., realize that he is a vile, worthless sinner) and must mourn (i.e., be gravely concerned for and broken over his worthlessness). After one achieves these two attitudes, he is ready to add a third ingredient—surrender of his rights, privileges, and desires to God. "After all," he then reasons, "who am *I* to have any rights or privileges?" So the B–attitudes continue in a logical sequence. No one can be meek who is not first poor in spirit and mourning.

The Example

Abraham

Read Genesis 13:1–13. How do we see meekness in Abraham in this passage? ____

____

____

David

Read 1 Samuel 16:1–13. What right or privilege was David promised in this passage? ____

____

According to the passage, would David be aware that he was one day to be the king? _______________

Saul, aware of David's popularity, talents, and brilliance, sensed that David was his rival to the throne. Setting out with three thousand men, he sought to find and kill David.

Read 1 Samuel 24:1–22. How do we see the meekness of David in the way he treated Saul's evil? ____

____

____

____

____

____

Jesus

Read Matthew 26:47–54. How do we see the meekness of Christ in this passage? ____

____

____

The Practical Application

The overriding thought in this lesson is evident in the question "How do we treat people who mistreat and torment us?" It's easy to admire and love those who admire and love us, but the real test of meekness is in our attitude and treatment of those who constantly attack us.

Apply Philippians 2:2–4 to the following people.

- The student who has just told a lie about you (and has done so many times before) ____

  ____

- How did Christ handle a similar situation in Matthew 27:12–14? __

  ____

  ____

- The student who seems to delight in calling you a humiliating name

  ____

  ____

What, according to Romans 12:14, should be our response? ________
____

Read each of the following verses and state how the meek are to respond to those who mistreat us, bug us, rub us the wrong way, or act stupidly and immaturely.

1 Corinthians 6:7—________________________________
____

Galatians 6:1— ________________________________
____

Colossians 3:12— ________________________________
____

1 Thessalonians 5:14–15—________________________
____

1 Peter 2:21–23— ________________________________
____
____
____

Jude 9— ____
____
____

The Promise

Read the following verses and note what God promises to those who think of themselves as nothing and who think of their tormentors as better than themselves.

Psalm 37:11— ________________________________
____

Psalm 147:6— ____

____

Psalm 149:4— ____

____

(This means that the Lord will actually make you a more attractive person! Retaliators are *not* attractive! They are bitter, angry people.)

Isaiah 29:19— ____

____

The Attainment

How can one become meek? First, remember that we can never make ourselves meek! Nothing but the Holy Spirit can make us poor in spirit; make us mourn because of our sinfulness; produce in us this true, right view of self; and give us the very mind and love of Christ toward others.

Those of us who claim to be Christians necessarily claim that we have the Holy Spirit indwelling us. Therefore, we have no excuse for not being meek! The man who is lost has an excuse because meekness is impossible for him. But if we have the Holy Spirit indwelling us, we have no excuse for not being meek.

Meekness is not something that you and I *do*; it is a character trait that the Spirit produces in us. It is the direct fruit of the Spirit (Gal. 5:22–23). What must we do to get it? We must

- meditate upon this b–attitude,
- look at ourselves as we truly are,
- look at the Lord as He is,
- humble ourselves and confess with shame our utter smallness and sinfulness; and
- rid ourselves of pride, which resents our being belittled and mistreated.

In short, we must hate the self, which is the cause of all of our trouble, so that He who has bought us with His own blood may possess us fully.

Notes From The Teacher's Lesson

Meekness

The ____________________ Ways Of God And Man

- God's Way Is Contrary To ______________________________
- God's Way Is Contrary To ______________________________
- God's Way Is Contrary To ______________________________

The ____________________ Of Meekness

Categorized As An ______________________________________

Defined

- Meekness Is Being ________________________________.
- Meekness Is Being ________________________________
- Meekness Is ________________________ All Of Your Rights.

It Is Manifested In The Exercise Of _______________ Under Control

Compared

- A Soothing ______________________________________
- A Gentle ____
- A Broken ____

Meekness is the mild, gentle attitude that accepts God's dealings as good with unquestioning submission and is manifested in power under control.

Characteristics Of A Meek Man

- No ______________________________
- Not ______________________________
- Not ______________________________
- No Spirit Of ______________________________

Stepping Toward Effective Leadership

- List specific practical ways in which you can practice the B–attitude of being meek.
- Using your Bible and a concordance, list Bible characters who exhibited this B–attitude. Beside each name, explain briefly how this B–attitude was evidenced in that person's life.
- Numbers 12:3 states, "Moses was very meek, above all the men which were upon the face of the earth." Study the life characteristics of Moses and list the qualities that prove that "meekness is not weakness."
- The Scriptures contain many paradoxes such as those discussed in this lesson. List other examples of such paradoxes.
- Explain the difference between negative pride (e.g., pride that causes one to "look down the nose" at other people) and positive pride (e.g., taking pride in one's work or being proud to claim the name of Christ).
- How can one be sensitive to the needs and feelings of others without being sensitive to the hurts and slights that he or she experiences from others? How can one ensure that in trying not to be sensitive to wrongs committed against him he does not become so callous and "thick skinned" that he has no feelings at all?
- Whenever you are slighted or offended, what steps can you take to avoid falling to the temptation to retaliate? How can you apply these principles in your home situation? In your school or youth group?

13

Blessed Are The Hungry And Thirsty

Have you ever been hungry? Not just having "the munchies" or a gastronomic craving for a snack, but *real hunger?*

Most Americans do not know what real hunger is. We are so blessed materially that we say we're hungry when we are only late for a meal. But even more important is the fact that most Americans—including far too many Christians—do not experience *spiritual* hunger or thirst. We are starving ourselves to death spiritually. Many of us are suffering from spiritual anorexia nervosa.

The Old Testament prophet Amos predicted just such a day. He wrote, "Behold, the days come, saith the Lord God, that I will send a famine in the land, not a famine of bread, nor a thirst for water, but of hearing the words of the Lord" (Amos 8:11).

Although most Americans *say* that they still believe in God, think that religion is important in life, etc., they show by their daily lives that they just aren't hungry for God or His Word. Their actions show, however, that they *are* hungry for money, wealth, and pleasure. Even when they experience some hunger or thirst for spiritual things, they generally try to satisfy the hunger by eating "spiritual junk foods"—things that taste good and satisfy their ego but that lack any real spiritual value.

Christian bookstores encourage such poor spiritual diets by stocking more trinkets than books, and many of the few books they do stock offer more fluff than substance, more cotton candy than meat. Some Christian bookstores have a small corner with a few shelves of books, and the rest of the building is filled with WWJD merchandise, Precious Moments figurines, and contemporary Christian music. Many of the books offer a superficial covering of Christianity over a basic worldly philosophy of "do good to others—feel good about yourself." The hottest sellers are works of "Christian" fiction that contain a smattering of Bible information (and all too often *mis*information). The few people who still read end up reading books *about* the Bible rather than reading the Bible itself.

As a result, Christians are starving for the Word—but they don't even know it!

If a baby is alive, it naturally hungers for its mother's milk. As it receives that essential nourishment, it grows. With natural growth and development, the baby eventually reaches a point at which the mother's milk by itself no longer satisfies the hunger pangs; the child demands semisolid food. Eventually, the child progresses naturally to the eating of meat and vegetables and other solid foods, just like normal adults. If the baby or the child does not make this natural progression of diet, the parents and doctors know that something is wrong, and they take corrective measures.

The same is true spiritually. The "newborn babe" (new believer) craves "the sincere milk of the word" (1 Peter 2:2), but as he or she grows and develops spiritually, such basics no longer meet the needs, at which point he or she begins to devour the deeper things of the Lord. As this normal spiritual development continues, the believer eventually is eating the meat, the deepest truths of Scripture. If one does not see this natural spiritual progression—especially if he does not see any signs of hunger or thirst—he knows that something is seriously wrong and corrective measures must be taken.

Do you hunger and thirst for the things of God? If so, are you content to feed on spiritual junk food, or are you craving the "milk of the word" and developing a growing taste for spiritual meat? If you *don't* hunger or thirst for spiritual things, you'd better examine yourself to see if you're even alive spiritually! Only corpses don't need food!

Let's examine the role of hunger and thirst in the life of a believer in this lesson.

Student Work

The fourth B–attitude states,

"Blessed are they which do hunger and thirst after righteousness: for they shall be filled" (Matthew 5:6).

The Attitude

Definition

To hunger and thirst after righteousness is to have a deep desire to be rid of sin and to be filled with the Holy Spirit.

The word *righteousness* in this verse does not mean salvation; it means freedom from sin and holiness toward God. *Hunger and thirst* means…

- a deep longing and aching,
- a consciousness of our desperate need, and
- something that keeps on until it is satisfied.

It is like actual physical hunger and thirst. It goes on increasing, making one feel desperate to satisfy it.

Explanation

Therefore, to hunger and thirst after righteousness means that one is acutely aware of his filthiness and unworthiness before God and, as such, he aches to be holy and pure before that God. He longs to be as righteous as Christ. His greatest desire in life is not for happiness, fun, comfort, money, or new cars. Rather, he wants to be rid of his filthiness and in perfect fellowship with his God.

Position

Again, the logical order of this B–attitude among the other B–attitudes is obvious. Earlier, we saw man's sinfulness. We considered his terrible problem of self—self–concern, self–reliance, self–interest, and self–centeredness. We considered how we should bemoan, regret, and hate our sinfulness. This, in turn, produces a meek spirit that realizes that we deserve no rights and privileges.

The fourth B–attitude introduces a slight change in approach. Having looked at ourselves somewhat negatively in the first three B–attitudes, our eyes now turn to a positive solution. We find our hearts crying out, "Oh, that I might be like God!"

The Example—David

How did David express this B–attitude in Psalm 42:1? ______________

____

Read Psalm 42:1–6. For each of the following three characteristics, write down what David had to say about them.

Poor In Spirit

____

____

____

____

Mourning

____

____

____

Hungering And Thirsting

____

____

____

____

The Practical Application

The important thought in this lesson is *being* rather than *knowing*. The issue is not whether you hunger for *knowledge* but whether you hunger *to be righteous*. As you have studied these lessons on the B–attitudes, have you just learned *about* the B–attitudes, or have you developed a longing to *have* them in your life?

Let's consider our appetites for a minute. What do you most like to do? What are your priorities in life?

List approximately how much time (in minutes or hours) you spend *per day* in each of the following activities:

_____Watching TV

_____Playing sports (including both practice time and actual games)

_____Goofing off with friends

_____Reading God's Word

_____Meditating on God and spiritual matters

_____Praying

_____Reading

_____Pursuing a hobby

_____Playing video games

_____Shopping

_____Listening to radio, tapes, or CDs

According to the time spent in each of the preceding activities, are you hungering and thirsting for your own happiness and pleasure or for righteousness? In your Bible class, have you found yourself longing to be poor in spirit, mourning, and meek, or have you just learned the *facts about* these three attitudes? Has any change occurred in your life since you began this series of studies, or have you just learned more facts to no practical effect?

The important thing to remember in this lesson is that *this year's study has not been designed to teach facts but to change lives!* Is it working out that way, or are you just learning the facts?

Think about it. You can *be* a leader. You can *be* a Christian with character. You can *be* mature. You can *be* the man with these attitudes.

Too often, however, we just look at these fine qualities as academic facts that we should *know*. We get the idea that we are just studying these lessons so that we will know *about* leadership and Christian character. Instead, we should be studying so that we can *be* Christian leaders with character.

The Promise

What does God promise the man who hungers and thirsts to be righteous? ____________________

What do you think that means? ____________________

How does Psalm 37:4 apply here? ____________________

The "filling" that is promised could indicate being filled with the Spirit. To be filled with the Spirit, a person must

- see himself as he really is (note the first three B–attitudes);
- confess his sin; and
- cry out to God to be filled with the Spirit presenting each part of his body to God for that filling.

The Attainment

How can we become hungry and thirsty for righteousness? The teacher's outline lists seven tests. Memorize them, but don't stop at that—*do them!* These lessons are to be lived, not merely learned. You live them by

- becoming poor in spirit,
- becoming mournful,
- becoming meek,
- avoiding everything that opposes righteousness,
- avoiding everything that tends to dull your appetite for righteousness,

- being faithful in church,
- praying for righteousness, and
- presenting each part of your body for filling by the Holy Spirit.

The important thing in the Christian life is to focus on *inward development,* not on just *outward conformity.*

Notes From The Teacher's Lesson

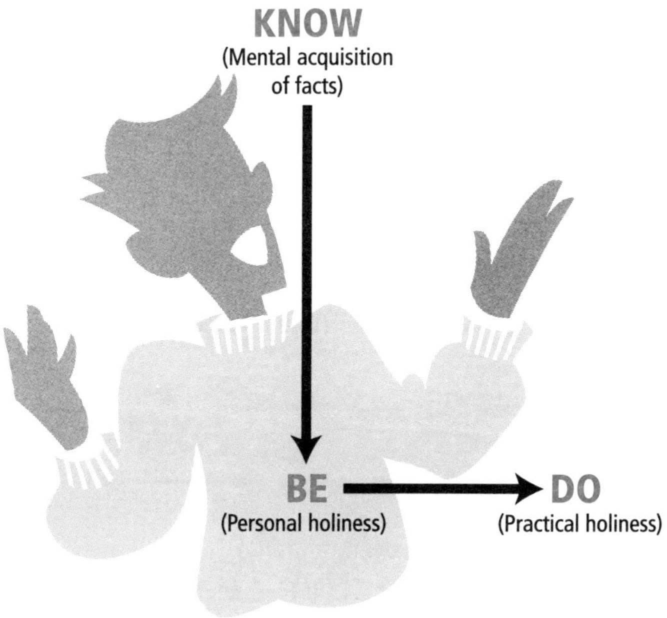

Hunger And Thirst For Righteousness

My only reason for ______________________ is that I might _______ so I can __________.

The Hunger Of The Unbeliever Is For ______________________ Things To Satisfy The Natural Thirst For God

The Hunger Of The Believer Is For _______________ To Satisfy Its Thirst

Satisfying The Hunger For Righteousness

- Love Him
- Know Him

  - Through His ______________________________________
  - Through ____

Testing For Hunger

- You Will Be ______________________________________
- You Will Be ______________________________________
- You Will Be ______________________________________
- You Will Avoid Everything Opposed to ________________
- You Will Avoid Anything That Tends To ______________
- You Will Be Faithful In ____________________________
- You Will Pray For _________________________________

Stepping Toward Effective Leadership

- List specific practical ways in which you can practice the B–attitude of hungering and thirsting for righteousness.

- Using your Bible and a concordance, list Bible characters who exhibited this B–attitude. Beside each name, explain briefly how this B–attitude was evidenced in that person's life.

- Define the physical ailment known as *anorexia nervosa.* How could the characteristics of the physical ailment parallel Christians that are spiritually starving? Suggest a proper treatment for this spiritual malady.

- Conduct a survey of your local Christian bookstore (or more than one if you have access to multiple Christian bookstores in your community). Approximately what percentage of the space is devoted to books? Of the books available, how many would you estimate focus on *self?* List the types of "trinkets" offered for sale. What types of music (i.e., traditional, gospel–country, or contemporary) have the most space? Overall, would you say that the bookstore sells primarily "fluff" or substance?

- Read and summarize the lessons of *Spiritual Intimacy* by Richard Mayhue.

- Read and summarize the lessons of *A Passionate Pursuit of God* by Tim Ritter.

- Read and summarize the lessons of *The Pursuit of God* by A. W. Tozer.

- If you have time to read all three of the preceding books, on what principles do they all agree? What principles does each offer that the other two do not mention? Why do you think that is so?

14

Blessed Are The Merciful

How you respond to someone who has wronged you and you have the upper hand in the situation reveals a lot about you. You could choose to get revenge, to give the other person exactly what they deserve, to exact the full penalty of the law. But is that the Christian response? No. We're to show mercy to others because God is merciful to us. God in mercy did not give us the punishment we do deserve; rather, He has given us numerous blessings that we did not deserve. We are to "recompense to no man evil for evil" (Rom. 12:17).

Does that mean that we as a society and nation are to let criminals and evil–doers "off the hook?" No, the Bible teaches that our rulers are to enforce the laws. They are to be a terror to evil–doers, using the force of the law, including the threat of punishment—even capital punishment, in some cases—to maintain civil peace and ensure justice. The ruler is "the minister of God, a revenger to execute wrath upon him that doeth evil" (Rom. 13:4). Clearly, the command to show mercy is for the individual, not for civil government.

In our dealings with others, we should demonstrate the attitude expressed in the following lines by English poet Alexander Pope:

> "Teach me to feel another's woe, to hide the fault I see;
> "That mercy I to others show, that mercy show to me."

Student Work

Lesson 9 referred to the B–attitudes as consisting of seven attitudes and one action. This fifth B–attitude is that action. Although we will refer to it primarily as an action, it is still an attitude. It could best be described as *an action that results from a right attitude.* The fifth B–attitude states,

"Blessed are the merciful: for they shall obtain mercy" (Matthew 5:6).

The Attitude

Definition

A general definition of *mercy* is given in the teacher's lesson. Here we look at the *practical* definition of being merciful.

What does it mean to be merciful? Is it an action, an attitude, or a combination of the two? Mercy is actually a combination in the following sense:

- it is an *attitude* of *pity* toward those who have personal problems,
- it is a *desire to relieve* the suffering and problems seen in others, and
- it is an *action bent on relieving* the suffering and problems of others.

Explanation

Mercy is thus seen as both an attitude and an action toward people with problems. It sees a problem beyond the loud, obnoxious personality. It sees a need beyond the lying tongue. It sees a troubled person beyond the ridiculing mocker. It has pity on the person in need. It wants to relieve the need and sets in motion actions designed to help the person.

Mercy is not an easy–going attitude. Some people mistake mercy for an easy–going disposition. Just because a person is easygoing does not mean that he or she is merciful. We have already learned that none of the B–attitudes is neutral. No one is born with these attitudes. Therefore, the person who is born with an easy–going temperament is not necessarily merciful.

Neither is mercy a flippant disregard of the law. Mercy does not overrule justice. Some people oppose capital punishment and would let all criminals off without punishment under the guise of mercy. *True mercy,* however, *never excludes justice.* God is merciful, but God also punishes the lawbreaker.

Position

- Again, the logical order of these B–attitudes is evident. You cannot have this fifth attitude until you have the other four that were listed before it. In fact, the first four attitudes help produce this fifth attitude.
- First, I am poor in spirit, I realize that I am nothing when compared with God. I see my filthiness and sinfulness. I feel worthless before a great and holy God.
- Second, seeing my condition, I mourn and cry, "O wretched man that I am! Who shall deliver me?!"
- Third, in meekness, I realize that I have no rights; I have surrendered them all to Christ. I consider others to be better than me.
- Fourth, I long to be rid of my sin and to be holy. I hunger and thirst to be like Christ. At that point, I am filled with the Holy Spirit. The result is manifested in the fifth B–attitude.

Fifth, I see other people differently; I see them as myself. How does Galatians 6:1–3 fit in here? ______

I now see that those who mistreat me are victims of the flesh. They are not simply men whom I dislike but men who are to be pitied. I want to help them overcome their problems.

The Example

The Good Samaritan

How do we see this attitude and action in the story of the Good Samaritan in Luke 10:30–36?

- An *attitude* of pity for a man's problem—____________________

- An *action* bent on relieving the problem—____________________

Christ

Luke 23:27–43 records three events on Christ's final day that display the three aspects of mercy. Match the three aspects with the events in this passage.

- Pity for other people's problems rather than His own— ____________

- A desire to relieve the problems of those who opposed Him—________

- An action bent on relieving someone's misery and suffering— ________

The Practical Application

- How does a merciful Christian react in the following situations?
  - A person calls you a fool— ____________________
  - A person constantly teases you with evil intent— ____________

A person who has made fun of you makes a bad public mistake (see Job 31:28–30— ______________________________

____

People act as they do because of inward problems and conflicts. Remember, the gospel places its primary emphasis upon *being* rather than *doing. Attitude* is more important than *action*; *attitude governs actions.* A Christian *is* something before he *does* something. Thus, right responses to mistreatment are the result of what you really are deep down inside. This same truth makes clear that individuals who mistreat others have at the root of their actions serious inward problems. Therefore, we must look beyond a man's actions to his real problem.

What is the probable root problem for each of the following people?

- A person who constantly tells lies about you or others— ______________________________
- A person who continually makes fun of you— ______________________________
- A person who constantly brags— ______________________________
- A person who is loud and overbearing— ______________________________

How does a merciful Christian treat such people? ______________________________

____

Why is this the Christian response? ______________________________

____

What is true of a Christian who does *not* see the deeper needs of those who mistreat him? ______________________________

____

The Attainment

How can one become merciful?

- First, by achieving the four previous attitudes! If you have not gained the first four attitudes, you cannot suddenly have a merciful attitude. These attitudes must come in order.

- Second, you must realize that people's problems and obnoxious ways are the result of their inner needs.

- Third, you must pray for them, asking God to forgive them and help them. (This prayer must be sincere; it cannot be forced or impious.)

- Fourth, you must show them all of the kindness possible.

Consider the following verses on this issue, and write out what each says about the subject:

Romans 12:18–21— ______________________________

____

____

Matthew 5:44— ________________________________

____

____

Remember, you can *act mercifully* but you cannot *be merciful* until you have all five attitudes within.

The Promise

"They shall obtain mercy" does not mean that God will save those who are merciful. Some people have taken this verse to show the way of salvation—that if we are to be forgiven of our sin, we must have a forgiving spirit. Such is *not* the case. The promise of this B–attitude has to do with *fellowship*, not *relationship* (salvation). If, when you sin, you see it and in repentance go to God and confess your sin, and there on your knees you realize that you have not forgiven someone else, you will have no confidence in your prayers. You will realize, as did David in Psalm 66:18, "If I regard iniquity in my heart, the Lord *will not hear me.*"

If you despise your brother or sister in Christ, you can ask God for forgiveness, but you will have no confidence in your prayers, and your prayers will not be answered. That is what this promise means. Only the merciful can confess their sins with confidence.

Notes From The Teacher's Lesson

Blessed Are The Merciful

God's Mercy To Us

- Mercy is not getting what you ______________________________.
- It Is ______________________ (Isa. 43:25; Ps. 103:12)
- It Is ______________________ (Ps. 103:3)
- It Is ______________________ (Heb. 8:12, 10:17)

Our Mercy Toward Others

You cannot extend mercy (forgiveness) to others until you have yourself received mercy (forgiveness).

The Principle In __________________________ (Mt. 18)

The Principle In __________________________ (Mt. 6:5–15)

The Principle In __________________________

- Stephen (Acts 7:60)
- Christ (Luke 23:34)

The Principle In ________________________ (Gen. 50:20)

The key to forgiveness is seeing the offender as an instrument of God in your life.

- Discover What Made The Relationship ________________
- Confess The ______________________________ To God
- Forgive The Other ______________________________
- Ask Forgiveness Of The ____________________________
- Make Up For Any __________ That You Wronged The Person

Stepping Toward Effective Leadership

- List specific practical ways in which you can practice the B–attitude of being merciful.
- Using your Bible and a concordance, list Bible characters who exhibited this B–attitude. Beside each name, explain briefly how this B–attitude was evidenced in that person's life.
- Explain the following quotation by Chrysostom, an early Christian Father: "Mercy imitates God and disappoints Satan."
- How does God temper justice with mercy in His dealings with His children? What does that teach you about your dealings with other Christians?
- How does the "Golden Rule" (see Matt. 7:12) reflect the principle of mercy?
- In Romans 12:1—where Paul tells us to "present your bodies a living sacrifice, holy, acceptable unto God, which is your reasonable service"—what did he mean when he prefaced that command with the words *by the mercies of God?*

15

Blessed Are The Pure In Heart

Some people think that when Christ fulfilled the law He did away with it, ushering in a new era in which believers have license to do whatever they please. Whenever anyone takes them to task for some alleged questionable action or behavior, they typically respond, "But we're under grace, not under the law, so I'm not doing anything wrong."

In reality, Christ stated in Matthew 5:17, "Think not that I am come to destroy the law, or the prophets: I am not come to destroy, but to fulfill.

In fact, rather than doing away with the standard for our behavior, Christ *raised* that standard even higher! He said that we should be concerned with more than an overt action of wickedness; we must also be concerned with the inner thoughts or attitudes that produce such evil actions.

"Ye have heard that it was said by them of old time, Thou shalt not commit adultery," Christ said. "But I say unto you, That whosoever looketh on a woman to lust after her hath committed adultery with her already *in his heart*" (Matt. 5:27–28, emphasis added).

Purity of actions is important for Christians, but purity of heart is even more critical. Keep this thought in mind as we study the following lesson on purity of heart and how to acquire it.

Student Work

We come now to the sixth B–attitude:

"Blessed are the pure in heart: for they shall see God" (Matthew 5:8).

The Attitude

Definition

Before we can understand this attitude fully, we must understand the meaning of several words in the verse.

Heart

The word *heart* here refers not to the organ that pumps blood through our veins but to the very center of our personality, the center of our being. The heart is the "real you." It is what you *are*; it is your character.

Pure

The word *pure* has a twofold meaning. First, it means "without hypocrisy, unmixed." It means single, as opposed to double.

✎ Matthew 6:22 speaks of the righteous person as having what kind of an eye? ______________________________

The next verse contrasts this kind of eye with the evil eye. So the singleness of soul corresponds to pureness of heart. You could say that it means "without folds"; it is open, hiding nothing. You can describe it as sincerity; being singleminded.

✎ Psalm 86:11 records that David's prayer had what kind of heart? ___
____

Such a heart is not divided. Isn't this one of the big problems we face? One part of us wants to know God and live for Him, but another part of us wants to please the world. We need a united heart, or a single eye. That is one meaning of *pure*.

The second meaning of *pure* is "cleansed, washed, without sin." According to Revelation 21:27, what is the only kind of person who will enter the New Jerusalem? ____________________

____

____

Therefore, *pure* is closely related to the word *holiness*. Just as Matthew 5:8 says that we must be pure to "see God," what do we read in Hebrews 12:14? ____________________

____

____

See

Does this verse mean that unless we are pure we will not be able to see God literally with our physical eyes? Or does the word *see* refer to seeing God indirectly, that is, by faith, seeing God through nature, the events in history, and God's working in our lives? ____________________

____

____

In all probability, both meanings are intended. First, unless a man is made pure by the blood of Christ, he will never see God literally in heaven. Second, as we become pure in character, motive, thought, and will (i.e., pure within), we will see God indirectly as He moves and works mightily in our lives.

Explanation

To be pure in heart includes two ideas as seen in the two types of seeing and the two definitions of *pure*.

Salvation

Pure relates to *salvation*. That is, I am washed, cleansed, and without sin in the sight of God through the blood of Christ. This condition is necessary for one to see God literally.

Pure also relates to inward *sanctification.* That is, I am without hypocrisy, and I am single in the sense that I have but one inner desire to please the Lord. Only through this kind of purity can I see God's mighty hand working in my life. This second kind of purity is the one on which this lesson focuses.

Position

This B–attitude is the sixth one in the sequence of Christ's sermon. Why does it come at this point? Perhaps we can see it best in the following diagram.

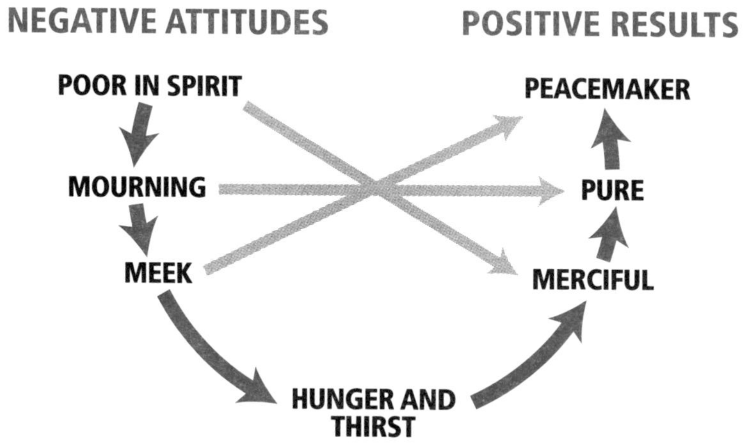

In the first three attitudes, we progress downward as we see ourselves as we really are. We finally reach the "end of our rope" with the fourth attitude. At that point, we begin to long for righteousness. We now want to know the power of God in our lives. From this point, we begin to rise (spiritually) as we become merciful, pure, and a peacemaker. The first three B–attitudes are concerned with negative aspects of our self, the fourth attitude is the turning point, and the next three attitudes are positive results of being "filled."

The interesting point is that "merciful" corresponds to "poor in spirit," "purity" corresponds to "mourning," and "peacemaking" corresponds to "meekness." Thus, as we are filled with the Spirit, we become merciful. (How else could one act who is poor in spirit?) Next, we become pure in heart (which is the direct result of mourning over our spiritual condition). Then, we act as a peacemaker because we are meek in our attitude toward others.

Thus, we see a divine order in the B–attitudes. You cannot possibly have the last three attitudes until you first develop the first three attitudes.

The Example

An amazing Bible fact is that no sin is recorded anywhere in Scripture against Daniel! Of course, we know that because he was human he must have sinned because 1 John 1:10 says, "If we say that we have ________ ____________________, we make him a liar and his word is not in us." So Daniel surely sinned. However, he evidently had a pure heart filled with pure motives. In other words, his character was pure. How do we see this fact in Daniel 1:8? ____________________

Read the rest of the story in Daniel 1:8–21. Did Daniel live up to his pure purposes? *Yes*____________________

What was the result? ____________________

As a result, Daniel saw the Lord through what great events in the following chapters of Daniel (specifically chapters two and six)? ____________

Needless to say, Daniel's promotion in a foreign land, his ability to understand and interpret dreams, and his vision of the seventy weeks (Daniel 9) were the direct result of his having a pure heart.

The Practical Application

Being pure in heart is not the same as being pure in outward actions. What men in the Bible were pure outwardly but were filthy inwardly (see Matthew 23:25, 27, 28)? ______________________________

How were they described outwardly? ______________________________

____

____

How were they described inwardly? ______________________________

____

____

From their bad example, we learn a great lesson. It is possible to do all of the *right* things (e.g., be saved, witness, read the Bible, be baptized, go to church faithfully, and tithe) and it is possible *not* to do all of the *wrong* things (e.g., dance, smoke, take drugs, drink alcohol, or curse) and still be filthy on the inside!

Remember the teacher's lesson on knowing, doing, and being? With which of these three are the B–attitudes concerned?______________

Consider the following questions about your inner being.

- How pure are your thoughts?
- What is the *real* reason you go to church?
- Why do you refrain from certain sins?
- What is your primary goal in life and the greatest desire of your life?
- Can you honestly say that you have a single, or united heart, or do you find yourself with mixed desires?

Is the Christian life essentially composed of positive ingredients such as Bible reading, prayer, witnessing, going to church, and tithing and the negative ingredients of separation of self from the world, the flesh, and the devil? Or does the Christian life also include the development of strong character within? ______________________________

____

On which have you focused your efforts—outward conformity to what a Christian is expected to *do* or inward development of what a Christian should *be?*

Remember: you must have *both* outward conformity *and* inward conformity to please God.

Notes From The Teacher's Lesson

The Pure In Heart

Three Kinds Of Purity

- Positional Purity—Our ______________________________
- Practical Purity—Our ______________________________
- Personal Purity—Our ______________________________

Definitions

- Heart—*kardia*, the inner man, or the master control center.
- Pure—*katharos*, to cleanse from filth or unmixed.

Purity Characterized

- Inner ____________________ To Sin
- Pursuit Of ____________________
- Pure ____________________

Acquiring A Pure Heart

- Often Look Into ____________________
- Receive Daily ____________________ Of Sin
- Allow The ____________________ To Work
- Walk With Those Who Are ____________________

Stepping Toward Effective Leadership

- List specific practical ways in which you can practice the B–attitude of being pure in heart.
- Using your Bible and a concordance, list Bible characters who exhibited this B–attitude. Beside each name, explain briefly how this B–attitude was evidenced in that person's life.
- Purity of heart will translate into purity of actions. Explain why this is true.
- Purity of actions includes personal and ecclesiastical separation. Using Scripture support, explain the proper Christian view for each of the following forms of separation: (a) separation from the world system, (b) separation from unbelievers, and (c) separation from erring or compromising believers.
- How can one *practically* "hate the sin but love the sinner"?
- Explain how the statement "Association begets assimilation" applies to your life.
- Read and summarize the truths shared in chapter twelve ("Companions") of R. A. Torrey's book *How to Succeed in the Christian Life.*
- Read and summarize what Ernest Pickering said about separation in *Biblical Separation: The Struggle for a Pure Church.*

16

Blessed Are The Peacemakers

In the Christian film *Truce in the Forest,* two military patrols—one American and one German—are separated from their main units and lost in the forest on Christmas Eve during the Battle of the Bulge. They have fired upon each other in one brief encounter, and one of the American soldiers has been shot and is in danger of dying unless he gets medical attention soon. The German patrol is more interested in getting back to their own lines than in pursuing the U. S. troops, but they need shelter from the steadily deteriorating weather.

The American patrol stumbles onto a tiny cottage in a small clearing. When they knock at the door, they are greeted by a widow and her young daughter who speak no English. Through signs and an occasional German word, however, the Americans explain their predicament, and the woman offers the soldiers shelter and invites them to join them in a Christmas Eve meal.

They are about to be seated at the table when a knock at the door startles them. The U. S. soldiers hide while the widow opens the door and goes outside. The German patrol has also found the cottage and asks for shelter. The tension rises as the Americans anticipate a close–quarters gun battle and the widow debates what to do. By helping the Americans she was already guilty of giving aid to the enemy—a capital offense! Finally, she tells the Germans that she has other guests whom they might not like, but she convinces them to stack their weapons outside. Reentering the cottage, she persuades the Americans to surrender their guns as well.

The Germans enter the cottage and, in a tense and awkward moment, sit down with their enemies, the American soldiers, for the Christmas Eve meal. During the meal, the wounded American screams in pain. One of the Germans reveals that he was a medical student in the United States before the outbreak of the war, and he offers to treat the soldier. He does so as the widow, her daughter, and the other soldiers sing Christmas carols, each patrol in its own language.

By the end of the film, the soldiers have gained a new respect for each other. Comparing notes, they help each other calculate the way back to their respective lines and part as friends rather than as enemies. The widow and her daughter have become peacemakers—at least for those two small groups of soldiers in that tiny, isolated part of the world in the midst of a terrible battle.

Believers are called upon to be peacemakers in the spiritual war that rages around us. First, we are each to make our own peace with God by receiving His gift of salvation through faith in His Son, Jesus Christ. Second, we are to help lead others to this peace by introducing them to the Prince of Peace. And third, we are to work to make peace between believers who are in conflict.

This role of peacemaker is far more important than that performed by the widow and her daughter in *Truce in the Forest*; it carries eternal consequences and includes a promise of God's blessing. Let's examine that role in the following lesson.

Student Work

We now come to the seventh B–attitude:

"Blessed are the peacemakers: for they shall be called the children of God" (Matthew 5:9).

The Attitude

Definition

A peacemaker is one who actively makes peace between opposing parties.

Explanation

To understand this lesson, we must differentiate between a peace*keeper* and a peace*maker*. A peace*keeper* is

- an easy–going person who seldom gets aroused;
- a compromiser who will do anything to keep people from getting upset with him; or
- an appeaser who pets, pampers, and pats everybody on the back.

He is like thick molasses or dripping honey. He does anything to avoid conflict.

A peace*maker*, however, is a person who *actively seeks to make true peace* between warring parties. First, he wants to see every man at peace with God. Then he seeks to settle hurt feelings and jealousies and arguments between bickering Christians. He joins no sides and does nothing to add fuel to the fire. Above all, he prays daily for those who are at odds with him or others.

Position

This B–attitude comes seventh in Christ's sermon because ultimately it is the product of the other six B–attitudes. We could look at the B–attitudes as falling into the following categories:

- Forget self: poor in spirit, mourn, meek;
- Desire righteousness: hunger and thirst for righteousness; and
- Concern for others: merciful, pure, peacemaker.

The first three B–attitudes deal with self and teach us to forget ourselves. What causes the most arguments, quarrels, and fights? Aren't they caused most often because we look at only what affects us rather than thinking of how things affect others? We wonder, "What is this going to mean to *me?*" "Am *I* getting a fair shake?" "Is he getting something more than *I'm* getting?"

That is the spirit that always leads to quarrels, disputes, gossip, and divisions. But the peacemaker has forgotten himself. He has become poor in spirit and thinks that his miserable, wretched self is not worth bothering about at all; he seeks, instead, to focus on the needs and problems of others.

Next, the peacemaker has developed an internal longing for righteousness. He no longer is as concerned with outward praise or glory. He wants only true holiness and conformity within.

Finally, the peacemaker has become concerned for others. As you can see, being merciful and pure in heart and peacemaking have to do with one's attitude toward others. Therefore, a peacemaker no longer talks about people who are offensive to him. He is concerned about them, and he wants to help them. When he sees jealousies, vengeful acts, bickering, and taking of sides, he stands solidly in the middle and seeks to reconcile both parties.

The Example

Read Colossians 1:20–22; Ephesians 2:14–16; and Romans 5:10 to answer the following questions.

Who was the greatest example of a peacemaker in the Bible? ______

____

Who were the two warring parties involved? ________________

What did He do to make peace? ______________________

____

(Note: *reconcile* means "to bring back into harmony.")

What is He called in Isaiah 9:6? ______________________

Practical Application

From the preceding information, does the peacemaker ever take sides and criticize the other party? ________ Do you ever find yourself taking sides with someone who has been wronged and find yourself criticizing the guilty party?

Does the peacemaker ever say, "That's not fair"? _______ Do you ever accuse teachers, referees, or parents of being unfair? Why does the peacemaker never yell, "Cheater" or "That's not fair"? What has happened to him that takes away that attitude? ______________________________

____

____

If you still find yourself looking out for your rights and yelling, "Unfair!" or "Cheater!" what does that then show about your attitudes? __________

____

____

The Promise

What promise is made to peacemakers? ______________________________

____

That is the one true characteristic in a child of God that so impresses the unsaved that they are convinced that we are God's children. We are not to be mushy, mealy–mouthed peace*keepers* but active peace*makers.* When unbelievers see Christians stop taking sides, forming cliques, criticizing their brothers, and splitting up over selfish offenses, they will begin to recognize us as God's children. Then we will have the greatest honor anyone can have—being called God's child.

Characteristics Of The Peacemaker

What are the characteristics of a true peacemaker? He evidences at least four characteristics. (These characteristics are the practical applications of the three general characteristics given in the teacher's lesson.)

He Has Learned Not To Speak

What does James 1:19 say about this point? ______________________________

____

In contrast, most of us are always determined to get in the last word! We have to say something smart back to the person who just blasted us. If we are peacemakers, however, not only do we refuse to speak back but also to repeat things that we know are harmful to others.

For example, when someone tells something on your best friend, what do you do? Do you run and tell your best friend? Is that true peacemaking? Of course not!

Remember, you are not a true friend when you tell your friend something unkind that was said about him. The peacemaker might feel like saying things, but for the sake of peace he does not. What does Proverbs 29:11 say about the Christian who brags, "I must express my mind; I don't keep anything in. I believe in telling it like it is"? ______________________

____

____

According to Proverbs 17:28, how will this same man be considered if he keeps his mouth shut? ______________________________

____

He Looks At Every Situation In The Light Of The Effect It Will Have On Christ And His Cause

Before he speaks or acts, the peacemaker thinks. He considers the effect that his comments will have for good or ill upon the cause of Christ.

He Looks Actively For Ways To Make Peace

What does Matthew 5:23–24 say that we should do to a Christian who has something against us? ______________________________

____

If, instead of doing that, we talk about him and pout because we know that he is unjustly criticizing us, are we being a peacemaker? __________ According to Matthew 18:15, if a friend actually mistreats you, what are you to do? ______________________________________

____

- According to Luke 17:4, what should we do to the fellow who continually torments us, and as soon as he repents, does it again—over and over?

  ____

He Spreads Peace Wherever He Goes

We do this by being selfless, lovable, approachable, friendly, and honest. Because self is forgotten, there is no sharp tongue. Because we are selfless, people feel at ease around us because they sense that we are genuinely interested in them.

How do you rate as a peacemaker?

Notes From The Teacher's Lesson

Blessed Are The Peacemakers

The ______________ Of Peace

- Not The Absence Of ______________
- Not A ______________

The ______________ Of Peace

- God Is The ______________ Of Peace (1 Cor. 14:33)
- Christ Is The ______________ Of Peace (Isa. 9:6)

The ______________ To Peace

- Selfishness ______________ (Jms. 4:1–2)
- Satan's ______________ (Jms. 3:14–16)

The ______________ Of Peace

- Make Peace ______________ Yourself
- Help Others Make Peace ______________
- Make Peace ______________; Bring Them Together

Stepping Toward Effective Leadership

- List specific practical ways in which you can practice the B–attitude of being a peacemaker.

- Using your Bible and a concordance, list Bible characters who exhibited this B–attitude. Beside each name, explain briefly how this B–attitude was evidenced in that person's life.

- Read of one family's opportunities to practice peacemaking in *Twelve–Part Harmony* by Pat and Jill Williams.

- List the lessons about peacemaking that you learn by reading Henry A. Virkler's book *Speaking Your Mind without Stepping on Toes.*

- Second Corinthians 5:20 says, "We are ambassadors for Christ...." In the diplomatic services, an ambassador must sometimes be a peacemaker between his own country and the country to which he is ambassador or a mediator for two other countries. Conduct a quick study of diplomacy and draw an analogy between an ambassador as peacemaker and the Christian as peacemaker.

HOLY

17

Blessed Are They Who Are Persecuted

The family and several of their friends drove several hours to hear the famous foreign pastor. He had hardly begun to speak when he asked all of the women and girls to leave the auditorium for a few minutes. After the last female had exited the room and the door had closed behind her, the speaker removed his suit coat and shirt. Turning around, he revealed his bare back to all of the men and boys in the room.

A collective gasp escaped from the male audience. The speaker's back was covered with numerous long and ugly scars incurred during his nearly fourteen years of imprisonment and torture by the Communists of Romania. He proceeded to describe in detail the horrors that he had experienced at their atheistic hands. Only then did the men present understand why he had sent the females from the room.

That speaker was Richard Wurmbrand, who was born in Bucharest, Romania, on March 24, 1909. He was arrested several times by the Nazis, who controlled Romania during World War II. He began an underground ministry to Russian prisoners of war who were being held in Romania.

Toward the end of the war, Soviet soldiers overran the country. After the war, the Communists retained control of Romania, and they hated Wurmbrand's work even more than had the Nazis. Romanian authorities kidnapped him in February 1948 and subjected him to brainwashing, threats against his family, and physical and mental torture. During that time, his wife, Sabina, was also arrested and forced to perform hard labor on the Danube Canal project for three years. The Communists told her that her husband was dead.

But Richard was still alive. He was released in 1956, and he immediately resumed his work in the underground church. He was rearrested in 1959 and sentenced to twenty–five years for preaching the gospel. Because of intense political pressure on Western governments by churches in America, however, they released Wurmbrand in 1964.

The following year, the Norwegian Mission to the Jews and the Hebrew Alliance paid a $10,000 ransom to win the release of Wurmbrand and his family from Romania. They moved to the United States, and he testified before the U. S. Senate Internal Security Subcommittee about the persecution of Christians behind the Iron Curtain.

In 1967, Wurmbrand published the first issue of a newsletter titled *Voice of the Martyrs* and began to set up offices of an international organization by the same name. During his life, he wrote eighteen books in English (and many others in Romanian), which were translated into thirty–eight languages. His most well–known book, *Tortured for Christ*, recounts his experiences in prison.

Richard Wurmbrand died on February 17, 2001, but his ministry of making the church aware of the believers who are being persecuted for Christ continues. That ministry is especially important for American Christians because we suffer relatively little for Christ whereas believers in other countries are giving their lives for Him.

Are *you* being persecuted for Christ? Are you willing to help other believers who are suffering such persecution for His name?

Student Work

We come now to the last of the B–attitudes:

"Blessed are they which are persecuted for righteousness' sake: for theirs is the kingdom of heaven. Blessed are ye, when men shall revile you, and persecute you, and shall say all manner of evil against you falsely, for my sake. Rejoice, and be exceeding glad: for great is your reward in heaven: for so persecuted they the prophets which were before you" (Matt. 5:10–12).

Persecution For The Wrong Reason

This B–attitude is not for everyone. Not everyone who happens to be persecuted has the promise of blessing. The promise "blessed" is for only those who are persecuted *"for righteousness' sake."*

Some people think that because they are persecuted, God will bless them and take care of them. That is not necessarily so. Much persecution is inflicted on Christians because of their own obnoxious ways or because they opened their mouth when they should have kept it shut! God will bless only persecution that results from righteousness.

Notice several things that this verse did *not* say.

It Does Not Bless Those Who Are Persecuted Because They Are Objectionable

Some people are persecuted because they have difficulty getting along with others. Some people are persecuted because they are seriously lacking in wisdom and therefore do or say foolish, unwise things. We can bring endless suffering upon ourselves because we have some foolish notion about witnessing or because we have a loud mouth. We do not always see the difference between prejudice and principle. Sometimes we take a stand on an issue out of prejudice and then, when we are criticized for it, assume that we are being persecuted.

It Does Not Bless Those Who Are Persecuted For A Cause

A difference exists between being persecuted for righteousness' sake and being persecuted for a cause. Granted, these two causes of persecution often become one, and many of the great martyrs were suffering for both righteousness' sake and a cause at the same time.

For example, some people suffer persecution for fighting abortion, liquor, drugs, tobacco, drunk driving, pornography, or other forms of immorality. Although we should fight these issues, do not think that the persecution that comes from our opponents in these fights is the same as that of which the Lord is talking in this B–attitude. We are not saying that a person should not stand for his moral principles; we are simply reminding you that the promise attached to this B–attitude does not apply to that type of persecution. If you choose to suffer for moral and/or political issues, go ahead and do so. But don't hold a grudge against God if you find that this B–attitude and its promise are not verified in your life. The B–attitude and its promise apply specifically to suffering for righteousness' sake.

It Does Not Bless Those Who Are Persecuted For Being Good, Noble, And Self–Sacrificing

Certainly, men should be outwardly good and noble, but those qualities are not the same as righteousness. (An unsaved person can have those qualities.) This verse does not say anything about the good and noble person's being persecuted or blessed, and for good reason. More likely than not, if you are good and noble, you will *not* be persecuted! The righteous *will* be persecuted, but not the good and the noble. The world usually persecutes only the righteous. Some people have made great sacrifices in life to help the poor, administer healing to diseased tribes, or rehabilitate alcoholics and drug addicts. Other people have sacrificed their fortunes, their health, and, in some instances, their lives for great humanitarian causes. These people, rather than being persecuted by the world, are generally praised and admired for their good works simply because they have made such sacrifices.

Persecuted For The Right Reason

Why, then, are Christians persecuted? For ______________________

____

What does *for righteousness' sake* mean if all of the preceding examples are not righteousness?

Being righteous really means being like the Lord Jesus Christ. Men are persecuted for being like Christ. In fact, those who are like Him will always be persecuted. What do the following verses say about this truth?

John 15:18— ______________________________________

____

John 15:20— ______________________________________

____

2 Timothy 3:12— ______________________________________

____

Examples Of Those Who Suffered For Righteousness' Sake

Read the following verses and name the man who was persecuted, not because he was difficult or obnoxious or overzealous but because he was simply righteous.

Genesis 4:1–8— ______________ What did he do that brought about his death? ______________________________

____

Exodus 16:1–4; 17:1–4—______________________________

1 Samuel 18:1–11— __________________________________

Daniel 3— ____

Daniel 6— ____

2 Corinthians 11:24–33— ____________________________

Who Does The Persecuting?

Both Scripture and secular history bear out the fact that some of the most grievous persecution suffered by Christians has been at the hands of religious people. Who caused Christ so much grief? ______________

____

The Jews bitterly persecuted the first Christians. The history of the church reveals the horrible persecution inflicted upon godly men by the Roman Catholic church. You will find that those who persecute you the most will not be the unsaved but those who are in the church or Christian school and claim to be saved!

Why Are The Righteous Persecuted?

Why are the righteous persecuted rather than the good and noble? What is it about righteousness that infuriates men, whereas mere goodness does not make them so mad?

The answer is simple. When a man is good, others think, *I am capable of that myself—if I only put my mind to it.* We admire the good because we think that we can be like them. But the righteous are persecuted because they are different. Jesus was persecuted not because He was good, but because He was different. Something about Him condemned the Pharisees. They thought that their righteousness looked cheap and dirty in contrast to Him. That was why they disliked Christ. The righteous do not have to *say* anything; they just condemn others by what they *are.*

Position Of This B–Attitude

As we have seen, a definite order is evident in these B–attitudes. This final B–attitude is really not so much an attitude as it is the *result* of possessing the other seven attitudes. The interesting point to note is that persecution follows the peacemaker. Imagine that! The one who actively seeks to bring peace is hated! The one who seeks to save men from hell is criticized, ridiculed, and maligned!

For righteousness' sake is perhaps a perfect description of the person who possesses the seven B–attitudes. The man who is outfitted with these seven inner attitudes is righteous (i.e., like Christ) and will be persecuted. So that this B–attitude is placed last in the list of the character traits that Christ requires of His leaders is fitting.

Conclusion

Our study of the character qualities that Christ wants to develop in you closes on a somber note. It doesn't end with promises of birds singing and flowers blooming. Instead, it closes with the promise that if a man is righteous he will face what Christ faced—persecution.

Answer the following questions about this issue. (Circle your answer. You may write any additional comments in the space beneath each question.)

- Are you willing to face a firing squad for Christ?
  Yes No
- Are you willing to go to a foreign country as a missionary?
  Yes No
- Are you willing to have your classmates turn against you?
  Yes No
- Are you willing to have your classmates tease you, and belittle you for Christ?
  Yes No
- Are you actively involved in evangelizing?
  Yes No
- Are you afraid of failure or persecution if you witness?
  Yes No
- Are you poor in spirit?
  Yes No
- Are you broken and mournful over your sinfulness?
  Yes No
- Are you meek, or do you still fight for your rights?
  Yes No
- Do you long to be righteous (filled with the Spirit)
  Yes No
- Are you merciful to those who are obnoxious?
  Yes No
- Are you pure in heart, hating sin?
  Yes No
- Are you a true peacemaker?
  Yes No
- Do you suffer persecution for righteousness' sake?
  Yes No

Do you know what it is to be persecuted for righteousness' sake? To become like Him, we have to become light. Light always exposes darkness; therefore, the darkness hates the light. We are not to be offensive, foolish, and unwise, and we are not to do anything that calls forth persecution. But just *being* like Christ makes persecution inevitable.

Paul wrote to the Philippians, "For unto you it is given in the behalf of Christ, not only to believe on Him, but also to suffer for his sake" (Phil. 1:29).

Do you rejoice and are you glad to suffer for Christ? Or do you cry, complain, and pity yourself?

Notes From The Teacher's Lesson

Blessed Are The Persecuted

Those Who Are Not ____________________ In Persecution

- The ________________________________ Person
- Those Who Are Persecuted _________________________ (Other Than The Cause Of Christ)
- The ___________________________________ Person

Those Who Are ____________________ In Persecution

- Those Who Are Persecuted For Righteousness Sake; ______________ ____

Examples

- The Apostles
    - James The Great—_________________________
    - Philip—_________________________ To A Cross
    - Matthew—_________________________
    - Mark—_________________________ Alive

- Matthias—Stoned And ______________________________
- Peter—______________________________ Upside Down
- Paul—______________________________
- Jude—______________________________
- Bartholomew—______________________________ To Pieces
- Thomas—Killed With A ______________________________
- Luke—______________________________
- Simon—______________________________
- Andrew—______________________________

- Under Nero And Marcus Aurelius
- During The Middles Ages And Early Reformation Eras

Stepping Toward Effective Leadership

- List specific practical ways in which you can practice the B–attitude of properly responding to being persecuted for righteousness' sake.

- Using your Bible and a concordance, list Bible characters who exhibited this B–attitude. Beside each name, explain briefly how this B–attitude was evidenced in that person's life.

- Watch and write a summary of the Christian film *Flame in the Wind.* In what geographic location and historical time period is the story set? What is the price that the "star" of the film must pay for his commitment to the faith? What price do other characters in the film have to pay? What character weaknesses are exhibited by other characters in the film who are not willing to pay that price?

- Visit the web site of Voice of the Martyrs at www.vom.org. Read the latest news about persecuted believers around the world. Make a map highlighting nations that officially persecute or permit the persecution of Christians. Following instructions given at the site, write a letter to a foreign Christian who is in prison for righteousness' sake.

- Write a history of the Voice of the Martyrs organization from its inception by Richard Wurmbrand to the present day.

- Why do you think that the U. S. government and the governments of other "Christian" nations in the West tend to disregard the overwhelming evidence of religious persecution in other countries? Write a letter to your U. S. senator and/or representative encouraging him or her to investigate specific instances of religious persecution in other countries. (Be very careful to give specific and accurate information in your letter.)

- Read and report to the class on the story of Pastor Laszlo Tokes in the book *In the Eye of the Romania Storm* by Felix Corley and John Eibner.

- Read selections from *Foxe's Book of Martyrs* and write a summary of the experiences recorded in those accounts.

- Read *In God's Underground* by Richard Wurmbrand.

- Research and write a brief biography of Richard Wurmbrand.

- Read *Testament from Prison* by Russian pastor Georgi Vins.

18

The Transforming Power Of The Spirit

Life had been a roller coaster ride for the disciples the past two months. They had witnessed Christ's popular acclaim as He entered Jerusalem. The people had shouted, "Hosanna!" They had waved palm fronds and spread the fronds and their outer garments as a carpet for Him to ride across. (This act was a practice that was reserved to show particular honor and respect for conquerors and great princes.)

But then things had turned ugly. Judas, one of their own, had betrayed Christ to the Jewish authorities for the measly price of a mere slave. Christ had been questioned, mocked, ridiculed, and tortured in a sham trial before finally being put to death in one of the cruelest, most humiliating ways—crucifixion. The disciples had fled for fear of their lives. Judas, in remorse, had hung himself.

But then everything changed. Christ had been resurrected from the dead! They had seen Him with their own eyes! He had appeared before them as they met in fear and secrecy. He had suddenly appeared in their midst right through a locked door! He had spoken comforting words to them.

But then after forty days, He had left them again. He had ascended into heaven in the clouds right before their very eyes. As He went up, He said, "But ye shall receive power, after that the Holy Ghost is come upon you: and ye shall be witnesses unto me both in Jerusalem, and in all Judaea, and in Samaria, and unto the uttermost part of the earth."

And then He was gone—just disappeared before their eyes. Then an angel appeared and said, "Why stand ye gazing up into heaven? This same Jesus, which is taken up from you into heaven, shall so come in like manner as ye have seen him go into heaven."

So He *was* coming back again after all! And the disciples thought of Christ's last words as He ascended. And those words reminded them that He had also taught them that "the Comforter, which is the Holy Ghost, whom the Father will send in my name, he shall teach you all things, and bring all things to your remembrance, whatsoever I have said unto you."

And now, on the day of Pentecost, the disciples were all gathered in Jerusalem. Then it happened! The Holy Spirit came upon them and filled them, and they testified of the gospel in the native tongues of all of the foreigners present. Peter delivered a stirring sermon the basic message of which was "Repent, and be baptized every one of you in the name of Jesus Christ for the remission of sins...." Three thousand souls were saved that day, and God continued to add converts to the church daily!

The Holy Spirit is still at work today, and He can work in *your* life, too—if you meet the conditions that we'll study in this lesson!

Student Work

This lesson looks at the ministry and power of the *third person* of the godhead in making us what God wants us to be. It's also your concluding lesson on the character of *The Inner Man.*

The One Necessary Ingredient

If spiritual maturity is our goal, then spiritual maturity is impossible without one absolutely necessary ingredient—an active Holy Spirit. Although the Holy Spirit *indwells* all believers, He is not *active* in all believers. Only as He is active will He perform His amazing character–building work and power in our lives. (By "active" we mean being filled with the Spirit.)

Note the power of the Holy Spirit in transforming the disciples' lives and personalities by comparing the disciples before and after they were filled with the Spirit.

Before The Spirit Came

- In Acts 1:4, the believers *waited* (inactive) for the Spirit. In John 20:19, they were ______________________________
- In John 20:2–9, they did not understand the ______________________

After The Spirit Came

- The believers became very active after the Spirit came. Read the following verses and list the things that the early church did.
  - Acts 2:4—______________________________
  - Acts 2:14–40— ______________________________
  - Acts 2:42—______________________________
  - Acts 2:43—______________________________
  - Acts 2:45—______________________________
  - Acts 2:46—______________________________
  - Acts 4:13, 31— ______________________________
  - Acts 4:33—______________________________

How The Spirit Becomes Active

Remember, it is not the Spirit *in* us but the Spirit working actively *through us* that transforms our character. Note that the Spirit is not automatically active in our lives. In fact, He is probably inactive in more Christians' lives than He is active!

Why The Spirit Is Inactive In Some Believers

At least three things hinder the working of the Holy Spirit. Read the following verses and identify those hindrances.

- Ephesians 4:30— ______________________________

- Ephesians 4:25–29, 31 list the things that do this to the Spirit. What are they? ______________________________

  ____

  ____

- 1 Thessalonians 5:19— ______________________________

  This word is usually associated with thirst and fire. Here, it obviously refers to fire. The Spirit, like a fire, can be extinguished by a refusal to go where He leads or a refusal to do what He wants.

- 1 Corinthians 6:19–20— ______________________________

  ____

This is a result of sin and impurity in one's life.

How The Spirit Becomes Active

From the preceding points we learn that the Spirit will not work in an environment of bitterness, strife, filthy talk, etc. He will not work in an environment of rebellion. And He will not work in an environment of sin and impurity. Thus, it becomes clear that if we are to be used of God by the Spirit, we must have the following qualities.

Yielded Bodies

What does Romans 6:13 say we must *not* do with the members (parts) of our body? ____

____

____

What does Romans 6:13 say we must *do* with the parts of our body? ___

____

____

How does the story of Elijah and the prophets of Baal illustrate this point?

____

____

____

Beholding Eyes

Read 2 Corinthians 3:18. As we all, ____________________________
______________________________as in a glass [the Word of God]
the ______________________________________, we are
______________________________________ (transformed) into
____
______________________________________ [the glory of God
by the ____.

How may we acquire likeness to Christ? By letting the Spirit transform us into His likeness. According to 2 Corinthians 3:18, how does the Spirit start working actively to do this? ____________________________

____

As we daily behold the Lord of Glory in the Word of God, the Spirit begins to work in His powerful way to transform our character and make us gradually ("from glory to glory") become like the One whom we are beholding. Thus, the switch that releases the Spirit's power within us is a clean, yielded body that is daily gazing at Christ in the Word of God.

What The Active Spirit Does

Once we release the Spirit of God in our bodies, what does He do?

He Transforms Us Into Christ's Image

- Read 2 Corinthians 3:18. What are we to behold daily? ______________
- In what do we behold Him? ______________
- What begins to happen when we behold Him? ______________
- Who changes (transforms) us? ______________

A law of nature is that we become like those we constantly observe. Thus, the more frequently we look at the Lord in the Word, the more quickly the Spirit transforms us.

He Gives Us The Characteristics Of Christ

- Galatians 5:22–23 lists nine characteristics of Christ that will be evident in the person in whom the Spirit is working. Read the verses and list those characteristics. ______________

  ____

He Brings About Gradual Change

- What phrase in 2 Corinthians 3:18 indicates that we do not become like Christ overnight? ______________

  ____

Conclusion

- To be like Christ, we have to fulfill a twofold responsibility. What is it?
  - ______________
  - ______________

The Spirit waits for these conditions to be met. Once they are met, what will He do? ____

____

Are you meeting these two conditions? The Spirit is waiting now to make you spiritually mature, but He will not work until you meet these conditions. As the God of heaven withheld the fire until Elijah had the altar ready, so God's Spirit is poised, waiting for us to make ready the altar of our lives.

Notes From The Teacher's Lesson

Spiritual Power

The ________________ Of The Fire (Elijah)

- Consuming Passion
- Contentment
- Obedient

The ________________ Of The Fire

The ______________________ Of Moses (Exod. 3:2, 4)

The ______________________ At Sinai (Exod. 19:18)

God Entered The ______________________ (Exod. 40:35, 38)

The ______________________ Of The Temple (2 Chron. 7:1)

The ________________ Of The Fire

At A Time Of ______________________________

When Elijah Obeyed God ______________________________

After The ______________________________ Had Been Repaired

When ______________________________ Was Placed On The Altar

As Elijah ________________________

Stepping Toward Effective Leadership

- List specific practical ways in which you can experience the power of the Holy Spirit.
- Using your Bible and a concordance, list Bible characters (*excluding Elijah!*) whose lives exhibited the power of the Spirit. Beside each name, explain briefly how the power of the Spirit was evidenced in that person's life.
- Conduct a study of the person and work of the Holy Spirit. (A good source of information on this topic is R. A. Torrey, "The Person and Work of the Holy Spirit," in *Power–Filled Living* [New Kensington, Pa.: Whitaker House, 1998].)
- What is the "consuming passion" of your life? Do you have a "magnificent obsession"? Analyze how you spend your time and money. Then list the priorities of your life as evidenced by the results of your analysis. Do you need to make any adjustments to ensure that you are "majoring" on the right things?

Unit 4

The Standards And Qualities Of Leadership

19

An Overview Of Leadership

The following eleven lessons are taken from *Spiritual Leadership* by J. Oswald Sanders. (The complete, unaltered text of this classic work is provided at the end of your textbook. We were given permission to reproduce it, but not to alter it. You will notice that he uses various Bible versions. Please use your version for comparison.) The student outlines guide you through the book and ensure that you have a grasp of Sanders' excellent material.

The quiz for each lesson and the test for Unit 4 are taken from the student outline, the text itself, and the notes from the teacher's lesson. Therefore, do not read the book just to find the answers to the questions asked in the student outline. Remember, all that we study this year is not only for the purpose of learning facts but also to let the Lord change our character and develop maturity within. What you make on the quizzes and the unit test is not nearly as important as what you become through these lessons.

The following student outlines contain a list of study questions. You can either write your answers on a separate sheet of paper or you can highlight the answers to the questions in the text of *Spiritual Leadership*. You might even write the question by the answer in the text of *Spiritual Leadership*. This activity will make the book more meaningful to you. In reviewing for the test, you might be required to write answers on the student outline; when that is necessary, a blank is provided for that purpose.

Spiritual Leadership, Chapters 1–3

Before proceeding with the rest of this lesson, read the first three chapters of *Spiritual Leadership*, which give an overview of Christian leadership. After you have read all three chapters, answer the following questions.

List the three chapter titles studied for this lesson, and state very briefly what each title means and a summary of its content.

Chapter	Title	Meaning Of Title	Summary Of Chapter
One			
Two			
Three			

Chapter One: An Honorable Ambition

1. When is ambition honorable?
2. Is all ambition noble and honorable?
3. According to Jeremiah 45:5, what kind of ambition would *not* be noble?

4. What is it, then, that makes ambition honorable and without which it is *not* honorable?
5. Finish the following statement: "It is not the office of the overseer (boss) but the ______________________________ of ______________________________ that is honorable and noble."
6. According to Mark 10:42–44, what must one who wants to be a leader do?
7. What does this requirement for leadership do to selfish ambition?
8. What two–fold mistake did James and John make?
9. What is the heavenly criterion for greatness?
10. What does the following statement mean: "Greatness of exaltation is in proportion to greatness of service humbly rendered"?
11. How did Christ exemplify the preceding statement?
12. What cost must one pay to be a leader?
13. What is the spiritual leader's greatest concern?
14. What does history honor *most* about a man?
15. What does history honor *least* about a man?

Chapter Two: The Search For Leaders

1. According to Psalm 75:6–7, how are men promoted?
2. According to 1 Samuel 13:14 and Ezekiel 22:30, for what is God constantly searching?
3. What kind of man, despite his shortcomings, does God use to the limit?
4. Why is such a man hard to find?
5. What three qualities are needed in the leadership of today's churches?
6. Does holding a position of importance make one a leader? (Why or why not?)
7. Who alone can confer true leadership on a man?
8. Why does God's Spirit use some men as leaders whereas He passes over others?

9. According to Samuel Brengle, what price must one pay if God's Spirit is to choose him for leadership?

10. Where must a man qualify for leadership before God will honor him in public?

Chapter Three: Natural And Spiritual Leadership

1. Leadership is ______________________________, the ability of one person to ______________________________.
2. Lord Montgomery defines leadership as comprising what two things?
3. Know President Truman's definition of leadership.
4. Of what man was the following statement true: he had a "capacity and will to rally men and women to a common purpose, and the character which inspires confidence"?
5. What kind of personality does the spiritual man use to influence others?
6. True–false: Few self–made spiritual leaders exist. Why or why not?
7. In what three ways does Oswald Sanders show the difference between natural and spiritual leadership?
8. Who said, "I believe it might be accepted as a fairly reliable rule of thumb that the man who is ambitious to lead is disqualified as a leader"?
9. What passage of Scripture comes to mind in the answer that St. Francis of Assisi gave to Brother Masseo?
10. Know the seven qualities that Lord Montgomery enumerated as necessary for a leader in war, each of which is as appropriate to those who will be generals in the *spiritual* war as it is to earthly warfare.
11. Know the nine questions that Dr. John Mott used to determine a leader's qualifications for leadership.
12. What was the central requirement that the apostles demanded of a deacon?

13. List the Scripture phrase in Acts 6:3 that best explains the following three qualifications for deacons:

Integrity–______________________________

Sagacity–______________________________

Spirituality– ____________________________

14. Of the items in the following list, which quality is the most essential ingredient in real leadership?

- A powerful personality
- The power to make clear decisions
- Humility
- The power to influence
- One who has his priorities straight
- Honesty
- Full of the Holy Ghost
- A man who loves God
- A man in God's will
- The ability to delegate responsibility

Notes From The Teacher's Lesson

Discovering Your Leadership Potential

Ambition—Right Or Wrong? (1 Tim. 3:1; Jer. 45:5)

The ____________________ When Paul Wrote

The ____________________ Of The Overseer

The ____________________ Of The Motive

Christ's ____________________ Of Greatness

Webster's Definition

- Ambition is a strong desire for ____________________________

  ____.

Christ's Definition (Mark 10:35–45)

- The Disciples Were Selfish And Worldly In Their ____________
- They Totally ______________ What Christ Had Come To Do.
- They Had No Idea Of What True ______________ Really Is.

How One Becomes A Leader

God Chooses ____

(1 Sam. 13:14, Jer. 4:25; 5:1; Ezek. 22:30)

God Chooses ____

- Pure And ____
- Standing Up For ____________________________________
- A Lowly ____
- Being Hated, _______________________________________
- Giving Up Earthly ___________________________________
- Being Filled With The _______________________________
- Fervent Prayer, Disciplined Study, And __________________

Stepping Toward Effective Leadership

- How can you know God's will? What steps are you taking to learn what He expects of you? Read James C. Petty's book, *Step By Step: Divine Guidance For Ordinary Christians*, and answer these key questions: How does God guide us? What part does wisdom play in determining God's will?

- Read *George Müller of Bristol* by Arthur T. Pierson, and explain the process by which God chose Müller for His service and then prepared him to fulfill that service. What leadership qualities did Müller's life exemplify?

- Read a biography of one of the following people and describe the leadership qualities that were evident in his or her life:

St. Francis of Assisi	Martin Luther
Hudson Taylor	Adoniram Judson
Florence Nightingale	George Whitefield
William Carey	John Wesley
Ronald Reagan	Thomas "Stonewall" Jackson
Robert E. Lee	George Washington

WEAKNESS
WEAKNESS
WEAKNESS
WEAKNESS
STRENGTH
STRENGTH
STRENGTH
STRENGTH

20

Discovering Your Leadership Potential

Preparatory assignment: Read chapter 4 of *Spiritual Leadership* for this lesson.

Your success or failure as a servant of the Lord may well be determined by your ability to discover the weaknesses of your life and improve upon them. The lesson that you are now beginning will help greatly in discovering both the strengths and the weaknesses of your life.

Chapter 4 of *Spiritual Leadership* is filled with questions that are designed to help you probe your character and discover your leadership potential. Your assignment for this lesson is as follows.

- Read the question(s) in each paragraph.
- Note our comments concerning the question(s),
- Write your answers to the questions on a separate sheet of paper under one of two columns. Label the first column "Areas Where I Am Strong" and the second column "Areas Where I Am Weak."
- Turn in your paper to the teacher.

Note: Simple "yes" and "no" answers are not acceptable.

Note that we have numbered each paragraph of questions from 1–22 beginning with the question "Have you ever broken yourself of a bad habit?" and ending with the question "Do you welcome responsibility?"

Although we have not restated the question on the student outline, we have given it a title corresponding to the area of responsibility that the question probes.

1. Habits/self–control. List under the "strong" column habits that you have broken and under the "weak" column habits that you need to break. If you want to keep your lists private, use a code name for each particular habit. Also, state whether you are strong or weak in this overall area of being master over yourself.
2. Emotions/temper. State your thoughts concerning how strong or weak you are in this area.
3. Mind/decisions. State how easy or hard it is for you to make up your mind about things and then stick to your decisions.
4. Criticism. State exactly how criticism affects you.
5. Disappointments. State how you accept and react to disappointments that you face (e.g., being denied the privilege of going somewhere that you really wanted to go or not being allowed to buy something that you really wanted to buy).
6. Influence/respect. State how you feel about this area as it relates to you.
7. Ability to control and discipline a group. State your feelings concerning this ability in your life.
8. Peacemaking. State your answer to this question under the appropriate column, recalling the material we studied in lesson 16.
9. Handling difficult situations. State your ability to talk to people about their needs and weaknesses without offending them.
10. Motivation. State under the "weak" column actual cases in which you showed this ability in this area.
11. Facing opposition. State how you react to people who oppose you and disagree with your viewpoint.

12. Friends. State whether you feel completely accepted by the majority of the "spiritual" students in the school. If you feel left out or unaccepted, place your answer in the "weak" column.

13. Praise/approval. State honestly your answer to the question asked.

14. Meeting strangers and important people. State your feelings when you meet such people or have to perform in front of them.

15. Friendliness. As best you can, state how you think strangers and outsiders feel about your friendliness. Put under the "strong" or "weak" column any comments you desire about this area of your life.

16. Concern. State under the "strong" column how you show concern for others. State in the appropriate column how concerned you are about the weaknesses, problems, physical needs, and spiritual needs of others.

17. Tact. Tact is the ability to tell people of their weaknesses and to correct them without hurting their feelings, being rude, or offending them. State in the appropriate column your feelings about whether you have tact.

18. Will/determination. State your strength or weakness concerning whether you give up easily.

19. Forgiveness. If you harbor resentment or ill feelings toward someone or if you pout and sulk when someone mistreats you, record this fact under the "weak" column. If you are strong in this area, state under the "strong" column *how* you are strong.

20. Optimism/pessimism. If you are optimistic, state this fact under the "strong" column. If you are pessimistic, indicate the fact in the "weak" column.

21. Goals/purposes. If you have definite spiritual goals for your life, list the top three such goals in the "strong" column. If you do *not* have goals, or if you think that you have some but can't name them, state so in the "weak" column.

22. Responsibility. State under the appropriate column your opinion about this area. Do you accept a job with enthusiasm and consider it

a great challenge to do your very best, or do you tend to run from hard jobs and fear failure? If you answer "yes" to the latter question, state your feelings under the "weak" column.

Now total the number of entries made in each column. Write the total in the following blanks.

- Number of areas in which I show *strength* = ____________________
- Number of areas in which I show *weakness* = ____________________

According to Sanders, the important thing is not just to do this exercise in self–analysis and then pay no further attention to it; rather, what should you do?____

____

____

____

In what person were all of these qualities present in their fullness? *Our Lord*

____

Notes From The Teacher's Lesson

Discovering Your Leadership Potential

Ingredients Of ______________________ (Acts 6:3)

Of ____________________ Report

Full Of The ____________________

Full Of ____________________

Titus—A Spiritual Leader (2 Cor. 8:16–22)

Interested In ____________________ (v. 16)

____________________ (v. 22)

Stepping Toward Effective Leadership

- Read and summarize the key principles of *How to Speak Your Mind without Stepping on Toes.* Which of those principles do you think is the most important in dealing with people?
- Leon Blum wrote, "I have often thought morality may perhaps consist solely in the courage of making a choice." Why does making a choice often require great courage? Describe a situation in which you had to have courage to make a particular decision. What were the results?
- Using the following quotation as a springboard, explain how one develops decision–making skills: "Every decision a man makes is based on a lifetime of decisions which either enhanced or diminished his character" (Edwin Louis Cole). What decisions are you making today that could affect the rest of your life? Have you sought the wisdom of the Lord in making that decision?
- "One of the tests of manhood," Edwin Louis Cole wrote, "is how a man handles pressure." How do you handle the pressure of competing time demands? Peer pressure? Temptation? Laziness?
- Does your school's guidance office offer an interest inventory assessment? If so, arrange to take it and see what it reveals about your interests and aptitudes. Could such a tool be used to help you determine your calling and purpose in life? If so, how? Could such a tool be inaccurate or misleading? If so, how? What steps could you take to avoid being misled by it? What other factors must you take into consideration in determining your calling?
- Read *The On–Purpose Person.* Define an "on–purpose person." Explain why the book's author selected a light switch turned on as the appropriate symbol of an on–purpose person.
- Write a two–page paper explaining and applying to your life the following quotation by Thomas Carlyle: "The man without a purpose is like a ship without a rudder—a waif, a nothing, a no man. Have a purpose in life, and, having it, throw such strength of mind and muscle into your work as God has given you."

HOLY
BIBLE

21

Scriptural Standards For Leadership

Preparatory assignment: Read chapters five and six of *Spiritual Leadership* for this lesson.

Chapters five and six of *Spiritual Leadership* examine Scripture standards for leadership as given by the apostles Paul and Peter. Chapter five gives Paul's perspective, which is therefore termed "Pauline." Chapter six gives Peter's perspective, which is therefore termed "Petrine." Read these two chapters carefully. Then underline and learn the material in the text that provides answers to the following questions.

Chapter Five: Pauline Sidelights On Leadership

Read 1 Timothy 3:2–7.

1. The leadership standards that Paul asserted in this passage are centuries old. Why are they still applicable in our modern society of computers and space–age technology?
2. List the six areas of leadership qualifications that Paul asserted in 1 Timothy 3:2–7.
3. List the quality or qualities needed in each of the six areas (see the italicized points in chapter five).

4. Explain what each quality means.

5. How do we know (from the text) that these qualities were qualities for leaders.

6. List six characteristics that, according to 1 Timothy 3:1–6 (KJV), we are *not* to have.

7. Why was *hospitality* one of the most necessary character traits in Paul's day?

8. How is a leader to relate to his children?

9. Which quality reflects the beauty and orderliness of God (which means being well mannered)?

10. What man, who was highly intellectual and possessed a brilliant knowledge of classical literature, could have been in front of the scholars of his day, and yet was known as a "man of one Book"—the Bible?

11. Explain the phrase "example is much more potent than precept" as it relates to the importance of a good reputation. ____________________

    ____

    ____

12. Who objected to making too much money and working too little?

13. What unsaved leader put forth the same qualifications as Paul?

14. What kind of man remembers the good that he has received rather than the good that he has done?

15. How did Paul practice good leadership in his treatment of new converts?

16. A new convert should not be thrust into a position of leadership too quickly, but neither should he be repressed. What is the danger in each case?

Chapter Six: Petrine Sidelights On Leadership

Read 1 Peter 5:1–7. Then read chapter six of *Spiritual Leadership* and answer the following questions.

1. In what illustration do we see the leadership and influence of Peter on the rest of the disciples?
2. What passage of Scripture relates Peter's list of leadership qualities?
3. Comparing Paul's list with Peter's list, which qualities do both men name, although they have different ways of expressing them?
4. Who is the "flock of God" that Peter mentioned?
5. What quality do we see in Peter in his opening words of this passage?
6. Finish this statement: "A shepherd's work cannot be done effectively without ____."
7. Verse two lists the first responsibility of a leader. What is it?
8. According to verse two, what do we learn about the leader's motivation? What should motivate him? What two things should *not* motivate him?
9. What acquaintance of Peter had the wrong motive for service?
10. "Filthy lucre" could suggest more than just money. According to Paul Rees, what else could be implied here?
11. According to verse three, a leader must not be what?
12. What man in 3 John failed as a leader in this area? *Diotrephes*
13. What does *clothed* mean in the context of this Scripture passage?
14. What is the reward of the leader?
16. What was unique about this reward?

Notes From The Teacher's Lesson

Scriptural Standards For Leadership (1 Thess. 5:14–17)

Discernment: A Leader Knows How to Deal With Different ______________ ______________ (v. 14)

- The Unruly— ______________
- The Easily Discouraged— ______________
- The Weak— ______________

Always Seeking Peace, Never ______________ (v. 15)

Joyous (v. 16)

Prays Much (v. 17)

A leader cannot get by without an effective prayer life.

Stepping Toward Effective Leadership

- Read *Leading with Integrity* by Fred Smith, Sr. As you read, list the spiritual and natural qualities that he discusses that should be evident in the life of a man of God.

- What are some fields *beyond the church* that call urgently for Christian leadership? Why are those fields in such dire need of Christian leaders?

- Interview your pastor to find out the major leadership positions in your church. For each position, list the qualifications of the church for the individual who holds that position. Beside each qualification, indicate whether it is a Scripture–mandated qualification or a practical qualification.

- How are leadership positions in your school like the leadership positions in a church? How are they different?
- Does your church have a formal, planned course or program for leadership training? If so, describe it. What steps (if any) is your youth department taking to ensure a new generation of qualified godly leaders? Are you a part of either of those programs?
- What leadership roles may women scripturally fill?
- Conduct a search of recent religious periodicals and summarize the ongoing controversy over the role of women in leadership roles in the church.

HUMI
OURAGE
CISION
WISDOM
VIS
DIS CIPLINE

22

Qualities Essential To Leadership, Part 1

Preparatory assignment: Read chapter seven of *Spiritual Leadership* in preparation for this lesson. Know the answers to the following questions. You are responsible for both questions on this student outline and information contained in the chapter that might not have been asked in the following questions.

1. List the thirteen qualities that Sanders names in chapters seven and eight as essential to leadership.
2. When God prepares a man for leadership, what does He always consider?
3. How was Paul able to accomplish his work?
4. Why did men follow Martin Luther so loyally?
5. God endowed Paul, Luther, Hudson Taylor, and Adoniram Judson with the gifts that each man would need for his assigned task, but He also endowed hundreds of other people with the same gifts. Yet, these men seemed to be a cut above the others. Why? What made the difference?

Discipline

6. What are the two kinds of discipline?
7. Which kind is best? Why?
8. What three things mark a young man as a future leader?

9. Finish this statement: A young man of discipline will "without reluctance undertake the ____________________________________ or the ____________________________________which others evade."
10. A disciplined leader's prayer will be "God, harden me against______
11. How do you see strong discipline in Dr. Thomas Cochrane?
12. What traits made Florence Nightingale memorable in history?
13. List the discipline habits of Samuel Chadwick and George Whitefield.

Vision

14. Who are seers?
15. What did each of the following great leaders see: Moses, Elisha, Charles Cowman?
16. Name the four things that comprise vision and describe each.
17. Why was William Carey greater than most other missionaries?
18. How does vision affect a man for leadership?
19. What's the difference between a pessimist and an optimist?
20. How does Browning describe the courageous optimist?

Wisdom

21. What is wisdom? ____
____
____

22. What single ingredient turns knowledge into wisdom? __________
____

Decision

23. What is the difference between a visionary and a true leader?
24. How did Abraham and Moses show their ability in making decisions?
25. What is usually the most difficult part in making decisions?

Courage

26. What is courage?
27. How did Martin Luther show courage?

28. When is courage seen at its highest?
29. What changed the fearful disciples of John 20 into the fearless disciples of Acts 4?
30. What gave the Israelites the courage to face Sennacherib's mighty army?

Humility

31. What characteristic made John the Baptist the greatest of those born of women?
32. Show how Paul increased in humility as he grew older.
33. Who said, "The ax cannot boast of the trees it has cut down"? What does that statement mean?
34. Of the six characteristics that you have studied in this lesson, which one do you believe is your strength? Which one do you think is your weakness?

Notes From The Teacher's Lesson

Qualities Essential To Leadership— ____________________

A Disciplined Person Learns From A ____________________

- He Has A ____________________ (Mt. 10:24)
- He Learns From A __________ (Mt. 20:17–18; Mk. 4:11–12, 33–34)
  - We Hear, But We Don't ____________________ (Mk. 8:17–18)
  - Learned Now, Take Root And ____________________
- He Learns About His ____________________

A Disciplined Person ____________________ *Himself*

"A leader is a person who has first submitted willingly and learned to obey a discipline imposed from without, but who then imposes on himself a much more rigorous discipline from within." *Spiritual Leadership*

Stepping Toward Effective Leadership

- Read a biography of one of the following people, and summarize the leadership qualities that characterized his or her life: Martin Luther, Hudson Taylor, Adoniram Judson, Florence Nightingale, George Whitefield, William Carey.
- Research the life of George Washington Carver, the great African–American scientist, and describe how his life exemplified the qualities of discipline, vision, wisdom, courage, and humility. How did each of the qualities play a part in his success?
- Explain the following statements by Edwin Louis Cole as they relate to leadership and your pursuit of it:
  - "Moral cowardice is the ruin of manhood."
  - "Soft men can't take rough times."
- According to Ron Kinkaid, "the average Christian now spends more than 175 minutes per day watching television, and less than ten minutes reading God's Word" (*The Secrets of Deciding Wisely*). What affect do you think this fact has on how the average Christian makes decisions? How do you measure up by this statistic? Are you average, above average, or below average in your TV viewing? In your Bible reading? What influences your decision–making processes more—TV or God's Word?
- Someone has listed the following elements of making godly decisions. Using Scripture support, explain the significance of each element to a believer's decision–making process.
  - Consecration
  - Information
  - Supplication
  - Consultation
  - Meditation
  - Decision
  - Expectation

INSPIRATION
EXECUTIVE ABILITY
FRIENDSHIP
PATIENCE
HUMOR
ANGER
TACT

23

Qualities Essential To Leadership, Part 2

Preparatory assignment: Read chapter eight of *Spiritual Leadership* for this lesson. After applying the material to your life, be ready to answer the following questions.

Humor

1. What can humor do for a sermon?
2. Of what must we be careful in our humor?

Anger

3. When is anger *right or appropriate?*
4. When is anger *wrong or inappropriate?*

Patience

5. How did Chrysostom describe patience?
6. In what area is patience most needed and most tested?
7. What great leader failed to be patient about another person's weakness?
8. In what three incidents do we see patience in Jesus?
9. What can we do that will keep us from losing patience with those who don't move as fast as we do?

Friendship

10. What was the secret of David's ability?

11. What can friendliness do that argument cannot do?

12. What man taught others to "rule by the heart"?

13. What does it mean to "rule by the heart"?

14. What verse shows how Christ ruled others by friendship and affection?

Tact And Diplomacy

15. What is tact?

16. What is diplomacy?

17. How did the shoe salesman show tact and diplomacy?

Inspiration

18. What pastor had an unusual ability to sway people without any apparent effort?

19. What Bible character displayed the ability to sway people to follow him?

20. What did this powerful biblical leader persuade the people to do?

Executive Ability

21. What does the word *judgment* reveal about God and a leader's executive ability?

22. What is executive ability?
    - Of the thirteen qualities listed in chapters seven and eight of *Spiritual Leadership*, in which are you strongest?
    - In which quality are you weakest?

Notes From The Teacher's Lesson

Qualities Essential To Leadership

Humor

- Humor Is Wrong When It Is In ______________________________
- Humor Is Wrong When The Humor ______________________________

Anger

- Right Anger (Jn. 2:15–17; Mk. 3:5; Mt. 21:13)
  - Someone Or Something Threatens That Which Is Holy And Pure ______________________
  - Someone Or Something ______________________________
- Wrong Anger—Anger That Is Centered ______________________

Patience

"The man who is impatient with weakness will be defective in his leadership." Spiritual Leadership

Friendship

- Based on ______________________________.

Tact And Diplomacy

The ability to handle delicate situations without arousing anger.

Inspirational Power

- An Inner ______________________________
- The Fullness Of The ______________________________

Executive Ability

The ability to organize and manage the Lord's work.

Stepping Toward Effective Leadership

- Explain the difference between being *efficient* and being *effective.* Which is the better result? Are you efficient? Are you effective? (Explain.)
- Discuss the significance to the Christian leader of the following statement by Winston Churchill: "We make a living by what we get, but we make a life by what we give."
- Read *Well Done!* by Dave Thomas, founder of the Wendy's fast–food restaurant. What lessons does he share about "treating people right"?
- What lessons do you learn about the proper/improper forms of anger from chapter eight, "Face Your Anger," in *Getting the Best of Yourself* by David W. Aycock? Which Bible characters does he use as examples of angry people?

24

The Holy Spirit—The Leader's Power

Preparatory assignment: Read chapter nine of *Spiritual Leadership* for this lesson. Know the answers to the following questions.

1. What is the only indispensable requirement for spiritual leadership?
2. What was the one requirement necessary to be a deacon in the early church?
3. What can gradually happen in a church, school, or other Christian organization that prevents the Holy Spirit from doing His work?
4. Finish the following statement: The Holy Spirit does not take control of any man or body of men ______________________.
5. List five people in Acts who were filled with the Spirit.
6. With what one mission is the Spirit preoccupied?
7. When a man is thus filled with the Spirit, with what will he be preoccupied?
8. According to Acts 20:28, how should men gain their leadership positions?
9. In simple terms, what does "filled with the Spirit" mean?
10. True–false: The word *fill* includes the idea of filling an empty glass with water.
11. What is the idea behind the word *fill?*
12. When is natural talent most potent and effective?
13. To be filled with the Spirit, what must one do?

Notes From The Teacher's Lesson

What Being "Filled With The Spirit" Means

Full Of The Spirit

Acts 4:8 ; 4:31; 6:3, 5; 7:55; 8:29; 8:39; 9:17; 10:9, 19; 11:24; 13:1, 4; 13:9–10; 13:52; 16:6–7; 20:22–23; 20:28

Meaning Of "Filled With The Spirit"

- Baptism Of The Spirit—The Act Whereby The Spirit Places ________ ____ (1 Cor. 12:13).
- Indwelling Of The Spirit—______________________________ ____________, When The Spirit Comes To Live In The New Believer.
- Filled With The Spirit—The Condition Wherein The Spirit, Who Is In The Christian, Has ______________________________.

How One Is Filled With The Spirit

- Salvation—The Spirit Must ______________________________
- Holiness—Indwelt Person Must ______________________________
- Longing—Indwelt Person Must ______________________________
- Yieldedness—Indwelt, Holy, Hungry Person Must ______________

The Results Of Being Filled With The Spirit And Prayer

- They Became Bold To ______________________________
- They Always Made The ______________________________
- They Were Burdened For ______________________________
- They Were Called Into ______________________________

They Were ____

They Were ____

Stepping Toward Effective Leadership

- Describe a specific person whom you believe to be Spirit filled. What evidences are present in that person's life that lead you to that conclusion?
- Defend and explain J. Oswald Sanders' statement that "each of us is as full of the Spirit as we really want to be."
- What role does the Holy Spirit play in each of the following leadership responsibilities?
  - decision making
  - hiring and directing the work of employees or subordinates
  - setting goals (both individually and corporately)

Unit 5

The Price Of Leadership

25

The Leader's Prayer Life

Preparatory assignment: Read chapter 10 of *Spiritual Leadership*, and know the answers to the following questions.

1. Which area of man's life, when one is questioned about it, will generally humble him most quickly? Why?
2. What was Samuel Chadwick's one regret?
3. What should a hectic, busy schedule cause one to do?
4. What did Martin Luther say about a busy schedule?
5. What is the only way for one to learn to pray?
6. In what one person would we think that prayer was unnecessary?
7. How prominent was prayer in Christ's life?
8. What does the prominence of prayer in Christ's life say to us about our need for it?
9. True or False? Prayer should be a pleasant, enjoyable experience.
10. What did J. H. Jowett say about prayer?
11. What verse shows the strain and drain that prayer had upon Christ both physically and emotionally?
12. List five ways that the New Testament describes prayer as a strenuous exercise.
13. When a man doesn't know what to say or how to pray about something, what happens?
14. Which ingredient of prayer will render prayer powerless?

15. According to Jude 20, how are effective prayers offered?
16. What does "praying in the Spirit" mean?
17. What are the three handicaps of a man of prayer?
18. In addition to those three handicaps, what other thing will the man of prayer have to overcome?
19. Which three warriors struggle on the battlefront of prayer?
20. When we pray for people who are bound by sin, for what two specific things should we pray?
21. What does Matthew 12 teach about prayer?
22. What is the only way to "bind the strong man"?
23. Who is the "strong man"?
24. What is the one way we can move and influence men?
25. Know Hudson Taylor's quotation.
26. What is revealed if God keeps burdening our hearts to pray?
27. What is the goal of prayer?
28. Correct the following statement: "Prayer moves men."

Using the prayer guide that your teacher will provide, pray every day for the next seven days. Record on the following chart when you begin and end your prayer time and the number of minutes you pray each day. Then add each day's total to arrive at a grand total of time prayed during the week.

Day	Time started	Time finished	Minutes prayed
Monday			
Tuesday			
Wednesday			
Thursday			
Friday			
Saturday			
Sunday			
Total time prayed during the week:			

Notes From The Teacher's Lesson

The Leader's Prayer Life

Why We Don't Pray

- Because ______________________________ Fights Us (Eph. 6:10–18)
- Because It Drains Our ______________________________ ______________________________ (Heb. 5:7; Col. 4:12; Jms. 5:16b)
- Because We Don't Always Know ____________________ (Rom. 8:26)

How To Become A Man Or Woman Of Prayer

- Know What ______________________________ About Prayer
- Follow The ______________________________

A ______________________________

C ______________________________

T ______________________________

S ______________________________

Stepping Toward Effective Leadership

- Read a book on prayer by one of the following authors, and explain what he taught on this subject: Bounds, Eastman, Hybels, Murray, Simpson, or Torrey. (See titles and other pertinent bibliographic information about these books in the Recommended Reading List.)
- Keep a prayer journal to account for your time of prayer each day and week.

- Make a prayer list on which you record each request, the date on which you begin praying for each particular request, and how the prayer is answered.

- Make a "Ministry Prayer Book." Divide the book into sections for your church's leaders, your school's leaders, and the missionary leaders whom your church supports. On the first page of each section, state the name(s) of the person(s) and ministry and attach a photograph of the person(s) involved in the ministry. Write to the person(s), asking specific needs they have or requests for which they would like you to pray. On the subsequent pages of each section, write down those needs or requests. Note each answered prayer.

- On a world map, indicate the locations where your church has missionaries or ministries that the congregation supports.

THE VANISHED HOUR
NO LONGER THINE, ONE
IN THY HANDS, THE NOW ON

26

The Leader And His Time

Preparatory assignment: Read chapters 11 and 12 of *Spiritual Leadership*, and know the answers to the following questions.

Chapter Eleven

1. Largely what determines a young person's character and career?
2. What do extremely busy leaders have that lesser men never have? Why?
3. What is the real problem with time?
4. Although we are not responsible for the amount of talent or ability that God has given us, for what *are* we responsible?
5. Finish the following statement: Time can be lost, but it can never be ________________________________. Explain what that means.
6. The average adult has how many hours to waste or use each week?
7. Allowing 138 hours in six days (from Monday, 6:00 a.m. until Saturday midnight), if a person sleeps 8 hours a night (M–F), eats 1 1/2 hours a day, and spends 8 hours a day in school, he still has 49 hours a week left over. Account for your 49 hours by marking how

much time you spend involved in the following activities. (Your total number of hours cannot exceed 49 hours.)

Watching TV ____________________

Sports (attending or participating/practicing) ____________________

Other school activities____________________

Doing homework ____________________

Talking on the telephone____________________

Church activities (do *not* include Sundays!)____________________

Praying ____________________

Having devotions ____________________

Working ____________________

Witnessing ____________________

Other activities (identify these) ____________________

Total: ____________________

8. What more than anything else probably produces more agitation and tension in daily life?
9. How did one man handle daily interruptions?
10. What two men were extremely disciplined in their use of time, and what did they do?
11. Although we might not be able to be that extreme, what do we learn from those two men?
12. What would you say was wrong with Sangster's use of time?
13. What is one of the devil's most potent weapons against the proper use of time?
14. How can one effectively overcome the tendency to procrastinate?

Chapter Twelve

1. Memorize Bacon's statement.
2. Read 1 Timothy 4:13. What did Paul challenge Timothy to do in that verse?

3. What two types of reading must a leader do?
4. What did John Wesley tell his younger ministers?
5. According to Tozer, why do most Christians find the reading of great books beyond them?
6. List five reasons why a Christian leader must read.
7. Finish the following statement: If it is true that a man is known by the company he keeps, it is not less true that ____________________
   ____
   ____
8. What must we do if our reading is to be profitable?
9. What does hasty reading produce?
10. What are the six rules of reading?

Notes From The Teacher's Lesson

A Leader And His Time

Three ____________________ To Being Young

- Abundant ____________________ (1 Tim. 4:7–8)
- More ____________________ (1 Tim. 4:13)
- Alert ____________________ (1 Tim. 4:15)

Stepping Toward Effective Leadership

- If the books you read measure your inner hunger and aspirations, what is in *your* heart?
- List the types of literature you read most.
- List the titles and authors of your five favorite books. Explain why each of them is one of your favorites.

- What do you think are the ten most influential books for Christians? Briefly describe each title you list and explain why you think it is so influential.

- Interview two influential Christian leaders in your church and/or school to determine which books influenced their ministry and how.

- Explain the difference between *efficiency* and *effectiveness.* Explain the following statement in relation to these two words: "It's not enough to do the job right; you must do the right job right."

- What does the following statement by H. G. Bohn mean? "One of these days soon becomes none of these days."

- Why are planning and prioritizing important for a Christian leader?

- Define *leisure.* How does leisure differ from "free" time?

- Explain and illustrate the following statement: "When you fail to plan, you are planning to fail."

- Make a "To Do" form on which you write and prioritize all of your weekly assignments and responsibilities. Mark off each task as you complete it. How does this exercise help you be a better steward of your time?

- Make a chart to keep track of how you spend your time. Break each day into ten–minute segments. After a week, analyze your findings to identify "time wasters" and to learn specific times when you are most apt to waste time. Develop ways to combat such time wasters.

- List at least ten things that you can do that are more productive than watching television.

- Why is the following statement a good yardstick by which to measure all activities? "To discern the value of an activity, ask yourself, 'Will this make a difference in five years?'"

- Read Luke 10:38–42. What does the incident recorded in this passage teach us about our priorities and competing time demands?

27

The Cost And Responsibilities Of Leadership

Preparatory assignment: Read chapters 13 and 14 of *Spiritual Leadership*, and know the answers to the following questions.

Chapter Thirteen

1. According to Quinton Hogg, what is the cost of every great achievement?
2. List the six costs of being a leader.
3. Which part of the price of leadership must be paid every day?
4. What is the absolute demand that God makes on leaders?
5. List two verses that tell of Christ's total self–sacrifice.
6. What are the marks of true spiritual leadership?
7. Why is the way of a leader lonely?
8. List examples of the Bible's lonely leaders.
9. True or false? The wise leader will seize every legitimate opportunity for recreation. Why or why not?
10. If a man is to make an impression on his generation, what must he be willing to do?
11. Explain the following statement: There is no virtue in flogging the tired horse to death.

12. How is humility most clearly seen?
13. Which of the B–attitudes are necessary to handle criticism properly? ____________________
14. Know the story of Drs. J. Gregory Mantle and A. B. Simpson.
15. What unusual statement does Sanders make about knowing God's will?

Chapter Fourteen

1. What is Christ's definition of leadership?
2. How does leadership in the spiritual realm differ from leadership in the world?
3. Why did God choose Joshua to lead Israel?
4. Which B–attitude is necessary in the person who disciplines others? Why?
5. Before one disciplines someone, what five things must he consider?
6. What makes a leader a good guide?
7. Which causes more failure—extra caution or courageous risks?
8. What kind of man is an initiator, and what does it mean to initiate?
9. What factor made it easier for Joshua and Elisha to accept the role of a leader?
10. Know the five responsibilities of a leader as set forth in this chapter.
11. How would you describe Archbishop Benson?

Notes From The Teacher's Lesson

Christ's Two Considerations For Discipleship

The Construction Worker

Note The ____________________

- Note The ____________________
  - Hate Your ____________________
  - Bear The ____________________
  - Come After ____________________
  - Forsake All ____________________

The __________________________ King

- The Power Of The ____________________________ Working In The Life Of A Yielded Body And
- The Power Of ____________________.

Stepping Toward Effective Leadership

- Explain the following excerpt from a poem by James Russell Lowell and how it might relate to the Christian leader:

  Greatly begin! Though thou have time
  But for a line, be that sublime—
  Not failure, but low aim, is crime.

- Are you a loner or a team player? Which tendency is better for people in leadership roles and why? What steps can a loner take toward becoming a team player? What steps can team players take to help loners join them?

- Henri Nouwen named the following among the greatest temptations for Christian leaders:

  - the temptation to be relevant,
  - the temptation to be popular, and
  - the temptation to be powerful.

  Explain how each of these temptations is detrimental to effective Christian leadership. What do the following Scripture passages tell us concerning how Christ led in each of these areas of temptation: John 6:26–31; Mark 5:41–43; John 6:53, 60–61?

- Read "The Amazing Power of a Bibliography," chapter 22 in W. Clement Stone's book (see Recommended Reading List). What does he say concerning this topic?

- How can failure be good for a leader? Read "The Benefits of Failure" in Henry Rogers' book (see Recommended Reading List) for material to support your answer.

28

Searching Tests To Leadership

Preparatory assignment: Read chapter 15 of *Spiritual Leadership*, and know the answers to the following questions.

Chapter Fifteen

1. Name the five things that test our leadership.
2. Define and explain compromise.
3. Know the four ways by which Moses was tempted to compromise and the form that that same test takes today.
4. What did God offer Moses that tested his desire for fame and power?
5. What made this test difficult for him to pass?
6. When is a true leader at his best?
7. What was Moses' "impossible situation" test?
8. How did Moses react in those circumstances?
9. What were Moses' three commands, all of which seemed foolish, and *why* did they seem foolish?
10. In what does God delight?

11. Why did John Mott encourage leaders to deal with impossible tasks rather than easy ones?
12. How does failure test a man's leadership?
13. What Bible character rose from failure to lead God's people?
14. Concerning failure, what was true of most Bible characters who became leaders?
15. What has the successful man learned about failure?
16. What two attacks did Moses receive from jealous followers?
17. Which B–attitude is necessary to overcome jealous attacks from others?
18. How did Moses manifest this B–attitude in the jealous attack of Miriam and Aaron?
19. What do we learn about God in the stories of Miriam, Aaron, and Korah?
20. Read Numbers 12. Who settled the jealousy? What was Moses' only response in the whole episode?
21. Read Numbers 16:1–35. What charge did Korah make against Moses? What was Moses' immediate reaction? How did Moses later save the congregation from destruction? What happened to Korah?

Notes From The Teacher's Lesson

Satan's Tests To Leadership

His Purpose Is To ______________________________

He Tests With ______________________________

- "Worship God Where ______________________________"
    - Use The World's ______________________________ To Worship God

- "If You Must Leave Egypt, ______________________
  Go Just Over The Border."
  - Don't Go ______________________ With Your Religion
- "Let The Men Go And Worship, But Let The Children And The Women Stay Behind."
  - Opposite Today—Religion Is For ______________________
- "Take Your Family If You Must, But Leave Your ______________________
  ____
  - Hold Something ______________________

Stepping Toward Effective Leadership

- Distinguish between good and bad forms of compromise. Explain why the temptation to compromise principles is a test to effective leadership.
- Explain why the statement "Set the standard high" is a good motto for a Christian leader. Describe how that statement can be applied to music, worship, academics, personal purity, and work quality.
- Explain and illustrate the saying "The test of your character is what it takes to stop you."
- What are some ways to avoid comparing your own work and ministry with that of others and possibly becoming jealous over the differences in your success, acclaim, etc., in contrast to that of others?
- Read John 21:20–22. What was Peter's problem in those verses? What did Christ tell him that was meant to correct the problem? What application can you make to your own life based on that advice?

29

The Peculiar Perils Of Leadership

Preparatory assignment: Read chapter 19 of *Spiritual Leadership*, and know the answers to the following questions.

1. Name the seven perils of leadership, any of which will destroy a leader.
2. What was Paul's great concern in 1 Corinthians 9:27? What is a castaway?
3. In what realm do the spiritual leader's greatest dangers lie?
4. What three tests will reveal if we are proud?
5. Explain in your own words each of the tests of pride.
6. Which test does each of the following examples illustrate?
   - John gets extremely angry when Ed says that John is lazy and can't sing (something that John has frequently said about himself).
   - John fires back at Ed's accusation by accusing Ed of the same thing.
   - Ed laughs when he hears that John has been chosen over him for the ball team. He accuses John of buttering up the coach.
7. What is egotism?
8. How does egotism differ from pride?
9. What is the real test of egotism?

10. What characteristic marks a jealous man?
11. What incident illustrates Moses' lack of jealousy?
12. What was the Corinthians' biggest problem?
13. Following personalities rather than God is a mark of what?
14. What danger does a leader face when men praise, follow, and love him?
15. Is it right to be admired and loved by one's followers?
16. According to Spurgeon, what does success tend to cause a man to do?
17. What did Spurgeon say could keep success from going to one's head?
18. What is the sin of infallibility?
19. Why does a leader face the temptation of infallibility?
20. What is the peril of indispensability?
21. How can elation defeat a leader?
22. When did Spurgeon usually experience his greatest depression?
23. What did Chadwick say about success and defeat?
24. What was Paul's great fear?
25. What form of pride does God hate most?
26. What is pride?
27. Finish the following statement: The leader is most successful who ____ ____

Notes From The Teacher's Lesson

Peculiar Perils Of Leadership

Popularity

When Some People Praise You, Always Remember What ____________ ____________ And From ______________________________.

Pride

- Egotism: Pride Manifested In Our ____________________
- Infallibility: Pride Seen In An Inability To ____________________
____
- Jealousy: Pride Manifested When ____________________
- Indispensability: Pride Manifested In One's Opinion ____________________
____
- Elation And Depression: Pride In Our Victories And Defeats

Stepping Toward Effective Leadership

- Do you complete what you begin? Or do you have several unfinished projects? Why? What steps can you take to finish what you start?
- Define and give examples of *procrastination.* What are the results or effects of procrastination? What steps can you take to avoid or overcome procrastination?
- How does the following statement relate to the expectations that leaders should "finish the job"? "It is hard to grow enthusiastic over mediocrity, settling for less than the best of which leaders and followers are capable."
- Are you basically an optimist or a pessimist? How do you deal with times of discouragement or depression? How can you balance elation and depression?
- Read 1 Samuel 30:6. According to this verse, how did David deal with times of discouragement? How do you think that David did that? How can you apply that verse to your own particular times of discouragement?

Unit 6

Case Studies Of Leadership

30

Nehemiah

Preparatory Assignments:

- Read chapter 20 of *Spiritual Leadership.*
- Read the entire book of Nehemiah.
- Answer the following questions about your readings.

1. Know the ten character qualities prominent in Nehemiah's life and the incident in his life in which we clearly see each quality.

2. Record the prayers of Nehemiah as found in the following references. Beside each reference, state the thing for which he prayed.

1:4–11 ______________________________

____

2:1–5 ______________________________

____

4:1–6 ______________________________

____

4:7–9 ______________________________

____

5:19 ______________________________

____

6:14 ______________________________

____

13:10–14 ______________________________

____

13:23–29 ______________________________

____

3. What was Nehemiah's job before he returned to Jerusalem? ______

____

Background information: Israel was in captivity under the ruler Artaxerxes. Ezra had returned to Jerusalem with the king's permission about 540 B.C. to rebuild the temple, which had been torn down when Israel fell into captivity. By 517 B.C., the temple was completed. Seventy–two years passed, and the Jews were still in captivity. In Babylon, Nehemiah received word about the conditions (especially about the condition of the walls) in Jerusalem from a Jew who had just returned from visiting that city. Nehemiah was brokenhearted and prayed that God would let him have the king's permission to return to Jerusalem to restore the walls. This information brings us to the first chapter of Nehemiah.

4. What was the name of the man who brought to Nehemiah news of the condition of the walls in Jerusalem? ______________________

5. What was the condition of the walls? ______________________

____

6. What happened in Nehemiah 2:1–8? ______________________

____

____

7. What three men laughed at Nehemiah and mocked him when they heard that he had returned to Jerusalem to rebuild the wall? ______

____

8. In chapter three, Nehemiah recorded the names of the ten gates that were rebuilt. Name them in the order in which they were finished.

- ______________________
- ______________________
- ______________________
- ______________________
- ______________________
- ______________________
- ______________________
- ______________________
- ______________________
- ______________________

9. Nehemiah faced all kinds of opposition, including…

- Mockery from (4:1–3) ______________________
- Conspiracy to stop him from (4:7–9) ______________________ ______________________
- Discouragement because of (4:10) ______________________ ______________________

10. Name the six main elements in the methods that Nehemiah used to restore the wall.
11. Know the four statements that Nehemiah made when the morale of his helpers fell.
12. What seven things did Nehemiah restore concerning their worship?
13. How do we see the organizational ability of Nehemiah?
14. What do you most admire about Nehemiah?

Notes From The Teacher's Lesson

Nehemiah

A Man Of ______________________________

A Man Of ____________ *Because He Knew* ____________

- He Gathered ______________________________
- He ______________ About The Information
- He Became ______________ About The Wall
- God Opened ______________ In The Direction Of The Burden
- God Did Not ______________ All Of His Will At One Time

Stepping Toward Effective Leadership

- The motto of the Boy Scouts of America is "Be prepared!" Explain how Nehemiah was prepared to make his request before the king ever asked him what was bothering him. What does 1 Peter 3:15 say about every believer's responsibility to "be prepared?"

- Trace the major events in the ongoing, centuries–old conflict between the Arabs and the Jews from the time of Abraham to the present day. Explain why all efforts to bring peace to that region are doomed to failure until the return of Christ. Does that mean that we should not work to bring peace to that region of the world? What does the Bible say that we should pray for in relation to that region (give the reference)?

- Nehemiah established an around–the–clock guard on the walls of Jerusalem as they were being repaired. What lesson does that teach us concerning believers' responsibility to arm ourselves and to keep a watchful eye against Satan? Which passage of Scripture gives details concerning the believer's armor and equipment in that conflict? Explain why we must always be watchful against Satan.

- Write an essay explaining and applying to the believer's life the following saying from a famous speech by Winston Churchill: "Never, never, never give up!"

- What discourages you most in your Christian life? What steps can you take to overcome those enemies?

- What types of things does Satan use to distract you from doing your God–given duty? How do you deal with such distractions?

- How did Nehemiah's planning and goal–setting skills help him stay "on task" and undeterred by his opposition? What goals do you have for life? For this year? For this month? For this week? For today?

- Nehemiah clearly was an "on–purpose person." Read *The On–Purpose Person* by Kevin McCarthy, and list principles from that book that you can apply to your own life.

31

Joshua—A Young Man With A Future

Have you ever seen an article or TV show titled something like "Whatever Happened to…?" The idea behind that type of article or program is that some people flash onto the scene as leaders in various fields—such as fashion or acting or politics—or they become heroes of one sort or another, but then they seem to disappear just as quickly. No one ever mentions them again. Until you see someone who reminds you of the person, and then you find yourself asking, "Hey, whatever happened to…? You know, the guy who…."

You'll soon find that that happens a lot with your high school friends. One day, about a dozen years after you graduate from high school, you'll run across your old high school yearbook and begin to page through it, reminiscing about the times and people and events of "the good old days." Invariably, you'll happen upon the picture of a classmate whom you've all but forgotten. Perhaps he was a BMOC ("big man on campus"), an officer in the student council, or a leader of a major student organization. But you've lost track of him. In fact, you've almost forgotten that he even existed. And you find yourself asking, "I wonder whatever happened to old Richard? I wonder what he's doing now? Do you think he fulfilled our prophecy when we students voted him "Most Likely to Succeed?" Sometimes the answers to such questions surprise us.

But at least one young person mentioned in the Bible didn't leave any doubt about how he turned out. Joshua was a young man with great promise. Although he had to struggle to overcome what to many young people would have been insurmountable disadvantages, Joshua had something more. He had Christian character. He learned from a mentor. And he became a leader who would be remembered for countless generations.

What made the difference in Joshua's life? What separated him from all of the other promising young men of his day? What ensured that in later years his friends and "classmates" wouldn't think of him and ask, "I wonder whatever happened to old Joshua?" Let's examine his life and find out!

Joshua became one of the Bible's greatest examples of leadership. He was just a youth when Moses led Israel out of Egypt. At that time, no one would have imagined that Joshua would grow up to be the man to take Moses' place. No one, that is, but God and Moses!

Student Work

From the teacher's lesson, you should be able to answer the following questions about the background facts about this young man with a bright future.

- Where was he born? ______________________________

- What did he probably endure while he lived there? ____________
  ____

- Of what general age was he at the time of the Exodus? (Exod. 33:11)
  ____

- What was his job as a youth? (Exod. 33:11) ______________
  ____

The following three facts about Joshua can be seen in his performance of this job.

1. *He must have had some admirable qualities.* Why can we assume this fact? ______________________________________
   ____

2. *He was willing to be a servant.* From this fact, what lesson can we learn about one of the most important qualities of leadership? __________
   ____

3. *He was truly dedicated to the Lord.* What phrase in Exodus 33:11 indicates spiritual discipline? ______________________________

____

What two types of discipline did Joshua experience in his youth? ______

____

____

____

His name was changed from ______________________________ to ______________________________(Num. 13:8, 16), which means ______________________________.

Joshua was dependable. What great responsibility did he accept and finish in Exodus 17:8–16? ______________________________

____

If Joshua had not been careful, he would have been defeated by pride. How did God use Moses to keep Joshua humble? ______________________________

____

____

What lesson do we learn about our successes from this incident? ______

____

Joshua was tested and stood alone. According to Numbers 13:1–16; 14:26–35, how was Joshua tested concerning his ability to stand alone?

____

____

____

Joshua was Spirit filled. According to Numbers 27:15–23, why did God select him to succeed Moses? ______________________________

____

What two things do we learn from this passage about how one becomes a leader? ______________________________

____

____

Notes From The Teacher's Lesson

Joshua

His Birth And Early Life

- Born In ________________________
- Strong Through ________________________

His ________________________ To The Lord (Exod. 33:11)

- An ________________________ Youth
- A Willing ________________________
- A ________________________ Youth

His ________________________ (Exod. 17:8–16)

His ________________________ Life (Num. 27:15–23)

Stepping Toward Effective Leadership

- Think of and describe an experience that occurred early in your life that helped prepare you for later service, responsibility, or leadership. How did you see God's hand at work in your life during and after that incident?
- Complete the inventory of leadership qualities (see "Measuring Yourself"). Follow the instructions given. Discuss the results with your teacher. Discuss with your teacher, principle, or guidance counselor other personality inventories and/or skills assessment tools that will help you learn about your leadership skills and qualifications.
- List the "giants" that stand in the way of your obeying God and doing His will. What steps can you take to defeat those giants?
- List and memorize verses that will equip you to stand alone in doing what you know is right. (Be especially sure to select verses that address specific problems with which you struggle.)

Measuring Yourself:
An Inventory Of Leadership Qualities

Name______________________________ Date ______________________

Joshua was a balanced young man. He was physically and spiritually strong, and the next three lessons will reveal that he was also emotionally stable and socially mature.

How do *you* rate in these areas? How good a leader would *you* be? You can get a good idea of your leadership qualities by rating yourself honestly on the following inventory. For each statement, circle the appropriate number to indicate how true the statement is of you. (For example, circle 1 if the statement is *almost never true* of you, 10 if it is *always true* of you, or another number between 1 and 10 as appropriate.)

Emotional Maturity

I accept criticism without being hurt or overly sensitive.

1 2 3 4 5 6 7 8 9 10

I am tolerant of the faults of others.

1 2 3 4 5 6 7 8 9 10

I refrain from repeating gossip.

1 2 3 4 5 6 7 8 9 10

I put the happiness and welfare of others above myself.

1 2 3 4 5 6 7 8 9 10

I face problems objectively and do not make excuses.

1 2 3 4 5 6 7 8 9 10

I get along well with people.

1 2 3 4 5 6 7 8 9 10

I am loyal to friends and employers.

1 2 3 4 5 6 7 8 9 10

I can make sound decisions fairly quickly and live with those decisions.

1 2 3 4 5 6 7 8 9 10

I have the courage of my convictions regardless of their popularity or rejection by others.

1 2 3 4 5 6 7 8 9 10

I can control my temper.

1 2 3 4 5 6 7 8 9 10

I work democratically with others; I am not authoritarian in leading them.

1 2 3 4 5 6 7 8 9 10

I do not ask for special favors.

1 2 3 4 5 6 7 8 9 10

I am not touchy or temperamental.

1 2 3 4 5 6 7 8 9 10

I am prompt and businesslike in keeping records.

1 2 3 4 5 6 7 8 9 10

I am dependable.

1 2 3 4 5 6 7 8 9 10

I am organized, and I plan well before I do something.

1 2 3 4 5 6 7 8 9 10

Total ____________ **÷ 16 =** __________

Social Maturity

I am cheerful.

1 2 3 4 5 6 7 8 9 10

I am tactful; I do not usually offend others.

1 2 3 4 5 6 7 8 9 10

I have a sense of humor, even when the joke is on me; I can laugh at myself.

1 2 3 4 5 6 7 8 9 10

I use good English when I speak and write.

1 2 3 4 5 6 7 8 9 10

I consider myself poised in most situations.

1 2 3 4 5 6 7 8 9 10

I enjoy my work.

1 2 3 4 5 6 7 8 9 10

I have varied interests.

1 2 3 4 5 6 7 8 9 10

I am enthusiastic and outgoing.

1 2 3 4 5 6 7 8 9 10

I am neat in appearance.

1 2 3 4 5 6 7 8 9 10

I keep my clothing and myself clean.

1 2 3 4 5 6 7 8 9 10

I like children and enjoy their company.

1 2 3 4 5 6 7 8 9 10

I can teach or assist using several skills.

1 2 3 4 5 6 7 8 9 10

I am able to work well as a member of a group; I'm a team player.

1 2 3 4 5 6 7 8 9 10

I assume responsibility and am conscientious in performing my duties.

1 2 3 4 5 6 7 8 9 10

I am familiar with the outdoors.

1 2 3 4 5 6 7 8 9 10

I am completely honest with both myself and others.

1 2 3 4 5 6 7 8 9 10

I keep people's confidences and share them with no one, not even to have others "pray about it."

1 2 3 4 5 6 7 8 9 10

I can see a job to be done and do it without having to be told.

1 2 3 4 5 6 7 8 9 10

I adapt easily to new situations.

1 2 3 4 5 6 7 8 9 10

I get involved in recreation and challenge others to follow my example.

1 2 3 4 5 6 7 8 9 10

Total ______________ ÷ 20 =___________

Health

I know my own limitations and can live within them.

1 2 3 4 5 6 7 8 9 10

I discipline myself in eating, sleeping, and using time.

1 2 3 4 5 6 7 8 9 10

I am in good health and exhibit vitality.

1 2 3 4 5 6 7 8 9 10

I can participate in a vigorous activity program.

1 2 3 4 5 6 7 8 9 10

Total ____________ ÷ 4 =__________

Spiritual Maturity

I know Jesus Christ as my personal Lord and Savior and enjoy a vital and growing relationship with Him.

1 2 3 4 5 6 7 8 9 10

Working with the Holy Spirit, I can lead a person to Christ using language and terms that a child could understand.

1 2 3 4 5 6 7 8 9 10

My life is a good example, the kind that I want others to follow.

1 2 3 4 5 6 7 8 9 10

I have a regular, daily time of fellowship with my Lord by reading the Word and praying.

1 2 3 4 5 6 7 8 9 10

I am concerned that each of my friends grows in his or her spiritual life.

1 2 3 4 5 6 7 8 9 10

I am able to relate the Word of God to my friends' everyday lives.

1 2 3 4 5 6 7 8 9 10

I know what it is to have my prayers answered.

1 2 3 4 5 6 7 8 9 10

Total ____________ ÷ 7 =__________

(Adapted from *Creative Counselling* by Joy McKay)

Scoring/Interpreting This Inventory

Add the numbers you circled in each of the four sections. Then divide the sum of each section by the number of questions in that section. The result will give you your average score for that section. Now rate your average for each section according to the following key:

If your average is...	Then...
8–10	You are good leadership material; keep up the good work, and ask the Lord to continue giving you the grace to serve Him even better in the future. Keep in mind that no one knows everything, so keep learning and growing in your leadership potential.
4–7	You still have room for a lot of growth and improvement. Keep working on yourself, and ask God to point out areas in which you need specific help. Seek out a mentor from among the godly people you know and trust to help you develop a plan for learning and growing in knowledge and skills.
1–3	You have a LONG way to go, so you'd better get busy now! Seek out a godly person who is willing to guide you in your growth in each of the categories covered by this inventory. Ask for his or her advice in identifying specific weaknesses in your life, then work to turn those weaknesses into strengths by God's grace.

32

Joshua—Lessons On Leadership

Preparatory Assignment: For the next several chapters, we will study thirty–three different lessons on leadership found in the life of Joshua as recorded in the book of Joshua. We find the first twelve lessons in the first chapter of Joshua. Read Joshua 1 carefully before proceeding with this lesson. Then use that passage (and other verses as noted) to answer the following questions.

1. A Leader Is Instructed By The Lord (vv. 1–9)

Which verse tells us that the Lord instructed Joshua? ____________

How does God instruct His servants today? ____________

____

What does that fact teach us that we must do if we are to know His instruction? ____________

____

____

2. A Leader Is Immortal When He Is In God's Will (v. 5)

What does the word *immortal* mean? ______________________

____

What phrases in verse 5 point out this fact? ______________________

____

____

So as long as Joshua was in God's will, nothing could stop him! And the same is true with us!

3. A Leader Must Be Strong (vv. 6–7)

We see here three reasons why Joshua had to be strong:

1. he would face giants,
2. he would face defeat and disappointment, and
3. he would face jealousy and greed when he divided the land.

In what two ways had Joshua already made himself strong in his youth?

____

4. A Leader Must Be Mentally Alert (vv. 6–7, 9, 18; 10:25; 23:6)

The word *courage* in these verses means "mentally alert." A leader must be intelligent, quick witted, and well read. What exercises in Bible class are designed to expand and sharpen the alertness of your mind? __________

____

____

5. A Leader Must Be Obedient (v. 7)

What phrase reveals this point? ______________________

____

____

What is promised to those who obey perfectly? ______________________

____

Name several ways by which we can "turn to the right hand or to the left" and thereby get out of God's will. ______________________________

____

____

6. A Leader Must Have A Personal Relationship With The Lord (v. 8)

What three commands does God give Joshua in this verse concerning his relationship to the Lord?

1. ______________________________________

2. ______________________________________

3. ______________________________________

What is promised to those who have this kind of relationship with the Lord? ______________________________________

____

7. A Leader Must Never Be Discouraged (vv. 9; 8:1; 10:25)

What phrase in these verses describes this quality? ________________

____

Dismayed means "to prostrate, to stretch out face down on the floor; to break down; to be discouraged." This command—do not be dismayed—is found sixteen times in the Bible! The Word commands us nineteen times to be courageous.

The Lord Jesus Christ was *disappointed* a number of times, but He was never *discouraged* (i.e., ready to give up).

What does Isaiah 42:4 say about this fact? ______________________

____

____

Instead of being discouraged, what must a leader do? (Read 1 Thessalonians 5:14 [*comfort* means "encourage." *Fainthearted*, or *feeble-minded*, means "easily discouraged."]) ______________________

____

____

8. A Leader Leads (v. 10)

How do we see Joshua leading in this verse? ______________________

____

____

9. A Leader Is An Organizer (v. 11)

How do we see Joshua's organizational skills in this verse? ___________

____

____

Good leaders attend to details, set and meet goals, and set and meet deadlines. Do you plan how you will do things, or do you just do things without forethought?

10. A Leader Is Positive (v. 11)

How do we see from this verse that Joshua had a positive spirit? _______

____

____

Leaders never take *no* or *I can't* for an answer. What was Joshua preparing these people to do? ____

If a leader isn't strong and positive, or if he lets the group control him (see point 8), what will happen? ______________________________

____

Many people never accomplish anything worthwhile for the Lord because they and their leaders have "I–can't–itis."

11. A Leader Has Faith (vv. 11–13)

What phrases in vv. 11–13 show Joshua's faith in God?

- Verse 11—____
- Verse 13—____

On what was his faith based? _________________________________

____

Faith is never guesswork; it is always based on concrete evidence. And the surest evidence that anyone can ever have is God's own promises.

12. A Leader Motivates (vv. 14–15)

To whom were these words (v. 12) addressed? ______________________

____

These two–and–a–half tribes were to live eventually across the river on the east side. The area west of the river, however, had to be conquered. Fierce giants and great warriors lived across the river. The two–and–a–half tribes were relieved to know that they had no enemy to drive out, and they felt no responsibility or desire to help their brother tribes conquer the west. *After all,* they thought, *we can't live there. Why should we shed* our *blood fighting for* their *land?*

Joshua had to show his ability to motivate these men to do what they had no desire to do. What did he command them to do? ______________

____

____

What was their reply (v. 16)? ______________________________

____

From this, we see Joshua's ability to get men to do what they did not really want to do! One of the greatest motivational forces is enthusiasm (a spirit of faith and excitement). Dull, dead people don't excite groups to action.

Notes From The Teacher's Lesson

Lessons On Leadership (Joshua 1:1-9)

1. A Leader Is ______________________ By The Lord (1:1–4)

- God Taught Him His ______________________ For His Life.
- God Gave Him ______________ On Which To Anchor His Faith.

2. A Leader Is ______________________________ (1:5)

3–5. A Leader Must Be ______________________________
______________________________ (1:6–7)

6. A Leader Must Have A ______________ With The Lord (1:8)

7. A Leader Must Never Be ______________________ (1:9)

Stepping Toward Effective Leadership

- Explain what author and teacher Jesse Stuart meant by the following statement: "I am firm in my belief that a teacher lives on and on through his students. Good teaching is forever and the teacher is immortal." How does 2 Timothy 3:14 relate to this saying? Make a list of the teachers who have most influenced your life and explain how they did so.

- Define the word *mentor*. Have you ever had a mentor? If so, who was it, and how did they help lead you? List the qualities that you think are important for a mentor. For whom could you be a mentor?

- List chronologically the plans whereby you will be properly trained to serve the Lord. What is your timetable for completing that training period? What steps should you be taking *now* to fulfill that long–range plan?

- Why is physical strength and good health important for a leader? What steps are you taking to ensure your strength and health? To guarantee mental alertness?

- Describe your devotional process. What Scripture–reading methods or plans do you use? What role do prayer, meditation, and Scripture memorization play in your devotional time? Do you use any other books or literature in your devotions? (If so, describe them.)

33

Joshua—Beginning The Campaign

Joshua, having received a commission from the Lord to lead the children of Israel to victory over the nations living in Canaan, was at last ready to cross the Jordan River. Chapter 2 of Joshua tells how he sent spies to reconnoiter Jericho and gather information to help in conquering the city. During the spies' reconnaissance, they were nearly discovered, but Rahab helped them avoid capture. In return for her kindness, they promised safety for her and her family during the coming campaign against Jericho.

In chapter 3, the people were ready for the miraculous crossing of the Jordan River. That is where we resume the story and learn more great lessons of leadership from Joshua.

Preparatory assignment: Read Joshua 3–8 carefully before continuing with this lesson.

Crossing The Jordan (Josh. 3–5)

Describe the crossing of the Jordan River by writing the details in the following blanks.

Joshua rose (when?) ____
and marched the people to the Jordan River, where they waited for (how long?) ________________________. The (who?) ____________________

then instructed the people about the crossing of the river. First, the (what?) ____________ and the (who?) _____________________ would lead the procession. Then the people would follow behind by (how much?) ____

When the people were ready, Joshua made a speech of encouragement. He commanded them to (do what?) ________________________________
Then he promised the people that God would—without fail—(do what?)
____
____
________________________________from before them. (See verse 10.)

When the (what?) ___________________ of the priests who carried the ark touched the waters of the river, the waters that came down from above (did what?) ____ and those that were below them (did what?) __________________________
____, and the people passed over near Jericho. As they passed over, those who bore the ark stood (how?) __________________ on (what?) _________________________ in the (what part?) _____________________ of the river until all of the people had passed safely over.

When everyone had finished crossing the river, the Lord commanded Joshua to (do what, according to 4:2–3?) __________________________
____ who were to (do what?) ____
____.

These stones were to be a (what, according to 4:6?) ______________ to the people in the days ahead so that they would not forget to tell their (who?) ______________________ about the miraculous crossing of the Jordan. Joshua did not only that but also set up (how many?) ________ stones in the midst of Jordan where the priests stood.

After these tasks were completed, the (who?) ____________________ who bore the ark came up out of the Jordan and the waters (did what?) ____ ____ (4:18).

On the tenth day of the first month, they encamped in (where?) ____________________. (This meant that their crossing of the Jordan had occurred on Nisan 10, the same date on which the passover lamb had been set aside and the same day on which, years later, Christ would make His triumphal entry into Jerusalem!)

What effect did the miraculous drying up of the Jordan River have on the kings of the Canaanites when word of it reached them (5:1)? ________ ____ ____

Four days later (Nisan 14), what did the Israelites do? ______________ ____

What provision ceased the next day? ____________________________ ____

When Joshua was by Jericho, he saw a (what?) ________________ near him with his (what?) ______________________________________
According to the man's own admission, who was he? ______________ ____

It was actually Jesus Christ Himself in human form! How did Joshua react? ____ ____

This is one reason we know that this man was not an angel! Every time men bowed before angels, the angels immediately commanded them not to worship them, for "Thou shalt worship the Lord thy God, and Him only shalt thou worship." The fact that this man allowed Joshua to worship him proves that he was God. What did Joshua call him? ________

Jericho And Ai (Josh. 6–8)

- According to 6:1, what had the citizens of Jericho, fearing Israel, done?
  ____

- What did God promise Joshua in 6:2? ____________________
  ____

- Provide the following details about the conquering of Jericho.
  - Who went first? ______________________________
  - Who sent second? ______________________________
  - Who went third? ______________________________
  - Who went fourth? ______________________________

- They were to march around the city in this order (for how long?) _____ _______with the priests blasting on the trumpets. The people, however, were not to make (what?) ____________________. On the seventh day, they were to march around the city (how many?) ____________ times. On the seventh time around, the priests were to blow on the trumpets and the people were to give a great (what?) ________________. The people followed these instructions, and when the people shouted, the walls fell down flat, and the people went into the city and (did what?) _________ ________________________________ all that was in the city (6:21).

- What had Joshua commanded concerning the capture and spoils of the city (6:17–19)? ______________________________
  ____
  ____
  ____

- Who violated this command? ____________________ What effect did that person's sin have upon the Israelites? ____________________
  ____
  ____

According to 7:6, what was Joshua's reaction to this defeat? ___________

____

____

He then prayed a prayer of mourning and contrition. If you study the prayer carefully, you can see Joshua's weaknesses. How do we see his weakness of unbelief in this prayer? ______________________________

____

____

____

What did God command Joshua in 7:10? ________________________

This is a reminder of the command in 1:9. God had told Joshua *never* to be ____

The word *dismayed* means "to prostrate, or to lie flat." And here Joshua was breaking that command!

What had to happen to Achan to correct the sin of the nation? ______

____

____

____

Imagine how hard it must have been for Joshua to carry out this command (especially if Achan was his friend). Yet, he did exactly what God had commanded.

Did Joshua quit? _____ What does God command a second time in 8:1?

____

This time, Joshua took (how many?) __________________ soldiers with him. (He had learned from his previous mistake when he had taken only [how many?] ________________________ soldiers.) They laid an ambush for the men of Ai, and this time Israel won the battle. How many of the people of Ai did they destroy? ____________________________________.

Joshua then built (what?) _______________________________to the Lord on Mount ________________. There, they (did what, according to 8:31?)

____

Joshua then wrote a copy of the (what?) ______________________
on the stones of the altar and (did what, according to 8:34?) ________
____

Leadership Lessons

Joshua chapters 3–8 give us ten more great lessons on leadership.

13. God Magnifies His Man (3:7; 4:14)

As we've already learned this year, leaders cannot be self–appointed. God must choose the man He wants. After choosing him, God will cause his followers to admire, appreciate, and respect him. The point to remember here is that as long as we try to magnify ourselves (by boasting, trying to outdo everybody else, or talking about our achievements), God won't use us. Let *Him* magnify those He intends to use. If God wants to use you for leadership, He will find ways to magnify you.

Why did God magnify Joshua in the eyes of the people? __________
____
____

14. A Leader Relates Everything To God's Word (3:9–10; 8:32)

How did Joshua do this? ______________________________
____
____

A true spiritual leader solves all problems with the Word, makes decisions according to the Word, finds God's will for his life in the Word, and gives reasons for all of his actions from the Word.

15. A Leader Recognizes The Real Leader (5:13–15)

Did Joshua think that he was the real leader of Israel? ___________
How do you know that? ______________________________
____

What will happen when we realize and remember that we are not the real leaders and that we are only God's servants? ______________________

____

____

16. A Leader Is A Detail Man (6:12–16)

Leaders have the ability to think through a plan to the point of taking care of every detail ahead of time. Men who lack leadership ability can think only of ideas; they can't work out the small details. How do we see Joshua thinking through and carrying out the smallest details in this account?

____

____

____

17. A Leader Admits Mistakes (7:6–9)

What mistake did Joshua make in this passage? ____________________

____

____

____

One of the greatest lessons we can learn is to say, "I was wrong." Most leaders get so used to being right that it is hard for them to admit that they've made a mistake. Actually, admitting a mistake often causes people to admire you *more* because they realize that you are honest and that you don't think of yourself as a god.

18. A Leader Must Be Firm (7:24–26)

How does this passage show firmness on the part of Joshua? __________

____

____

____

One of the hardest tasks for a leader is to set rules and then ensure that they are enforced consistently. A leader will often let friends get by the rules because he doesn't want to be unpopular with them. Yet, rules must not only be made but also strictly enforced; otherwise, the leader will not have the respect of the people.

19. A Leader Tries Again (8:1–2)

How do we see this quality in Joshua? ______________________________

____

____

Leaders are not quitters. Leaders will be defeated many times and they will have a lot of setbacks, but their spirit is never broken. They know that God will ultimately give them the victory. According to 7:10, what is a leader never to do? ______________________________

____

20. A Leader Learns From His Past Mistakes (8:3)

From what mistake did Joshua learn a lesson? ______________________

____

____

____

Mistakes are always embarrassing and discouraging. However, we should view them as challenges. The leader who is greatly used of God is not the man who lets mistakes defeat him. He's the man who lets mistakes *challenge* him and *teach* him how to win the next time.

21. A Leader Finishes The Job (8:26)

How do we see Joshua "finishing the job" in this passage? ____________

____

____

One of the greatest temptations of a leader is to say, "That's good enough." Remember, *good enough* is never good enough! God expects and demands that whatever we do for Him is done completely, wholeheartedly, and with every ounce of energy and enthusiasm we can muster. Jobs begun for Him must be finished. How would this lesson apply to worldly amusements in our lives? ______________________________

____

____

How would this lesson apply to preparing for this class? ___________

____

____

____

____

What, then, is the sin of saying, "That's good enough?" ___________

____

____

____

22. A Leader Gives God The Credit, Praise, And Glory (8:30–31)

How did Joshua do this? ___________________________

____

____

____

What earlier incident in Joshua 5 made it easier for Joshua to give God the credit? ___________________________

____

____

We must never forget that any accomplishment in which God uses us is not of our doing. Whatever is accomplished through us is totally God's doing.

Do these ten leadership qualities describe you? Are you the kind of man or woman whom God can use? Think about it!

Notes From The Teacher's Lesson

Lessons On Leadership

13. God ____________________ His Men (Josh. 3:7; 4:14)

14. A Leader Relates Everything To ____________ (Josh. 3:9–10; 8:32)

15. A Leader Recognizes The ____________________ (Josh. 5:13–15)

16. A Leader Is A ____________________ Man (Josh. 6:12–16)

17. A Leader ____________________ (Josh. 7:6–16)

18. Leaders Must Be ____________________ (Josh. 7:24–26)

19. A Leader Tries ____________________ (Josh. 8:1–2)

20. A Leader Learns From ____________________ (Josh. 8:3)

21. A Leader ____________________ The Job (Josh. 8:26)

22. A Leader Gives God the ____________________(Josh. 8:30–31)

Stepping Toward Effective Leadership

- List ten areas of your life where you are most likely to say, "Oh, that's good enough." What steps can you take to avoid being satisfied with *good enough* in each of those areas?

- Visit a library to locate and read the poems "The Broken Wheel" and "Good Enough" by famous American folk poet Edgar A. Guest. What message was Guest trying to communicate through each of these poems, and how does that message relate to this lesson?

- One principle in this lesson is that "A leader relates everything to God's Word." If you are a baseball fan, read Michael O'Connor's book *Sermon on the Mound* and then explain how the author related baseball to God's Word. What spiritual lessons do you learn from the book?

- Why is attention to details so important for a leader? What activities or exercises will help you increase your skill of attending to details?
- Explain how the following saying relates to effective leadership: "If at first you don't succeed, try, try again."
- Someone used to say frequently, "Oh, that's good enough for government work." What does that saying communicate about the quality or efficiency of government employees? How did that reputation develop? Do you think it is justified? (Why or why not?)

34

Joshua—Continuing The Campaign

Preparatory assignment: Continuing our study of the leadership qualities found in the life of Joshua, we discover twelve more lessons in Joshua 10–16. Read each of these chapters carefully before continuing with this lesson.

23. A Leader Has The Ear And The Heart Of God (Josh. 10:1–14)

Adonizedek, king of ____________________, was upset over two things:

Israel's victory over ____ and

Israel's alliance with the people of ________________________________.

Therefore, he called together the following four kings to form a united alliance of their own:

- __________________________, king of Hebron;
- __________________________, king of Jarmuth;
- ______________________, king of Lachish; and
- ____________________________, king of Eglon.

These five kings went out to wage war against ________________. In turn, these men sent messengers to ______________________, which was Joshua's headquarters, and asked him to ____________________

____

____.

Joshua agreed, gathered his mighty men of war, and headed for the battlefield.

While Joshua was enroute to the battle, the Lord spoke to him and said,

____

____

____

Three important events took place during this battle:

1. ______________________________________them with giant ________________ all the way from ____________________ to ____.

2. More were killed by the ____________________ than by combat.

3. Joshua made what fantastic request when he reached Azekah? _____

____

____

God granted his request. How long did this occur? ________________

____

____

Verse 14 is the key verse in this lesson on leadership: "…that the Lord hearkened unto the voice of a man." Here we see the great power of prayer that every great spiritual leader possesses. What does 1 John 3:22 promise? ____

____

According to 1 John 3:22, what requirement must God's man meet if he is to receive this promise? __________________________________

____

All effective spiritual leaders have power in prayer. In fact, their powerful prayer life is what sets them above other men and makes them leaders.

24. A Leader Is Merciless To God's Enemies (Josh. 10:15–28)

"Mopping up" operations began as the war ended. What did Joshua do to the five kings after he had captured them? ______________________

____

____

From this event, we learn a lesson concerning sin and worldliness. How are we to treat sin? ______________________________

____

What seven ways do the following verses show us to treat sin?

1. 1 John 1:9—______________________________
2. Psalm 38:18— ____________________________
3. Psalm 97:10— ____________________________
4. 2 Timothy 2:19— __________________________
5. 1 Thessalonians 5:22—_____________________
6. Colossians 3:5— __________________________
7. Romans 6:6— _____________________________

Have you taken this attitude toward sin? Do you hate it? Do you utterly destroy it? Or do you, like Achan, save back the best parts to enjoy?

25. A Leader Accomplishes No More Than God Wants But No More Than He Tries (Josh. 10:29–42)

Joshua 10:29–41 describes Joshua's continuing practice of "*Good enough* is never good enough." He destroyed all of the enemy wherever he went.

Which phrases show the completeness of his victories over each of the following places?

- Libnah (v. 30)—____________________
- Lachish— ____________________
- Horam—____________________
- Eglon—____________________
- Hebron— ____________________
- Debir—____________________

The entire Negev and Shephelah (valley) regions—____________________

____

Yet, according to verse 42, who really gained all of these victories? _____

____

Here we learn a great lesson: as we fight temptation and worldliness each day, we can overcome them only as God gives us the power. But God will not give us the power unless we make a definite attempt to overcome them. God gave Joshua victory—but only as He saw Joshua moving forward in battle.

26. A Leader Will Face Opposition (Josh. 11:1–5)

Who opposed Joshua by the waters of Merom? ____________________

____

____

____

Here we learn another great lesson: the more victories we gain, the more we will be opposed! For example, if you take a stand for God and honestly seek to live a separated Christian life, you will be scrutinized and criticized and opposed. Carnal students will delight in watching your life to find just one tiny inconsistency for which they can castigate you.

Carnal students aren't gossiped about; it's the spiritual students who are put down. As we have already seen, Nehemiah faced the same problem. He could have stayed in the palace of Artaxerxes and never been criticized. But just as soon as he went to Jerusalem and made public his plan to build something for the Lord, he immediately faced gossip, criticism, and hatred. So it is with every person who tries to accomplish anything worthwhile for the Lord. Take a stand against wrong in your school or community, and you will be opposed, and sometimes the source of your opposition will surprise you!

27. A Leader Never Retires (His Work Is Never Finished) (Josh. 13:1)

How do we see this lesson in 13:1? ______________________________

____

____

The young Christian who wants to serve the Lord must be willing to work long and hard while others play and rest. A youth pastor must be willing to get up early and go to bed late. He must be willing to have a crowd of teens in his house until midnight, go to bed with the house still dirty, be aroused at 3:00 a.m. with the news that a member of the church is dying, and then be at work by 8:00 the next morning after rising early for prayer.

28. A Leader Rises To The Challenge (Josh. 14:1–15)

Caleb, who (along with Joshua) had helped spy out the land of Canaan years before, made a special request of Joshua. Caleb was now _________ ___________ years old, and he remembered a particular mountain that the twelve spies had seen forty–five years earlier when they were scouting the land. (See Numbers 13:1–33 for that story.) On that mountain, the spies found the children of ___________ (Num. 13:28, 33). These men were ________________________, and in contrast to them the Israelites were as ____________________________. Now, Caleb, at a ripe old age, requested what? ____

____

Joshua granted Caleb's request, and you can guess what happened! (Read Joshua 15:14.) So, we see in Caleb another lesson in leadership: no problem is too great for God to overcome. Leaders are men and women who are able to believe God for anything that He has promised them.

Notes From The Teacher's Lesson

Lessons On Leadership

23. A Leader Has The ______________________________ Of God (Josh. 10:1–14)

If You Are To Be Effective With Men, You Must Have The ______ ____.

24. A Leader Is ______________ To God's Enemies (Josh. 10:15–28)

The Enemy Of God Should Be The Enemy Of ______________

25. A Leader Accomplishes No More Than God Wants But No More Than He ____________________________ (Josh. 10:29–42)

We Must Do __________________________ God Will Do His.

26. A Leader Will Face ____________________________ (Josh. 11:1–5)

Great Blessings Are Followed By Great ____________________.

27. A Leader Never _________________ Because His Work Is Never Finished (Josh. 13:1)

28 A Leader Rises To The ______________________ (Josh. 14:1–15)

True Leaders Are Not __________________ By Great Obstacles, Rather They Are Challenged To Conquer.

Stepping Toward Effective Leadership

- In George Washington's "Farewell Address" to the nation following his service as our president, he warned the people against "entangling alliances." Why do you think he included that warning? How can we see the effects of ignoring that warning in subsequent U. S. history? How does his advice echo the lesson that Joshua and Israel learned from their experience with the Gibeonites?

- God will never do for you what He has already equipped and empowered you to do; He expects you to exert some of your own efforts, using what He's given you. How does that truth ring true in this lesson?

- Explain the following saying in relation to this lesson: "Pray as if everything depended on God; work as if everything depended on you."

- Although the following statement is not found anywhere in the Bible, is it true or false? (Why?) "God helps those who help themselves."

- Conduct a study of the Amorites, Hittites, Perizzites, Jebusites, or Hivites, and contrast them with Israel.

- In light of what this lesson teaches about the man of God never retiring, describe a senior citizen with whom you are acquainted who is busy in the Lord's service. Contact a mission agency to ask them about opportunities they might have by which "senior saints" can continue to serve God in their "golden years."

- Study the lyrics of the song "I Want that Mountain." Relate the words to both Caleb's request and our own modern–day challenges.

35

Joshua—Possessing The Land

During World War II, as the demand for military officers increased with the expansion of our two–front war and as increasing numbers of officers were killed in action, the U. S. armed forces began to step up its officer training program dramatically. If a recruit or draftee had a college degree, he was automatically considered as officer material. After all, he had proven that he had the discipline to stick it out through the rigors of college—the tough academic standards, the razzing and hazing dished out by classmates, and often the grueling demands of athletic competition—so he could surely help lead those who hadn't had such experience.

The military leaders took such inductees and rushed them off to a special officer training program—Officer Candidate School. Because the demand for officers was so critical, they condensed the program, graduating record numbers of officers in record time. To many of the OCS graduates, they hardly seemed to get into the program before they found themselves in positions of leadership, required to direct the work and conduct of groups of soldiers in areas of knowledge and experience totally new to them. And the soldiers in their commands were looking expectantly to them for leadership to get them through the war—at least alive, if not with honor.

Although many good leaders came from this special training program, not all of the OCS graduates were really prepared or capable of the leadership that was demanded of them. Some of them came to their men with a cocky, know–it–all attitude. Others came like wimps, not even hiding from their men their gross ineptitude. As a result, such officers became known among the common soldiers as "ninety–day wonders." Even the lowliest private had enough sense to know that a mere ninety–day crash course was insufficient to make leaders of people who didn't already possess the basic qualities necessary for leadership. Only under the stressful demands of warfare did some of these "ninety–day wonders" gain the experience they needed to be the leaders they were intended to be. Many of them passed the trial of fire and led their units to great deeds and, eventually, victory over Nazi Germany and the warlords of Japan. Some of them, however, were miserable failures whose ineptitude cost the lives of the soldiers under them.

True leadership doesn't just happen. It doesn't come as a result of taking a crash course titled "How to Be a Leader of Men in Ten Easy Lessons." It comes over sometimes long, trying periods of time during which God molds the boy into a man and a follower into a leader.

Student Work

You are about to complete a year–long course during which you have studied the essential characteristics and qualities of a spiritual leader. But merely completing this course has not made you a spiritual leader, although we hope and pray that it has helped. The real test of your leadership will come *after* you leave this class. Will you go out as a "ninety–day wonder" who knows it all and is convinced that you can make it on your own—and who soon falls on his face and drags others down with him? Or will you go out in humility, asking God to guide you into the proper application of the principles you've learned about during this course and to give you the discernment to see the opportunities He has for you to exercise the lessons you've learned?

As we continue our study of Joshua, we find that Joshua was able to apply the lessons of leadership that he had learned. And he continued learning. He recognized the fact that there are no "know–it–alls" in this life. He knew that, as Depression–era humorist Will Rogers stated, "We're all ignorant—just on different subjects." He looked to God for guidance in leading Israel to complete victory over and possession of the Promised Land.

The smoke of battle has cleared, the enthusiasm and exhilaration of victory has subsided, and the everyday tasks of cleaning up, building houses, establishing a government, etc., must be accomplished.

We learn the last five lessons on leadership in this setting. Before continuing with this lesson, read carefully Joshua 17–24.

Notes From The Teacher's Lesson

Lessons On Leadership

29. A Leader ______________________________ In People (Josh. 17:15, 17–18)

- You Must Learn To __________________ Discouragements And The Pessimism Of Your Followers.

30. A Leader Plays No ______________________ (Josh. 18:4–6)

- A Leader Must Always Strive To Be __________________ ________________________________ In His Work.

31. A Leader Strives For __________ And Doesn't Accept Gossip (Josh. 22:11ff; Tim 35b)

- Never Accept Gossip As True Without __________________ ____.

32. A Leader Is ____________________________ (Josh. 23:6)

33. A Leader Brings Followers To A Point Of A ______________ ____________ (Josh. 24:15)

"Choose You This Day Whom You Will Serve."

Stepping Toward Effective Leadership

- Read Francis Havergal's book *Kept for the Master's Use*, which is based on her hymn "Take My Life." Examine and study the lyrics of that hymn carefully. What lessons does the song teach concerning spiritual leadership and personal spirituality?

- Use a commentary to conduct a study of Romans 12:1–2. How does that passage of Scripture relate to the principles of effective spiritual leadership that we've studied this year?

- List the principles of leadership that have made the greatest impression on your life during our studies this year. In what practical ways have those lessons influenced your life this year? What changes have you made in your life and plans as a result of this study?

Spiritual Leadership

by J. Oswald Sanders, Moody Press, copyright 1967. Used with permission.

Foreword

This book has grown out of two series of messages delivered to the leaders of the Overseas Missionary Fellowship at conferences in Singapore in 1964 and 1966. It was then suggested that these messages should be amplified and shared with a wider public. The author has acceded to this request.

The principles of leadership in both the temporal and spiritual realms are presented and illustrated both from Scripture and from the biographies of eminent men of God. Not every reader will have access to many of the biographies from which these illustrations are drawn, and this has encouraged the author to include apposite incidents from the lives of men whose leadership has been more than usually successful. Wherever possible, sources are indicated. In the case of Scripture references, that translation has been used which appeared to the author to be most accurate and luminous.

The material has been presented in a form that is calculated to be of help even to younger Christians in whose hearts the Holy Spirit is working to create a holy ambition to place all their powers at the disposal of the Redeemer. If there is something, too, that will rekindle aspiration and crystallize a fresh purpose in the hearts of those further along the road of leadership, the aim of the book will be realized.

—J. Oswald Sanders

Contents

1

An Honorable Ambition

To aspire to leadership is an honourable ambition.

—1 Timothy 3:1, New English Bible

Seekest thou great things for thyself? Seek them not.

—Jeremiah 45:5

Paul's affirmation that aspiration to leadership is an honorable ambition will not be accepted by all Christians without a measure of reservation. Should it not be the office that seeks the man, rather than the man the office? Is it not perilous to put an ambitious man into office? Is there not more than a modicum of truth in the claim that ambition is "the last infirmity of noble minds"? Was not Shakespeare expressing a profound truth when he made Wolsey say:

Cromwell, I charge thee, fling away ambitions,
By that sin fell the angels; how can man then,
The image of his Maker, hope to profit by't?

We cannot deny that there is an ambition which warrants these strictures. But there are ambitions that are noble and worthy and to be cherished. When the two passages at the head of this chapter are held in constant tenson by one who desires to be effective in the service of God and realize the highest potential of his life, there need be little fear for the outcome of that ambition.

In appraising the honorable ambition of which Paul speaks, several factors must be kept in mind. We are apt to view his categorical statement in the light of the honor and prestige which in our day accrue to those in positions of Christian leadership. When Paul wrote, however, conditions were much different. Then the office of bishop, or overseer, far from being a coveted, easy position, often involved great dangers and heavy responsibilities. Not infrequently hardship, contempt and rejection were its rewards. In times of persecution the leader drew the fire, and he was the first to suffer.

When read in the light of these conditions, Paul's statement does not seem so fraught with danger as might at first appear. Mere place–seekers and charlatans would have little heart for such an onerous assignment. Under these discouraging circumstances, Paul felt it right and necessary to provide some incentive to leadership and to give a word of praise to those who were willing to incur the risks involved. Hence his statement: "To aspire to leadership is an honourable ambition."

This very situation is repeated today. It was the leaders of the church in China who suffered most at the hands of the Communists. It was the pastor of the Little Flock in Nepal who suffered years of imprisonment, while his church members were early released. In many countries even today, spiritual leadership is no sinecure.

It should be observed that it is not the *office of overseer* but the *functions of overseeing* that Paul asserts is honorable and noble. This is the most privileged work in the world, and its glorious character should be an incentive to covet it since, when sought from highest motives, it yields both present and eternal dividends. In Paul's times, only deep love for Christ and genuine concern for His church would provide men with a sufficiently powerful motive to aspire to this office. But in most lands today Christian leadership confers prestige and privilege; and unworthy ambition may easily induce self–seeking and unspiritual men to covet office.

It is this very fact that makes Jeremiah's counsel to Baruch so pertinent: "Seekest thou great things for thyself? Seek them not." He is not warning against ambition per se, but against *self–centered* ambition—"great things *for thyself*." A desire to be great is not necessarily in itself sinful. It is the motivation that determines its character. Our Lord did not discount or disparage aspiration to greatness, but He did pointedly expose and stigmatize unworthy motivation.

All Christians are under obligation to make the most of their lives, to develop to the utmost their God–given powers and capacities. But Jesus taught that any ambition that centers around and terminates on oneself is wrong. In an address to ordinands, Bishop Stephen Neill had this to say: "I am inclined to think that ambition in any ordinary sense of the term is nearly always sinful in ordinary men. I am certain that in the Christian it is always sinful, and that it is most inexcusable of all in the ordained minister."[1]

On the other hand, an ambition which has as its center the glory of God and the welfare of His church is not only legitimate but positively praiseworthy.

Our word *ambition* derives from a Latin word meaning "canvassing for promotion." A variety of ingredients may be present in ambition—to be seen and approved by men, to be popular, to stand well among one's contemporaries, to exercise control over others.

Ambitious men enjoy the power which money or authority brings. Such carnal ambitions were roundly rebuked by the Lord. The true spiritual leader will never canvass for promotion.

To His ambitious disciples Jesus enunciated a new standard of greatness: "You know that those who are supposed to rule the heathen lord it over them, and their great men rule as despots over them; but this is not to be the case among you. Whoever wants to be great among you must be your servant, and whoever wants to hold first positions among you must be *everybody's slave*" (Mark 10:42–44, C. B. Williams N. T.)

The context of this revolutionary conception strips the mask from selfish ambition and reveals its true nature. Jesus had been unburdening Himself to His intimate friends, sharing with them the foreknowledge of His impending suffering and death (vv. 33–34). Scarcely had the words fallen from His lips before James and John, callously indifferent to His moving plea for fellowship and understanding, said: "Grant us to sit, one at your right hand and the other at your left, in your splendor" (v. 37). They coveted a crown of glory but were not ready for a crown of thorns. Coronation interested them, but not crucifixion. Pomp and power were much to be preferred to sharing the fellowship of His sufferings. Is it much different today? They had to learn, as we, that the glory is reached only by way of the cross.

While there is nothing inherently wrong in aspiring to be great from high motives, there is everything wrong in desiring to be *greatest.* This was the sinful ambition of James and John who resorted to shabby intrigue, exploiting the affection of their doting mother to secure their temporal advancement. Surreptitiously they endeavored to forestall and exclude their closest friends from the positions of privilege and power in Christ's kingdom.

In this they made a twofold mistake. First, they envisaged Christ's kingdom as one of earthly pomp and splendor. Second, they thought greatness consisted in place and position. These considerations made them desire to become His chief ministers of state. Their thinking was still fashioned by worldly standards. Not until the purging flame of the Holy Spirit had consumed their carnal ambition in the Pentecostal conflagration did they reach the true place of spiritual leadership. A similar thirst for power and prominence still plagues the church and negates spiritual power. Diotrephes is not dead.

Refusing to be diverted by the ambitious request of His two friends, Jesus used the occasion to teach them an important and timeless lesson. "Ye know not what ye ask," He said. "Can ye drink the cup that I drink of? and be baptized with the baptism that I am baptized with?" "We are able," they replied, with boundless self–confidence but little self–knowledge. "To sit on my right hand and on my left hand is not mine to give," Jesus answered, "but it shall be given to them for whom it is prepared" (vv. 38–40, AV).

Jesus was teaching them, and us, that worldly conceptions of greatness and leadership cannot be carried over into His spiritual kingdom. In that kingdom there is a complete reversal of earth's values. In heaven, gold is used for road–metal. "Those for whom it is prepared" are those who have prepared themselves for it. And what is the necessary preparation? "He must be everybody's slave." Not the number of one's servants, but the number whom one serves, is the heavenly criterion of greatness and the real preparation for leadership. Greatness of exaltation is in proportion to greatness of service humbly rendered. Greatness is not circumstantial, it is inherent.

Our Lord perfectly exemplified His own precept: "The Son of man did not come to be served but to serve" (v. 45 C.B. Williams). "I am among you as the servant that waits on you" (Luke 22:27).

At the beginning of any study of spiritual leadership, it is essential that this divinely enunciated master–principle be clearly understood and firmly embraced. True greatness, true leadership, is achieved not by reducing men to one's service but in giving oneself in selfless service to them. And this is never done without cost. It involves drinking a bitter cup and experiencing a painful baptism of suffering. The true spiritual leader is concerned infinitely more with the service he can render God and his fellowmen than with the benefits and pleasures he can extract from life. He aims to put more into life than he takes out of it.

"one of the outstanding ironies of history is the utter disregard of ranks and titles in the final judgments men pass on each other," said Samuel Brengle. "The final estimate of men shows that history cares not an iota for the rank or title a man has borne, or the office he has held, but only the quality of his deeds and the character of his mind and heart."[2]

"Let it once be fixed that a man's ambition is to fit into God's plan for him, and he has a North Star ever in sight to guide him steadily over any sea, however shoreless it seems," wrote S. D. Gordon. "He has a compass that points true in the thickest fog and fiercest storm, and regardless of magnetic rocks."

Although Count Zinzendorf was strongly drawn to classical pursuits and tempted by rank and riches, his attitude and ambition were summed up in one sentence: "I have one passion, it is He, He alone." He renounced selfish ambition and became the renowned founder and leader of the Moravian church. His followers drank deeply of the spirit of their leader and circled the world with the gospel. Their missionary activity had the unique distinction, in days when missionary work was on a very limited scale, of bringing into being an overseas church with three times as many communicants as in their home churches. One member out of every ninety–two became a foreign missionary.

Because we children of Adam want to become great,
He became small.
Because we will not stoop,
He humbled Himself.
Because we want to rule,
He came to serve.

2

The Search For Leaders

Promotion cometh neither from the east, nor from the west, nor from the south. But God...putteth down one, and setteth up another.

—*Psalm 75:6–7*

Give me a man of God—one man,
Whose faith is master of his mind,
And I will right all wrongs
And bless the name of all mankind.
Give me a man of God—one man,
Whose tongue is touched with heaven's fire,
And I will flame the darkest hearts
With high resolve and clean desire.
Give me a man of God—one man,
One mighty prophet of the Lord,
And I will give you peace on earth,
Bought with a prayer and not a sword.
Give me a man of God—one man,
True to the vision that he sees,
And I will build your broken shrines
And bring the nations to their knees.
—*George Liddell*

God and man are constantly searching for leaders in the various branches of Christian enterprise. In the Scriptures, God is frequently represented as searching for a man of a certain type. Not men, but a man. Not a group, an individual.

"The Lord hath sought him *a man* after his own heart" (I Sam. 13:14).

"I beheld, and lo, there was *no man*" (Jer. 4:25).

"Run ye to and fro through the streets of Jerusalem and see...if ye can find *a man* ...that executeth judgment, that seeketh the truth; and I will pardon it" (Jer. 5:1).

"I sought *a man*...that should...stand in the gap" (Ezek. 22:30).

Both Scripture and the history of Israel and the church attest that when God does discover a man who conforms to His spiritual requirement, who is willing to pay the full price of discipleship, He uses him to the limit, despite his patent shortcomings . Such men were Moses, Gideon and David, Martin Luther, John Wesley, Adoniram Judson, William Carey, and a host of others.

The supernatural nature of the church demands a leadership which rises above the human. And yet, has there ever been a greater dearth of God–anointed and God–mastered men to meet this crucial need? In a sense it has always been true that this type of dedicated leadership has been in short supply, for the simple reason that its demands are too stringent.

"The Church is painfully in need of leaders," lamented William E. Sangster. "I wait to hear a voice and no voice comes. I love the back seat in Synod and Conference. I would always rather listen than speak—but there is no clarion voice to listen to."[1] The overriding need of the church, if it is to discharge its obligation to the rising generation, is for a leadership that is authoritative, spiritual and sacrificial. *Authoritative*, because people love to be led by one who knows where he is going and who inspires confidence. They follow almost without question the man who shows himself wise and strong, who adheres to what he believes. *Spiritual,* because a leadership that is unspiritual, that can be fully explained in terms of the natural, although ever so attractive and competent, will result only in sterility and moral and spiritual bankruptcy. *Sacrificial,* because modeled on the life of the One who gave Himself a sacrifice for the whole world, who left us an example that we should follow His steps.

The church has always prospered most when it has been blessed with strong and spiritual leaders who expected and experienced the touch of the supernatural in their service. The lack of such men is a symptom of the malaise that has gripped it. The clarion voices that used to make the pulpit the paramount influence in the land are tragically few. In a world aflame, the voice of the church has sunk to a pathetic whisper. It is the binding duty of those in positions of leadership to face up to the situation and do all in their power to see that the torch of a truly spiritual leadership is passed on to the younger men.

Leadership is often viewed as the product of natural endowments and traits of personality—intellectual capacity, force of will, enthusiasm. That such talents and scholastic attainments do greatly enhance leadership is beyond question, but these are not the factors of paramount importance in the spiritual leader. "The real qualities of leadership are to be found in those who are willing to suffer for the sake of objectives great enough to demand their wholehearted obedience."

Spiritual leaders are not made by election or appointment, by men or any combination of men, nor by conferences or synods. Only God can make them. Simply holding a position of importance does not constitute one a leader. The only method is that of *qualifying* to be a leader. Religious position can be conferred by bishops and boards, but not spiritual authority, which is the prime essential of Christian leadership. This comes—often unsought—to those who in earlier life have proved themselves worthy of it by spirituality, discipline, ability and diligence. Men who have heeded the command: "Seekest thou great things for thyself? Seek them not," and instead have sought first the kingdom of God. Spiritual leadership is a thing of the Spirit and is conferred by God alone. When His searching eye alights on a man who has qualified, He anoints him with His Spirit and separates him to his distinctive ministry (Acts 9:17; 22:21).

Samuel Logan Brengle was one of the truly great leaders of the Salvation Army. A man of scholarship as well as of singular spiritual power, he outlined the road to spiritual authority and leadership in challenging words: "It is not won by promotion, but by many prayers and tears. It is attained by confessions of sin, and much heartsearching and humbling before God; by self–surrender, a courageous sacrifice of every idol, a bold, deathless, uncompromising and uncomplaining embracing of the cross, and by an eternal, unfaltering looking unto Jesus crucified. It is not gained by seeking great things for ourselves, but rather, like Paul, by counting those things that are gain to us as loss for Christ. That is a great price, but it must be unflinchingly paid by him who would be not merely a nominal but a spiritual leader of men, a leader whose power is recognized and felt in heaven, on earth and in hell."[2]

This is the type of man for whom God is searching, on whose behalf He desires to show Himself strong (II Chron. 16:9). But not all who aspire to leadership are willing to pay so exacting a price. However, God's conditions must be complied with in secret before He will honor a man in public. Our Lord made it clear to James and John that there is a sovereignty about leadership in His kingdom. The highest positions are reserved for those who have qualified in secret. It is this element of sovereignty that begets awe and a great humility in those to whom leadership is entrusted.

It remains to be said that there can be such a thing as inverted leadership. If those in positions of power and influence fail to lead their people into the spiritual uplands, they will unconsciously yet nonetheless surely lead them down into the lowlands, for none can live to himself.

Give me men to match my mountains,
Give me men to match my plains,
Men with empires in their purpose,
Men with eras in their brains.

3

Natural And Spiritual Leadership

When I came to you,...my speech and my preaching was not with enticing words of man's wisdom, but in demonstration of the Spirit and of power.

—*1 Corinthians 2:1, 4*

Leadership is influence, the ability of one person to influence others. One man can lead others only to the extent that he can influence them. This fact is supported by definitions of leadership by men who have themselves wielded great influence.

Lord Montgomery defines it in these terms: "Leadership is the capacity and will to rally men and women to a common purpose, and the character which inspires confidence."[1] The outstanding examplar of this quality was Sir Winston Churchill, especially in the darkest hours of World War II.

Dr. John R. Mott, a world leader in student circles, gave as his definition: "A leader is a man who knows the road, who can keep ahead, and who can pull others after him."[2]

President Truman's definition is: "A leader is a person who has the ability to get others to do what they don't want to do, and like it."

General Charles Gordon once asked Li Hung Chang, an old Chinese leader, a double question: "What is leadership? And how is humanity divided?" He received this cryptic answer: "There are only three kinds of people in the world—those that are movable, those that are immovable, and those that move them."

Spiritual leadership is a blending of natural and spiritual qualities. Even the natural qualities are not self–produced but God–given, and therefore reach their highest effectiveness when employed in the service of God and for His glory. The definitions above concern leadership in general. While spiritual leadership partakes of these qualities, there are other elements that supplement and take precedence over them. Personality is a prime factor in natural leadership. "The degree of influence will depend on the personality of the man," wrote Lord Montgomery, "the 'incandescence' of which he is capable, the flame which burns within him, the magnetism which will draw the hearts of men towards him."[3]

The spiritual leader, however, influences others not by the power of his own personality alone but by that personality irradiated and interpenetrated and empowered by the Holy Spirit. Because he permits the Holy Spirit undisputed control of his life, the Spirit's power can flow through him to others unhindered.

Spiritual leadership is a matter of superior spiritual power, and that can never be self–generated. There is no such thing as a self–made spiritual leader. He is able to influence others spiritually only because the Spirit is able to work in and through him to a greater degree than in those whom he leads.

It is a general principle that we can influence and lead others only so far as we ourselves have gone. The person most likely to be successful is one who leads not by merely pointing the way but by having trodden it himself. We are leaders to the extent that we inspire others to follow us.

At a large gathering of the leading Protestant missions in China, the question of qualifications for leadership was being discussed. There was vigorous debate on the subject. Mr. D. E. Hoste, General Director of the China Inland Mission, sat quietly listening until the chairman asked if he had anything to say on the subject. From all over the auditorium came murmurs of approval at the invitation, for his contributions to a discussion were always listened to with more than ordinary interest.

With a twinkle in his eye, he said in his curiously high–pitched voice: "It occurs to me that perhaps the best test of whether one is a qualified leader is to find out whether anyone is following him."[4]

Natural leadership and spiritual leadership have many points of similarity, but there are some respects in which they may be antithetical. This is seen when some of their dominant characteristics are set over against one another.

Natural	**Spiritual**
Self–confident	Confident in God
Knows men	Also knows God
Makes own decisions	Seeks to find God's will
Ambitious	Self–effacing
Originates own methods	Finds and follows God's methods
Enjoys commanding others	Delights to obey God
Motivated by personal considerations	Motivated by love for God and man
Independent	God–dependent

While conversion does not normally make leaders of people who would never become such otherwise, Church history teaches that in the hour of full surrender the Holy Spirit sometimes releases gifts and qualities that have long remained latent and dormant. It is the prerogative of the Spirit to bestow spiritual gifts which greatly enhance the leadership potential of the recipient.

This was Dr. A. W. Tozer's conviction:

> A true and safe leader is likely to be one who has no desire to lead, but is forced into a position of leadership by the inward pressure of the Holy Spirit and the press of the external situation. Such were Moses and David and the Old Testament prophets. I think there was hardly a great leader from Paul to the present day but was drafted by the Holy Spirit for the task, and commissioned by the Lord of the Church to fill a position he had little heart for. I believe it might be accepted as a fairly reliable rule of thumb that the man who is ambitious to lead is disqualified as a leader. The true leader will have no desire to lord it over God's heritage, but will be humble, gentle, self–sacrificing and altogether as ready to follow as to lead, when the Spirit makes it clear that a wiser and more gifted man than himself has appeared.[5]

In the biography of William E. Sangster, a private manuscript found after his death illustrates this contention. He was writing of his growing conviction that he should take more part in the leadership of the Methodist church in England.

> This is the will of God for me. I did not choose it. I sought to escape it. But it has come.
>
> Something else has come too. A sense of certainty that God does not want me only for a preacher. He wants me also for a leader—a leader in Methodism.
>
> I feel a commissioning to work under God for the revival of this branch of His Church—careless of my own reputation; indifferent to the comments of older and jealous men.
>
> I am thirty–six. If I am to serve God in this way, I must no longer shrink from the task—but *do* it.
>
> I have examined my heart for ambition. I am certain it is not there. I hate the criticism I shall evoke and the painful chatter of people. Obscurity, quiet browsing among books, and the service of simple people is my taste—but by the will of God, this is my task. God help me.

> Bewildered and unbelieving, I hear the voice of God say to me: "I want to sound the note through you." O God, did ever an apostle shrink from his task more? I dare not say "No" but, like Jonah, I would fain run away.[6]

That spiritual leadership and authority cannot be explained solely on the grounds of natural ability is strikingly exemplified in the life of St. Francis of Assisi. On one occasion Brother Masseo, looking earnestly at Francis, began to say: "Why thee? Why thee?" He repeated it again and again as if to mock him.

"What are you saying?" cried Francis at last.

"I am saying that everybody follows thee, everyone desire to see thee, hear thee, obey thee, and yet for all that, thou art neither beautiful, nor learned, nor of noble family. Whence comes it that it should be thee whom the world desires to follow?"

When Francis heard these words, he was filled with joy, raised his eyes to heaven and, after remaining a long time absorbed in contemplation, knelt praising and blessing God with extraordinary fervor. Then he turned to Brother Masseo:

"Thou wishest to know? It is because the eyes of the Most High have willed it so. He continually watches the good and the wicked, and as His most holy eyes have not found among sinners any smaller man, nor any more insufficient and sinful, therefore He has chosen me to accomplish the marvelous work which God hath undertaken; He chose me because He could find none more worthless, and he wished to confound the nobility and grandeur, the strength, the beauty and the learning of this world."[7]

Much may be learned from the wisdom of men who have made their mark as leaders. Two men already quoted had tests by which they determined the leadership potential of men they were interviewing.

Lord Montgomery enunciated seven ingredients necessary in a leader in war, each of which is appropriate to the spiritual warfare: (1) He should be able to sit back and avoid getting immersed in detail. (2) He must not be petty. (3) He must not be pompous. (4) He must be a good picker of men. (5) He should trust those under him, and let them get on with their job without interference. (6) He must have the power of clear decision. (7) He should inspire confidence.[8]

Dr. John R. Mott moved in student circles and his tests covered different territory: (1) Does he do little things well? (2) Has he learned the meaning of priorities? (3) How does he use his leisure? (4) Has he intensity? (5) Has he learned to take advantage of momentum? (6) Has he the power of growth? (7) What is his attitude to discouragements? (8) How does he face impossible situations? (9) What are his weakest points?[9]

Since leadership is essentially the power of one man to influence another, it is well to consider the almost limitless possibilities of a single life, for good or ill. Both Scripture and experience affirm that no one can be neutral, either morally or spiritually. On lives that come within the range of our influence we leave an indelible impress, whether we are conscious of it or not. Dr. John Geddie, for example, went to Aneityum in 1848 and worked there for God for twenty–four years. On the tablet erected to his memory these words are inscribed:

When he landed, in 1848, there were no Christians.
When he left, in 1872, there were no heathen.

When the burning zeal of the apostolic church resulted in converts multiplying at an extraordinary rate, the Holy Spirit taught a striking lesson on the nature of spiritual leadership. The exigencies of the work made such heavy demands on the apostles that the creation of a lower echelon of leaders to care for the neglected poor and widows became necessary. These must be carefully selected, so the apostles specified the type of man to be chosen: "Wherefore, brethren, look ye out among you seven men of honest report, full of the Holy Ghost and wisdom, whom we may appoint over this business" (Acts 6:3).

Is it without significance that the central requirement is that they be "full of the Holy Ghost," even for what might be termed a secular service? They were to be men of *integrity*, of honest report; of *sagacity*, full of wisdom, of *spirituality*, full of the Spirit. Spirituality is not easy to define but its presence or absence can easily be discerned. It has been called the diffused fragrance which has been assimilated in the garden of the Lord. It is the power to change the atmosphere by one's presence, the unconscious influence which makes Christ and spiritual things real to others.

If this is the standard for those who occupy the lower offices of the church, what of those who aspire to the higher? Spiritual ends can be achieved only by spirutual men who employ spiritual methods. What a far–reaching change could be effected in our churches and Christian organizations if this priority was strictly observed! Secular men, be they ever so gifted and charming in person, have no place in the leadership of the church, even in temporal matters.

The essential ideas of true spiritual leadership are gathered up in these words of John R. Mott:

> I have in mind the use of the word leadership which our Lord doubtless had in mind when He said, "He who would be greatest among you shall be the servant of all"—leadership in the sense of the largest unselfishness; in the sense of unwearying and unceasing absorption in the greatest work of the world, the building up of the kingdom of our Lord Jesus Christ.[10]

4

Criteria Of Leadership Potential

Send men...every one a leader....

—Numbers 13:2, RSV

Since qualities of natural leadership are by no means unimportant in spiritual leadership, there is value in seeking to discover leadership potential both in oneself and in others. Most people have latent and undeveloped traits which, through lack of self–analysis and consequent lack of self–knowledge, may long remain undiscovered. An objective study of the following suggested standards of self–measurement could result in the discovery of such qualities where they exist, as well as the detection of incipient weaknesses which would unfit one for leadership.

Have you ever broken yourself of a bad habit? To lead others, one must be master of oneself.

Do you retain control of yourself when things go wrong? The leader who loses self–control in testing circumstances forfeits respect and loses influence. He must be calm in crisis and resilient in adversity and disappointment.

Do you think independently? While using to the full the thought of others, the leader cannot afford to let others do his thinking or make his decisions for him.

Can you handle criticism objectively and remain unmoved under it? Do you turn it to good account? The humble man can derive benefit from petty and even malicious criticism.

Can you use disappointments creatively?

Do you readily secure the cooperation and win the respect and confidence of others?

Do you possess the ability to secure discipline without having to resort to a show of authority? True leadership is an internal quality of the spirit and requires no external show of force.

Have you qualified for the beatitude pronounced on the peacemaker? It is much easier to *keep* the peace than to *make* peace where it has been shattered. An important function in leadership is conciliation—the ability to discover common ground between opposing viewpoints and then induce both parties to accept it.

Are you entrusted with the handling of difficult and delicate situations?

Can you induce people to do happily some legitimate things which they would not normally wish to do?

Can you accept opposition to your viewpoint or decision without considering it a personal affront and reacting accordingly? Leaders must expect opposition and should not be offended by it.

Do you find it easy to make and keep friends? Your circle of loyal friends is an index of the quality and extent of your leadership.

Are you unduly dependent on the praise or approval of others? Can you hold a steady course in the face of disapproval and even the temporary loss of confidence?

Are you at ease in the presence of your superiors or strangers?

Do your subordinates appear at ease in your presence? A leader should give an impression of sympathetic understanding and friendliness that will put others at ease.

Are you really interested in people? In people of all types and all races? Or do you entertain respect of persons? Is there hidden racial prejudice? An antisocial person is unlikely to make a good leader.

Do you possess tact? Can you anticipate the likely effect of a statement before you make it?

Do you possess a strong and steady will? A leader will not long retain his position if he is vacillating.

Do you nurse resentments, or do you readily forgive injuries done to you?

Are you reasonably optimistic? Pessimism is no asset to a leader.

Are you in the grip of a master–passion such as that of Paul who said: "This *one thing* I do"? Such a singleness of motive will focus all one's energies and powers on the desired objective.

Do you welcome responsibility?

R. E. Thompson suggests these tests of our attitudes to people as an indication of our capacity for leadership:

Do other people's failures annoy us or challenge us?

Do we use people or cultivate people?

Do we direct people or develop people?

Do we criticize or encourage?

Do we shun the problem person or seek him out?[1]

It will not be sufficient merely to engage in this exercise in self–analysis superficially, and pay no further heed to the discoveries made. Something must be done about it. Why not take some of the points of conscious weakness and failure and, in cooperation with the Holy Spirit who is the Spirit of discipline, concentrate on strengthening or correcting them?

These desirable qualities were all present in their fullness in the symmetrical character of our Lord, and each Christian should make it his constant prayer that they might more rapidly be incorporated into his own personality.

5

Pauline Sidelights On Leadership

An overseer, then, must be above reproach, the husband of one wife, temperate, prudent, respectable, hospitable, able to teach, not addicted to wine or pugnacious, but gentle, uncontentious, free from the love of money. He must be one who manages his own household well, keeping his children under control with all dignity...and not a new convert, lest he become conceited.... And he must have a good reputation with those outside the church.

I Timothy 3:2–7, NASV

Who is better qualified to catalog the requisites of spiritual leadership than the peerless leader, Paul? In addition to the richness of his own experience, he enjoyed the illumination and inspiration of the Holy Spirit. Spiritual standards do not change from generation to generation, but remain the same in the space age as at the birth of the church. None of the qualities here enjoined by Paul are optional extras, but indispensable requirements.

It is generally held that the two words used of leaders in the church—*bishops* and *elders*—were applicable to the same person. *Elder* had reference to his dignity and status, while *bishop* related to his function or duty. In other words, one word had reference to his person, the other to his work. This is borne out by such passages as Acts 20:17, and 28, where Paul addresses the same people first as elders and then as bishops. The present connotation of *bishop* was a considerably later development.

The paragraph at the head of this chapter specifies the qualifications to be expected in a spiritual leader, in several spheres and relationships.

Social Qualifications

In respect to those within the church, he is to be *above reproach*. His character is to be such as will not leave him open to attack or censure. Colloquially stated, detractors will not have a "rung to stand on." If a charge were preferred against him, it would fall to the ground because his life would afford no grounds for reproach. He must give no opening for his adversary even to launch a smear campaign.

As to those without the church, he is to be *of good reputation*. The person who associates with a Christian in daily secular life and work or in extrachurch activities often has the clearest insight into the genuineness of his Christian character. The reason for this requirement is obvious. An elder known to the author was a businessman who sometimes took preaching appointments on the Lord's Day. His employees used to say that they could always tell when he had been preaching on Sunday, because he was unusually bad–tempered on Monday. He did not influence his employees toward Christ.

Despite their criticisms, non–Christians generally respect the high ideals of Christian character and, when they see them actually reproduced before them in a holy life, covet a similar experience. It is this very fact which lends point to their criticisms. The character of an elder should be such as commands the respect of the outsider, inspires his confidence and arouses his aspiration. Example is much more potent then precept.

Moral Qualifications

In a world in which moral principles come under subtle and constant attack, a leader must be blameless in that respect. He is to be *"one wife's husband,"* in a society where this is far from being the norm. There are several interpretations of this phrase, but whatever else it means, it certainly indicates that he must be blameless in his moral life. He must set a high standard in the marital relationship in his faithfulness to a sole marriage partner. He must be a man of unchallengeable morality.

He must also be *temperate*, "not addicted to wine," with all that is involved in that statement. The word signifies "one who lingers by his wine," with the probable result of becoming drunk and disorderly. A drunken man is disgraced in ordinary society, and how much more in the Christian church. A leader must allow himself no indulgence in secret that would undermine his character or mar his public witness.

Mental Qualifications

He should be *prudent*, sound–minded. This word indicates "the well–balanced state of mind resulting from habitual self–restraint," and refers to the inner character which results from daily self–discipline. Jeremy Taylor termed this quality "reason's girdle and passion's bridle."[1] The Greeks placed great value upon it. To them it was the state of mind which was disciplined, not swayed by sudden impulse, that did not fly to extremes but was the mean between them. For example, courage is the mean between rashness and timidity; purity is the mean between prudery and immorality. The leader who possesses this desirable quality is in control of every part of his nature.

As to his outer conduct, he must be *respectable*, decorous. The word is *kosmos,* the order that emerged out of chaos at the fiat of God. A well–ordered life is the outcome of a well–ordered mind. The life of the leader should be so ordered as to reflect the beauty and orderliness of God.

Mentally and spiritually, he should be *able to teach.* The word implies not only ability but readiness to teach; a desire and constraint to impart to others the truth which the Holy Spirit has taught him from the Scriptures. If he is to teach, he himself must be a student of the Scriptures. "Any man who shows himself incapable of successfully teaching others is not qualified for the eldership," says H.A. Kent. The spiritual leader is responsible for teaching those under him to a greater or lesser degree, and his instruction must have the support of a blameless life.

Samuel Brengle lamented:

> Oh, for more teachers among us; leaders who know how to read hearts and apply truth to the needs of the people, as a good physician reads his patients and applies remedies to their ills. There are soul–sicknesses open and obscure, acute and chronic, superficial and deep–seated which the truth as it is in Jesus will heal. But it is not the same truth for each need, any more than the same medicine for every disease. That is why we should most diligently study the Bible and pray for the constant and powerful illumination of the Spirit.[2]

John Wesley was a man who possessed these mental qualities to a high degree. He never indulged in a cheap disparagement of the intellect and was always seeking to raise the intellectual as well as the moral and spiritual condition of those around him. His own intellectual powers were of the highest order; had he chosen, he could have been in the front rank of the scholars of his day. He had a wonderful knowledge of literature. An eminent preacher declared that he knew of no sermons that evince so intimate a knowledge of classical and general literature as those of Wesley. And yet he was known as a "man of one Book." He was a shining example of consecrated intellect.

Personality Qualifications

The Christian leader must not be *pugnacious,* but genial and *gentle.* Not a contentious controversialist, but one who is sweetly reasonable. These contrasting words give an attractive angle to the character of the ideal leader. Of the word *gentle,* R. C. Trench says, "It is the spirit which rectifies and redresses the injustices of justice." The person who possesses this quality, according to Aristotle, "remembers good rather than evil, the good one has received rather than the good one has done." He will be actively considerate and forbearing rather than merely uncontentious; irenic in disposition, always seeking a peaceful solution to a thorny problem or an explosive situation.

Then, too, he must be *hospitable,* a friend of strangers. This ministry will not be regarded as an irksome imposition, but instead as a privileged service done for his Lord. In the early book, *The Shepherd of Hermas,* it is stated that a bishop "must be hospitable, a man who gladly and at all times welcomes into his house the servants of God."

When Paul wrote, hospitality of this kind was much more essential than in our own times, although this is still a desirable grace in a leader—and in a leader's wife, for it is she who has to bear much of the load. In the days of the early church, inns were few, and those few were both dirty and immoral. Visiting Christians or teachers could not resort to the homes of the heathen. As persecution spread, upon entering another city, Christians were liable to be hunted down and sold as slaves. It was therefore essential that church members, and especially leaders, should extend hospitality to them. There must be an open door for fellow Christians and non–Christians too.

A friend of the author who had large business responsibilities as well as heavy church commitments made it a practice to keep an open home for visitors or the unprivileged on the Lord's Day. Besides making a fine contribution to the life and atmosphere of the church, his own spiritual leadership was enhanced, his life enriched and others blessed.

Covetousness and its twin, *love of money,* are disqualifying factors. In the exercise of his spiritual ministry, the leader must never be swayed by considerations of financial reward. He will be as willing to accept an appointment with a lower remuneration as one with a higher.

Fletcher of Madeley was described thus by Wesley: "As unblamable a character in every respect I have not found, either in Europe or America; and I scarce expect such another on this side of eternity." Previous to Fletcher's going to Madeley, with which his name is inseparably linked, it is told that his benefactor, Mr. Hill, informed him that he could have the living in Dunham in Cheshire, adding: "The parish is small, the duty is light, the income is good (400 per annum), and it is situated in a fine healthy sporting country!"

"Alas, sir," replied Fletcher, "Dunham will not suit me. There is too much money and too little labor."

"Few clergymen make such objections," remarked Mr. Hill. "It is a pity to decline such a living, as I do not know that I can find you another. Would you like Madeley?"

"That, sir, would be the very place for me."

"My object is to make you comfortable in your own way," said Mr. Hill. "If you prefer Madeley, I shall find no difficulty in persuading the present vicar to exchange it for Dunham, which is worth more than twice as much."

In that small church this man who was innocent of covetousness and devoid of the love of money exercised a remarkable ministry; and through his biography his influence is still being felt in this generation.

Domestic Qualifications

The Christian leader who is married must demonstrate his ability to rule his home in a godly way—"one who manages his own household well, keeping his children under control with all dignity." Is it not failure in this realm that has caused many ministers and missionaries to fall short of the highest in their leadership? "Dignity" is a better rendering than "gravity" in the Authorized Version, since it avoids the picture of unsmiling sternness while still retaining the idea of due respect.

To attain this ideal, a man must have a wife who fully shares his spiritual aspirations and is willing to make the necessary sacrifices. Many a gifted man has been lost to high office and spiritual effectiveness because of the unsuitability of the wife he has chosen. If a man has not succeeded in exercising a benevolent and happy discipline in his own family, is there reason to expect that he will do better with the family of God? If his home is not well ordered nor his children well controlled, his ability to offer worthy hospitality will be greatly restricted, and his influence on other families diminished.

The clear implication is that, while caring for the interests of the church or other spiritual activity, the leader will not neglect the family which is his personal and primary responsibility. In the economy of God, the discharge of one God–given duty or responsibility will never involve the neglect of another. There is time for the full discharge of every legitimate duty. Paul implies that the ability of a man to exercise spiritual authority over others is evidenced by his ability to exercise a wise and loving discipline in his own home. Leadership has often been forfeited through failure in this realm.

Maturity Qualifications

Spiritual maturity is indispensable to good leadership. There is no place for a novice, a new convert, in positions of responsibility. The word is our *neophyte*, and means "newly planted," a figure taken from nature. A plant needs time to take root and come to maturity, and the process cannot be hurried. It must take root downward before it can bear fruit upward. In harmony with this figure, Bengel said that novices usually have "an abundance of verdure. The convert is not yet pruned by the cross." In I Timothy 3:10, referring to the qualifications of a deacon, Paul urges, "Let these also first be tested." This will prove their worthiness or otherwise for a position of responsibility in the church.

When Timothy became pastor of the church at Ephesus, it had already been in existence for more than a decade. It had enjoyed a galaxy of gifted pastors and teachers, so there were many men of mature experience in it; hence Paul's insistence on the necessity of this quality in its leaders.. In the light of missionary experience in the guidance of emerging churches, it is interesting to note that Paul, always realistic, does not demand this qualification in the case of the recently established Cretan church, for there were no such men available (Titus 1:5–9). The ideal cannot be insisted on in the early stages of church–building; but every care should be taken in the selection of those asked to assume responsibility to ensure that they are stable in character, spiritual in outlook and not ambitious for position.

Paul advances a valid and convincing reason for this requirement: "Lest being lifted up with pride, he fall into the condemnation of the devil." A recent convert lacks the spiritual maturity and stability essential to wise leadership. It is unwise to give key positions too early even to those who manifest promising talent, lest it spoil them. The history of the church and missions is strewn with tragic illustrations of this possibility. Such an appointment would be in the best interests of neither the new convert nor the church. Human nature being what it is, the novice would stand in great danger of being inflated with a sense of his own importance by too sudden an elevation to a place of authority over his fellows. But while he should not be given a key position too soon, the promising convert should be afforded a widening opportunity to serve at humbler and less prominent tasks that would develop both natural and spiritual gifts. He should not be advanced too fast, lest he become puffed up. Neither should he be repressed, lest he be discouraged.

In harmony with this ruling, as William Hendriksen points out, Paul did not appoint elders in every place on his first missionary journey, but only after he had revisited the churches and satisfied himself of the spiritual progress of those whom he appointed (Acts 14:23). Nor was Timothy ordained immediately on his conversion. Although his conversion took place on Paul's first journey, he was not ordained until the second journey at the earliest.[3]

"It is the mark of a grown–up man, as compared with a callow youth, that he finds his center of gravity wherever he happens to be at the moment, and however much he longs for the object of his desire, it cannot prevent him from staying at his post and doing his duty," wrote Dietrich Bonhoeffer. This is just what a new convert finds it difficult to do. It is a characteristic which accompanies a growing maturity.

The above requirements for leadership in the Christian church are recognized as essential even in worldly circles. William Barclay quotes a pagan, Onosander by name, who gave this description of the ideal commander: "He must be prudently self–controlled, sober, frugal, enduring in toil, intelligent, without love of money, neither young nor old, if possible the father of a family, able to speak competently, and of good reputation."[4] The similarity to Paul's list is striking. If the world demands such standards of its leaders, is it too much to expect all these and more of leaders in the church of God?

6

Petrine Sidelights On Leadership

Now may I who am myself an Elder say a word to you my fellow Elders? I speak as one who actually saw Christ suffer, and as one who will share with you the glories that are to be unfolded to us. I urge you then to see that your "flock of God" is properly fed and cared for. Accept the responsibility of looking after them willingly and not because you feel you can't get out of it, doing your work not for what you can make, but because you are really concerned for their well–being. You should aim not at being "little tin gods" but as examples of Christian living in the eyes of the flock committed to your charge. And then, when the chief shepherd reveals himself, you will receive that crown of glory which cannot fade.

You younger members must also submit to the Elders. Indeed all of you should defer to one another and wear the "overall" of humility in serving each other. God is always against the proud, but he is always ready to give grace to the humble. So, humble yourselves under God's strong hand, and in his own good time he will lift you up. You can throw the whole weight of your anxieties upon him, for you are his personal concern.

I Peter 5:1–7, Phillips Translation

Peter was the natural and accepted leader of the apostolic band. What Peter did, the others did. Where Peter went, the others went. "I go afishing," said Peter. "We also go with thee," rejoined his friends. His mistakes, which sprang mostly from his incurable impetuosity, were many; but his influence was great and his leadership unchallenged. To ponder his advice, written to spiritual leaders in the years of maturity, is a valuable exercise. He enunciates to the guides of a persecuted church some of the timeless principles which relate to every type of spiritual leadership.

The veteran shepherd reminds them of their primary responsibility to the flock committed to their care: "See that your 'flock of God' is properly fed and cared for" (5:2). Undertones of his never–to–be–forgotten private interview with the chief Shepherd after his tragic failure are not difficult to detect (John 21:15–17). Indeed, in this passage he seems to be living again the experiences of those early days. He well knew that those who were passing through deep trial, as were "the strangers of the dispersion" (1:1) to whom he was writing, needed the highest type of pastoral care. With this in view he wrote to the elders.

It should be noted that Peter did not write as chief of the apostles, but as "a fellow Elder," one who was bearing similar responsibilities. He spoke to them not from above, but from alongside—a good vantage ground for the exercise of leadership. He treated them as being on an equality with himself. He wrote, too, as a witness of the sufferings of Christ, one whose heart had been chastened by his own failure, broken and conquered by Calvary's love. A shepherd's work cannot be done effectively without a shepherd's heart.

First, Peter deals with the leaders' *motivation.* The spiritual leader is to assume and discharge his responsibility uncoerced, not under compulsion, but "willingly and not because you feel you can't get out of it." Conditions prevailing at the time Peter wrote were such as could have daunted the stoutest heart, but he urges the leaders not to hold back on that account. Nor were they to serve merely out of a sense of duty or through the pressure of circumstances, but under the loftier constraint of divine love.

This pastoral ministry was to be exercised "according to...God." (5:2, ASV), not according to their own preferences and desires.

> Peter says to the elders, "Shepherd your people *like* God." Just as Israel is God's special allotment, the people we have to serve in the church or anywhere else are our special allotment; and our whole attitude to them must be the attitude of God; we must shepherd them like God. What a vision opens out! What an ideal! And what a condemnation! It is our task to show people the forbearance of God, the forgiveness of God, the seeking love of God, the illimitable service of God.[1]

Service to which God calls must not be refused because of a sense of unworthiness or inadequacy. Whoever could be worthy of such a trust? And as for inadequacy, it should be remembered that Moses' plea for exemption on that ground, far from pleasing God, kindled His anger (Exodus 4:14).

The spiritual leader must be *disinterested* in gain in his service. "Doing your work not for what you can make" out of it, "not for shameful gain" (RSV). Peter had not forgotten the corrupting power of covetousness on his companion Judas, and he was concerned that his fellow elders should be entirely free from avarice. The leader is not to be affected in his service or decisions by any considerations of financial or other gain. When people see he is genuinely disinterested, his words will carry greater weight.

Dr. Paul Rees suggests that greed for money is not the only thought contained in the Greek words "shameful gain."[2] The phrase might as appropriately be applied to greed for popularity or fame, an equally insidious temptation. Prestige and power are often coveted more than money.

"I am not sure which of the two occupies the lower sphere, he who hungers for money or he who thirsts for applause," wrote Dr. J. H. Jowett. "A preacher may dress and smooth his message to court the public cheers, and labourers in other spheres may bid for prominence, for imposing print, for grateful recognition. All this unfits us for our task. It destroys his perception of the needs and perils of the sheep."[3]

The Christian leader must not be *dictatorial.* "Not as domineering over those in your charge" (5:3a, C.B. Williams). An ambitious leader can easily degenerate into a petty tyrant with a domineering manner. "Even a little authority is prone to turn the seemly walk into the offensive strut." No attitude could be less becoming for one who professes to be a servant of the Son of God who humbled Himself.

He must set a *worthy example* for his flock. "Proving yourselves models for the flock to imitate" (5:3b, C.B. Williams)—words reminiscent of Paul's exhortation to Timothy: "Be thou an example of the believers, in word, in conversation, in charity, in spirit, in faith, in purity" (I Tim. 4:12). Peter reminds the elders of the spirit in which their ministry was to be exercised—the shepherd spirit. The word *feed* implies the compete task of the shepherd. Lest they should assume prerogatives not rightly theirs, he reminds them that it is God's flock, not theirs, and it is to Him they are finally accountable. He is the chief Shepherd, they are his undershepherds.

If it is "according to God," this shepherding ministry will surely include intercession. The saintly Bishop Azariah of India once remarked to Bishop Stephen Neill that he found time every day to pray by name for everyone in a position of leadership in his extensive diocese. Small wonder that during his thirty years of office the diocese trebled in its membership, and greatly increased in spiritual effectiveness.[4]

The leader is to be "clothed with humility." The word *clothed* occurs only here and refers to the white garment or apron worn by a slave. The leader is to *don the slave's apron.*

Was Peter recalling the tragic night when he refused to take the towel and gird himself and wash his Master's feet? He must guard them against a similar tragedy. Pride ever lurks at the heels of power, but God will not encourage proud men in His service. Rather will He oppose and obstruct them. But to the undershepherd who is humble and lowly in heart, He will multiply grace. In verse 5 Peter exhorts that the leader *act humbly* in his relations with others. But in verse 6 he challenges him to *react humbly* to the disciplines of God. "Therefore humbly submit to God's strong hand" is Charles B. Williams' rendering, bringing out the significance of the passive voice of the verb. "Allow yourselves to be humbled" conveys the correct idea.

As an inducement to the highest type of leadership, Peter holds out another powerful incentive: "When the Head Shepherd appears, you will win the unfading garland of glory" (5:4, Beck). *Unfading* here means "unwithering." The coveted wreath of laurel or parsley would soon fade or wither, but not the garland of amaranth, the reward of the faithful leader.

The undershepherd may also derive comfort from the fact that he will not be left by the chief Shepherd to shoulder his burdens alone. He can experience a transference of anxiety. "You can throw the whole weight of your anxieties upon him for you are his personal concern" (5:7, NEB). And it is the cares incidental to leadership of which Peter is speaking. *Anxiety* implies "distraction of mind and heart in view of conflicting emotions." But the undershepherd need have no fear that the cares of his flock of God will be too heavy for him. By a definite act of mind and will, he can transfer the crushing weight of his spiritual burdens to the powerful shoulders of the God who cares.

7

Qualities Essential To Leadership I

A bishop, then, must be...

I Timothy 3:2

In preparing a man for leadership God always has in view the sphere of service to which He purposes to call him. He is able therefore to adapt the means to the end and endow him with gifts of nature and grace that will best fit him to fulfill his commission. Without the superb equipment and unique training which were granted to him, Paul would never have achieved the incredible results he did within the space of one short life.

God prepared Adoniram Judson to pioneer His work in Burma by endowing him with the appropriate qualities—self–reliance balanced by humility, energy restrained by prudence, patience, self–forgetfulness, courage and a passion for souls.

Martin Luther the great Reformer was described as a man easy of approach; totally without personal vanity; so simple in his tastes that men wondered how he could sustain life on so little; abounding in solid sense, playful humor and mirthfulness; honest as the day, transparently sincere. Added to this was his undaunted courage, inflexible conviction and passion for Christ. It is small wonder that he bound men to him with bonds of steel.[1]

Professor G. Warneck described Hudson Taylor in terms that indicated how appropriately God had endowed him for his work of pioneering in China: "A man full of faith and the Holy Ghost, of entire surrender to God and His call, of great self–denial, heartfelt compassion, rare power in prayer, marvelous organizing faculty, indefatigable perseverance, and of astounding influence with men, and withal of childlike simplicity himself."

In each case these men were endowed with gifts which uniquely equipped them for the special tasks to which they were later called. But that which raised them above their fellows was the degree to which they developed these gifts and graces through devotion and self–discipline.

We shall consider the general qualities which go to make a man a spiritual leader, and which require to be continually developed by the possessor.

Discipline

This quality is placed first, for without it the other gifts, however great, will never realize their highest possibilities. Only the disciplined person will rise to his highest powers. The leader is able to lead others because he has conquered himself.

The words *disciple* and *discipline* derive from the same root. A leader is a person who has first submitted willingly and learned to obey a discipline imposed from without, but who then imposes on himself a much more rigorous discipline from within. Those who rebel against authority and scorn self–discipline seldom qualify for leadership of a high order. They shirk the rigors and sacrifices it demands and reject the divine disciplines that are involved. Many who drop out of missionary work do so not because they are not sufficiently gifted but because there are large areas of their lives which have never been brought under the control of the Holy Spirit.

Many who take courses in leadership in the hope of attaining it fail because they have never learned to follow. They are like the boys who were playing war in the street. When a passerby inquired why they were so quiet and were doing nothing, one lad replied, "We are all generals. We can't get anyone to do the fighting."

Dr. Donald G. Barnhouse drew attention to the striking fact that the average age of the 40,000 biographies in the *American Who's Who*—the 40,000 who really run America—was just under twenty–eight. This throws into relief the important fact that the discipline in early life which is prepared to make sacrifices in order to gain adequate preparation for the life–task paves the way for high achievement.

A great statesman made a speech that turned the tide in national affairs. "May I ask how long it took you to prepare that speech?" asked an admirer. "All my life has been a preparation for what I said today," was the reply.

The young man of leadership caliber will work while others waste time, study while others sleep, pray while others play. There will be no place for loose or slovenly habits in word or thought, deed or dress. He will observe a soldierly discipline in diet and deportment so that he might wage a good warfare. He will without reluctance undertake the unpleasant task which others avoid, or the hidden duty which others evade because it evokes no applause or wins no appreciation. A Spirit–filed leader will not shrink from facing up to difficult situations or persons, or from grasping the nettle when that is necessary. He will kindly and courageously administer rebuke when that is called for; or he will exercise necessary discipline when the interests of the Lord's work demand it. He will not procrastinate in writing the difficult letter. His letter–basket will not conceal the evidences of his failure to grapple with urgent problems. His prayer will be:

God, harden me against myself,
The coward with pathetic voice
Who craves for ease and rest and joy.
Myself, arch–traitor to myself,
My hollowest friend,
My deadliest foe,
My clog, whatever road I go.
—Amy Carmichael

Few men were more faithful and courageous in loving rebuke or in speaking frankly to people, when they or the work of God required it, than Fred Mitchell, who was British Director of the China Inland Mission and Chairman of the English Keswick Convention. Though unusually sensitive and affectionate in nature, he did not shirk the unpleasant interview. When he had something of this nature to say, it was always done in prayerfulness and with love, but not everyone was able to accept the admonition in the same spirit. He confided that he had suffered greatly when in a few cases his faithfulness had resulted in the estrangement of a friend.

As he drew toward the close of his life, it was observed by a friend that "he changed considerably. Although he did not avoid performing an unpleasant task when necessary, he would spend more time in prayer beforehand." Often when he had to deal with a matter of discipline, or cut across the desires of others, he would write a letter and then keep it for several days. Sometimes on rereading it, he was assured it was right to send it, and it would be mailed. Sometimes it would be destroyed and another one written.[2]

When Dr. Thomas Cochrane, Founder of the World Dominion Movement, was being interviewed for the mission field, he was asked, "To what position of the field do you feel yourself specially called?" He answered, "I only know I should wish it to be the hardest you could offer me"—the reply of a strongly disciplined man.

Lytton Strachey wrote of Florence Nightingale:

> It was not by gentle sweetness and womanly self–abnegation that she brought order out of chaos in the Scutari Hospitals, that from her own resources she had clothed the British army, that she had spread her dominion over the serried and reluctant powers of the official world; it was by strict method, by *stern discipline,* by rigid attention to detail, by ceaseless labor, by the fixed determination of an indomitable will. Beneath her cool and calm demeanor, there lurked fierce and passionate fires.

Samuel Chadwick, the great Methodist preacher and Principal of Cliff College, made a great impact on his generation. He disciplined himself with rigor, rising at six in the morning and having a cold bath, summer and winter. He accustomed himself to do with little sleep. His study light was seldom extinguished before two in the morning. This rigorous program was but the outward expression of his inner discipline.[3]

All through his life, George Whitefield was an early riser; his usual hour for rising throughout the year was four o'clock. He was equally punctual in retiring at night. As the clock struck ten, no matter who were his visitors or what conversation was going on at the moment, he rose from his seat, and, advancing toward the door, he would say good–naturedly to his friends, "Come, gentlemen, it is time for all good folks to be at home."[4]

> Barclay Buxton of Japan used to urge Christians to lead disciplined lives whether they were in business or evangelistic work. This included discipline in Bible study and prayer, in tithing their money, in use of their time, in keeping healthy by proper food and sleep and exercise. It included the rigor of disciplined fellowship among Christians who differed from each other in many ways. This discipline was to equip them to carry responsibility. He then urged them to take their place on committees and to fulfill their responsibility by careful thought, work and judgment. All these were the disciplines of his life, and his urgings for others came because of experience.[5]

These pieces of biography serve only to illustrate the fact that

The heights by great men reached and kept
Were not attained by sudden flight;
But they, while their companions slept,
Were toiling upward in the night.

Because the leader is himself so strongly disciplined, others sense this and are usually willing to respond cooperatively to the discipline he expects of them.

There is another little–emphasized element in discipline that merits attention. It is the discipline of being willing to receive from others as well as to give to others. There are some who delight in sacrificing themselves for others, who are quite unwilling to allow others to reciprocate. They are unwilling to place themselves under obligation to others. Yet this is a very powerful way of exercising helpful leadership. To neglect it is to rob both oneself and others.

It is told of Bishop Westcott that at the end of his life he said that he had made one great mistake, for while he had always been willing to do for others to the limit of his ability, he had never been willing to let others do for him, and as a result some element of sweetness and completeness was missing. He had not allowed himself the discipline of receiving many kindnesses which could not be repaid.

Vision

Those who have most powerfully and permanently influenced their generation have been the "seers"—men who have seen more and farther than others. Men of faith, for faith is vision. This was true of the prophets or seers of the Old Testament times. Moses, one of the greatest leaders of all time, "endured as seeing him who is invisible." His faith imparted vision. Elisha's servant saw with great vividness the vastness of the encircling army. Elisha saw the invincible environing host of heaven who were invisible to his servant. His faith imparted vision.

Powhattan James in his biography of George W. Truett, the great Baptist leader, wrote:

> The man of God must have *insight* into things spiritual. He must be able to see the mountains filled with the horses and chariots of fire; he must be able to interpret that which is written by the finger of God upon the walls of conscience; he must be able to translate the signs of the times into terms of their spiritual meaning; he must be able to draw aside, now and then, the curtain of things material and let mortals glimpse the spiritual glories which crown the mercy seat of God. The man of God must declare the pattern that was shown him on the mount; he must utter the vision granted to him upon the isle of revelation.... None of these things can he do without spiritual insight.[6]

This was a characteristic of Charles Cowman, founder of the Oriental Missionary Society. "He was a man of vision. Throughout his life he seemed to see what the crowd did not see, and to see wider and fuller than many of his own day. He was a man of far horizons."[7]

Vision includes *foresight* as well as insight. It was said of President McKinley that he was a great statesman because he had the faculty of putting his ear to the ground and listening for things that were coming. It is a different figure of speech, but it conveys the same idea. He turned his listening into vision. He saw what lay ahead. A leader must be able to envision the end result of the policies or methods he advocates. Responsible leadership always looks ahead to see how policies proposed will affect not only present, but succeeding generations.

The great missionary pioneers were without exception men of vision. Carey was seeing the whole world on the map while his fellow preachers were preoccupied with their own little parishes. Henry Martyn saw India, Persia and Arabia—a vision of the Muslim world—while the church at home was engrossed in its petty theological squabbles. Of A.

B. Simpson his contemporaries said, "His life–work seemed to be to push on alone, where his fellows had seen nothing to explore."

Speaking to Douglas Thornton of Egypt, Mr. Baylis his senior missionary remarked: "Thornton, you are different to anyone else I know. You are always looking at the end of things. Most people, myself included, find it better to do the next thing." Thornton's answer was: "I find that the constant inspiration gained by looking at the goal is the chief thing that helps me to persevere."[8] An ideal, a vision, was absolutely necessary to him. He could not work without it. And this explained the largeness of his views and the magnitude of his schemes.

Concerning Thornton's contribution to the Student Volunteer Movement it was said: "He was the greatest prophet the Student Movement has ever had. He looked in to the future and then devised his schemes." It was typical of his outlook to write to the leaders of his society:

> I have been to the American Press at Beirut and seen there the result of the seven Arabian scholars after lifelong study, and I tell you it is as a drop in the ocean. We need a hymnology in Arabic, a whole range of topical theological works, an army of controversial tracts.[9]

Eyes that look are common. Eyes that see are rare. The Pharisees *looked* at Peter and saw only a poor unlettered fisherman, totally insignificant , not worthy of a second look. Jesus *saw* Peter and discovered the prophet and preacher, saint and leader of the unique band of men who turned the world upside down.

Vision includes *optimism and hope.* No pessimist ever made a great leader. The pessimist sees a difficulty in every opportunity. The optimist sees an opportunity in every difficulty. The pessimist, always seeing difficulties before possibilities, tends to hold back the man of vision who desires to push ahead. The cautious man has his part to play in helping his optimistic leader to be realistic as well. But he must watch lest his native and now ingrained caution clips the wings of the man God intends to soar. The cautious man draws valuable lessons from history and tradition, but he is in danger of being chained to the past. The man who sees the difficulties so clearly that he does not discern the possibilities will be unable to impart inspiration to his followers.

Browning described the courageous optimist:

One who has never turned his back,
But marched breast–forward,
Never doubting clouds would break,
Never dreamed, though right were worsted,
Wrong would triumph.

Vision imparts *venturesomeness,* the willingness to take fresh steps of faith when there is seeming void beneath. Of Archbishop Mowll of Sydney it was said:

> It was a mark of his greatness that he was never behind his age, or too far ahead. He was up at the front, and far enough in advance to lead the march. He was always catching sight of new horizons. He still had a receptive mind for new ideas at an age when many were inclined to let things take their course.[10]

Only vision makes a visionary.
Only wisdom makes a wiseacre.
The combination of both is irresistible.
A vision without a task makes a visionary.
A task without a vision is drudgery.
A vision with a task makes a missionary.[11]

Wisdom

"Wisdom is the faculty of making the best use of knowledge, a combination of discernment, judgment, sagacity and similar powers.... In Scripture, right judgment concerning spiritual and moral truth" (Webster).

Wisdom is more than knowledge, which is the accumulation of facts. It has a personal connotation and implies sagacity. It is more than human acumen, it is heavenly discernment. It is knowledge with insight into the heart of things, and knows them as they really are. It involves the knowledge of God and of the intricacies of the human heart. It is much more than knowledge; it is the right application of knowledge in moral and spiritual matters, in meeting baffling situations and in the complexity of human relationships. "Wisdom is nine–tenths a matter of being wise in time," said Theodore Roosevelt.[12] Most of us are "too often wise after the event."

This quality imparts necessary balance to a leader and delivers him from eccentricity and extravagance. Knowledge is gained by study, but when the Spirit fills a man, He imparts the wisdom to use and apply that knowledge correctly. "Full of wisdom" was one of the requirements for even subordinate leaders in the early church (Acts 6:3).

Knowledge and wisdom, far from being one,
Have ofttimes no connection. Knowledge dwells
In heads replete with thoughts of other men:
Wisdom, in minds attentive to their own.
Knowledge is proud that he has learned so much,
Wisdom is humble, that he knows no more.

The place of wisdom in leadership was indicated in the statement of D. E. Hoste:

> When a man, in virtue of an official position demands obedience of another, irrespective of the latter's reason and conscience, this is the spirit of tyranny. When, on the other hand, by the exercise of tact and sympathy; by prayer, spiritual power and sound wisdom one is able to influence and enlighten another, so that he through the medium of his own reason and conscience is led to alter one course and adopt another, that is true spiritual leadership.[13]
>
> Paul's prayer for the Christians at Colosse should constantly be on the lips of those bearing spiritual responsibility: "That ye might be filled with the knowledge of his will *in all wisdom* and spiritual understanding" (Col. 1:9).

Decision

When all the facts are in, swift and clear decision is the mark of the true leader. The man who possesses vision must do something about it or he will remain a visionary, not a leader. While he will be quick to reach decision, it must be a decision based on sound premises. Lord Montgomery includes the power of clear decision in his seven ingredients of military leadership.

Once a spiritual leader is sure of the will of God, he will go into immediate action, regardless of consequences. In pursuing his goal, he will have the courage to burn his bridges behind him. He must be willing to accept full responsibility for consequent failure or success, and not place any blame that might accrue on a subordinate.

Abraham showed himself a man of swift and clear decision when faced with the crisis of the capture of Sodom and his nephew Lot. In his relations with Lot, Abraham manifested both active and passive sides of spirituality. In his unselfish yielding of his right to the choice of pasturelands, Abraham had displayed the passive graces of godliness. But when faced with this crisis, he displayed immediate decision and initiative. With great bravery he pursued the enemy with his pitifully inferior band of armed servants and, inspired by his faith in God, gained a resounding victory over his enemies.

Moses qualified to become the leader of Israel only when, after counting the cost, he made the momentous decision to abandon the treasures and pleasures of Egypt and identify himself with Israel in their sufferings and afflictions. It was his faith that nerved him to make such a far–reaching decision (Heb. 11:24–27).

Each of the worthies immortalized in Hebrews 11 was a man of vision and decision. First they all saw the vision. Then they counted the cost, made their decision and acted on it. The same is true of the great missionary leaders. Carey saw a vision in Kettering and made his decision in the light of it, although the difficulties in realizing his vision loomed up to heaven. He gave effect to his vision in India. David Livingstone saw the vision in Dumbarton, made his decision, overcame all obstacles and proceeded to bring it to fulfillment in Africa. Circumstances cannot frustrate such men, or difficulties deter them.

The true leader will resist the temptation to procrastinate in reaching a decision, nor will he vacillate after it has been made. These tendencies are fatal to leadership. Usually, a sincere though mistaken decision is better than no decision at all. In this connection it was said of Charles Cowman that he was a man of one purpose. He kept his eyes fixed on one great object. With him, a vision of possibility became action. The moment he found it possible to do a thing, he was uneasy until it was in course of execution.

A young man who was beginning his work with the coast guard was early called to take part in a desperate assignment. A great storm had arisen and a ship was signaling its distress. As the men began to move the big boat to the rescue, the young man, frightened at the fierceness of the gale, cried out to the captain, "We will never get back!" Above the storm the captain replied, "We don't have to come back, but we do have to go out." In most decisions the difficult part is not in knowing what we ought to do; it is in being willing to pay the price involved.

Courage

Courage of the highest order is demanded of a spiritual leader—always moral courage and frequently physical courage as well. Courage is "that quality of mind which enables men to encounter danger or difficulty with firmness, or without fear or depression of spirits."

Martin Luther possessed this important quality in unusual measure. It has been asserted that he was perhaps as fearless a man as ever lived.[14] When he set out on his momentous journey to Worms he said, "You can expect from me everything save fear or recantation. I shall not flee, much less recant." His friends, warning him of the grave dangers he ran, sought to dissuade him. But Luther would not be dissuaded. "Not go to Worms!" he said. "I shall go to Worms though there were as many devils as tiles on the roofs."[15]

When Luther appeared before the emperor, he was called on to recant. They insisted that he should say in a word whether he would recant or no. "Unless convinced by the Holy Scripture, or by clear reasons from other sources, I cannot recant," he declared. "To Councils or Pope I cannot defer, for they have often erred. My conscience is a prisoner to God's Word."

When again given an opportunity to recant, he folded his hands: "Here I stand, I can do no other. God help me." A few days before his death, recalling this incident, Luther described his feelings: "I was afraid of nothing; God can make one so desperately bold. I know not whether I could be so cheerful now."

But not all are courageous by nature as Luther was, and this fact is both explicit and implicit in Scripture. The highest degree of courage is seen in the person who is most fearful but refuses to capitulate to it. However fearful they might have been, God's leaders in succeeding generations have been commanded to be of good courage. Had they been without fear, the command would have been pointless. The responsibility for his own courage is placed on the leader himself, for, since he is indwelt by the Spirit of power, there is possible attainment.

Contrast these two records: "The doors were shut where the disciples were assembled for fear of the Jews" (John 20:19) and "They saw the boldness of Peter and John" (Acts 4:13). These were the same disciples confronted by the same Jews at an interval of only a short time. Whence this new courage? Inspiration gives the answer: "They were all filled with the Holy Spirit." And when the Holy Spirit is ceded control of the whole personality, He imparts "Not the spirit of fear, but of power . . ." (II Tim. 1:7).

The courage of a leader is demonstrated in his being willing to face unpleasant and even devastating facts and conditions with equanimity, and then acting with firmness in the light of them, even though it means incurring personal unpopularity. Human inertia and opposition do not deter him. His courage is not a thing of the moment, but continues until the task is fully done.

People expect of their leaders courage and calmness in crisis. Others may falter and lose their heads, but not they. They strengthen their followers in the midst of shattering reverses and weakening influences.

Faced with Sennacherib's ruthless hordes, Hezekiah calmly made his military preparations and then set about strengthening the morale of his people. "Be strong and of good courage," he exhorted them. "Do not be afraid or dismayed before the king of Assyria and all the horde that is with him.... With his is an army of flesh; but with us is the Lord our God, to help us and to fight our battles. *And the people took confidence from the words of Hezekiah*" (II Chron. 32:7–8, RSV). This was leadership indeed.

Humility

In the realm of politics and commerce, humility is a quality neither covered nor required. There the leader needs and seeks prominence and publicity. But in God's scale of values humility stands very high. Self–effacement, not self–advertisement, was Christ's definition of leadership. In training His disciples for their coming positions of authority, He told them they must not be pompous and overbearing like the Oriental despots, but humble and lowly like their Master (Matt. 20:25–27). The spiritual leader will choose the hidden pathway of sacrificial service and the approval of His Lord rather than the flamboyant assignment and the adulation of the unspiritual crowd.

In the early days of his ministry, one might have concluded that the greatness of John the Baptist lay in his fierce denunciation of the evils of his day, in the burning eloquence and blistering words which pierced and exposed the hearts of his contemporaries. But the secret that made him the greatest of those born of woman is to be found in his unconscious but infinitely revealing affirmation: "He must increase, but I must decrease" (John 3:30). In this one sentence his spiritual stature is revealed.

The humility of the leader, as his spirituality, should be an ever growing quality. It is instructive to notice Paul's advance in the grace of humility with the passing of the years. Early in his ministry, as he reviewed his past and now abhorred record, he acknowledged: "I am the least of the apostles, I am not meet to be called an apostle" (I Cor. 15:9). Sometime later he volunteered: "I am less than the least of all saints" (Eph. 3:8). When his life was drawing to a close and he was preparing to meet his Lord, He mourned: "I am the chief of sinners" (I Tim. 1:15).

In his *Serious Call,* William Law exhorts:

> Let every day be a day of humility; condescend to all the weaknesses and infirmities of your fellow–creatures, cover their frailties, love their excellencies, encourage their virtues, relieve their wants, rejoice in their prosperities, compassionate their distress, receive their friendship, overlook their unkindness, forgive their malice, be a servant of servants, and condescend to do the lowliest offices of the lowest of mankind.

On one occasion Samuel Brengle was introduced as "the great Dr. Brengle." In his diary he wrote:

> If I appear great in their eyes, the Lord is most graciously helping me to see how absolutely nothing I am without Him, and helping me to keep little in my own eyes. He does use me. But I am so concerned that *He* uses me and that it is not of me the work is done. The axe cannot boast of the trees it has cut down. It could do nothing but for the woodsman. He made it, he sharpened it, and he used it. The moment he throws it aside, it becomes only old iron. O that I may never lose sight of this.[16]

The spiritual leader of today is in all probability one who yesterday expressed his humility by working gladly and faithfully in the second place. Out of his wisdom, Robert Morrison of China wrote: "The great fault, I think, in our missions is that no one likes to be second. Perhaps the advantages predominate, but I have not been able to see them."

8

Qualities Essential To Spiritual Leadership II

Likewise must the deacons be....

—I Timothy 3:8

Humor

Since man is in the image of God, his sense of humor is a gift of God and finds its counterpart in the divine nature. But it is a gift which is to be controlled as well as cultivated. Clean, wholesome humor will relax tension and relieve a difficult situation more than anything else. It can be of untold value in a leader, both for what it does for him and for the use it can be in his work.

Samuel Johnson advised that "a man should spend part of his time with the laughters." Archbishop Whately the great apologist wrote: "We ought not only to cultivate the cornfield of the mind but the pleasure grounds also." Agnes Strickland claimed that "next to virtue, the fun in this world is what we can least spare."[1] A retired missionary was greatly dreading going to live in a home for retired missionaries. But in writing some months later, he said he had never been in a place where there was so much holy fun.

Charles H. Spurgeon was once chided for introducing humor into his preaching. With a twinkle in his eye he replied: "If only you knew how much I hold back, you would commend me." In justification of humorous touches in his pulpit, he wrote: "There are things in these sermons that may produce smiles, but what of them? The preacher is not quite sure about a smile being a sin, and at any rate he thinks it less a crime to cause a momentary laughter than a half–hour of profound slumber."

Helmut Thielecke wrote:

> Should we not see that lines of laughter about the eyes are just as much marks of faith as are the lines of care and seriousness? Is it only earnestness that is baptized? Is laughter pagan? We have already allowed too much that is good to be lost to the church and cast many pearls before swine. A church is in a bad way when it banishes laughter from the sanctuary and leaves it to the cabaret, the nightclub and the toastmasters.[2]

Humor is a great asset in missionary life. Indeed it is a most serious deficiency if a missionary lacks a sense of humor. A Swede was urged by his friends to give up the idea of returning to India as a missionary because it was so hot there. "Man," he was urged, "it is 120 degrees in the shade!" "Vell," said the Swede in noble contempt, "ve don't always have to stay in the shade, do ve?"

A. E. Norrish, a missionary to India, testifies:

> "I have never met leadership without a sense of humour; this ability to stand outside oneself and one's circumstances, to see things in perspective and laugh. It is a great safety valve! You will never lead others far without the joy of the Lord and its concomitant, a sense of humour."[3]

Douglas Thornton was often more amusing than he tried to be. He had a delightful way of mixing up two kindred proverbs or idioms. Once he told his companions that he always had two strings up his sleeve. They then asked him if he also had another card to his bow. Such things enliven heavy committee meetings and create wholesome laughter.[4]

In half a century of experience as a minister, F. J. Hallett claimed he had found that in the actual work of a parish, the most successful man is he who possesses a keen sense of humor in combination with God's grace. Humor lends pungency, originality and eloquence to sermons.

Of one great preacher it was said that he used humor as a condiment and a stimulant. At times paroxysms of laughter would rock his audiences, but he never permitted sacred things to be involved. He would quickly swing to the sublime, and his humor did not degenerate into frivolity.

A good test of the appropriateness of our humor is whether we control it or it controls us. Of Kenneth Strachan, General Director of the Latin America Mission, it was said: "He had a keen sense of humor, but he had a sense of the fitness of things. He knew the place for a joke and his humor was controlled."[5]

Anger

This sounds like rather a strange qualification for leadership. In another context it could be quoted as a disqualifying factor. But was this quality not present in the life of the supreme Leader? "Jesus looked on them with anger" (John 2:15–17). Righteous wrath is no less noble than love, since both coexist in God. Each necessitates the other. It was Jesus' love for the man with the withered hand that aroused His anger against those who would deny him healing (Mark 3:5). It was His love for His Father, and zeal for His glory, that kindled His anger against the mercenary traders who had turned His house of prayer for all nations into a cave of robbers (Matt. 21:13).

Great leaders who have turned the tide in days of national and spiritual declension have been men who could get angry at the injustices and abuses which dishonor God and enslave men. It was righteous anger against the heartless slave traders that caused Wilberforce to move heaven and earth for the emancipation of slaves.

F. W. Robertson was similarly stirred by righteous anger on one occasion. Describing his reaction he said: "My blood was at the moment running fired, and I remembered that once in my life I had felt a terrible might; I knew and rejoiced to know that I was inflicting the sentence of a coward's and a liar's hell."[6] Martin Luther claimed that he "never did anything well until his wrath was excited, and then he could do anything well."

But such anger is open to abuse, and few can entertain it without allowing it to degenerate into sin. Paul argues the possibility of righteous anger in his exhortation "Be angry and sin not." Holy anger is free from selfishness. Anger which centers upon self is always sinful. To be sinless it must be zeal for the rights of truth and purity, with the glory of God as its objective.

Thou to wax fierce
In the cause of the Lord!
Anger and zeal
And the joy of the brave,
Who bade thee to feel,
Sin's slave?

Bishop Butler analyzed the conditions under which righteous wrath degenerates into sinful anger:

When, from partiality to ourselves, we imagine an injury done to us when there is none.

When this partiality represents it to us greater than it really is.

When we feel resentment on account of pain or inconvenience without injury.

When indignation rises too high.

When pain or harm is inflicted to gratify that resentment, though naturally raised.

When we are angry with sin in our own lives, we will be most likely to experience righteous anger at the sin in others.[7]

Patience

A liberal endowment of this quality is essential to sound leadership. Chrysostom called patience the Queen of Virtues. The popular use of the word is too passive to adequately convey its full significance in the original. William Barclay has this to say of its meaning as used in II Peter 1:6: "The word never means the spirit which sits with folded hands and simply bears things. It is victorious endurance, masculine constancy under trial. It is Christian steadfastness, the brave and courageous acceptance of everything life can do to us, and the transmuting of even the worst into another step on the upward way. It is the courageous and triumphant ability to bear things, which enables a man to pass breaking point and not to break, and always to greet the unseen with a cheer."[8]

It is in personal relationships that patience meets its most stringent test. Paul broke down in patience in his dealing with John Mark. Hudson Taylor once made this confession: "My greatest temptation is to lose my temper over the slackness and inefficiency so disappointing in those on whom I depended. It is no use to lose my temper—only kindness. But oh, it is such a trial."[9] Many other leaders experience the force of this temptation, but how clearly does this bring into relief the marvelous patience of our Lord with doubting Thomas and unstable Peter and traitorous Judas!

One manifestation of this quality in a leader consists in his not running too far ahead of his followers and thus discouraging them. While keeping ahead, he stays near enough for them to keep him in sight and hear his call forward. He is not so strong that he cannot show a strengthening sympathy for the weakness of his fellows. "We who are strong *ought* to bear with the failings of the weak" (Rom. 15:1, RSV). The man who is impatient with weakness will be defective in his leadership. The evidence of our strength lies not in streaking ahead but in a willingness to adapt our stride to the slower pace of our weaker brethren, while not forfeiting our lead. If we run too far ahead, we lose our power to influence.

Of his father, Dr. A. J. Gordon, Ernest Gordon wrote:

> Criticism and opposition he endured without recrimination. "A Christian should be a patient, undaunted, undiscouraged torchbearer for Christ. If a storm of abuse should chance to break on him, he is to stand in statue–like indifference to it all, holding forth the word of life. If blasts of ridicule dash him in the face, he is to take it silently and imperturbably as the bronze figure takes the tempest. It is the man who stands who moves the world."[10]

Great patience may have to be exercised by a leader in the implementation of cherished plans which he believes to be in the best interests of the work for which he is responsible. D. E. Hoste said:

> I shall never forget the impression made upon me by Hudson Taylor in connection with these affairs. Again and again he was obliged either to greatly modify or lay aside projects which were sound and helpful but met with determined opposition, and so tended to create greater evils than those which might have been removed or mitigated by the changes in question. Later on, in answer to patient continuance in prayer, many of such projects were given effect to.[11]

Friendship

"The crowning glory of his leadership was that he was a friend of man. He loved the man next to him and he loved mankind."[12] This tribute to Dr. A. B. Simpson illustrates the fact that the spiritual leader will be a lover of men and will have a large capacity for friendship. David's peerless command of men sprang from his genius in gathering around him men of renown who were ready to die for him. So fully did he capture their affection and allegiance that a whispered wish was to them as a command (II Sam. 23:15–16). They would die for him because they knew he would die for them.

Paul, too, had this gift for friendship. "Paul had a genius for friendship. No man in the New Testament made fiercer enemies, but few men in the world have had better friends. They cluster around him so thickly that we are apt to lose their personality in their devotion."[13]

There are men like General Charles de Gaulle whose greatness is the greatness of isolation. On the contrary, Paul's greatness and successful leadership lay in no small measure in his ability to capture and to hold the intense love and loyalty of the friends with whom he freely mixed. True, he involved his friends in all sorts of risks for Christ's sake and the gospel's, but they followed him cheerfully because they were assured of his love for them. His letters glow with a warmth of appreciation and personal affection for his fellow workers.

Another important ingredient in leadership is the faculty of being able to draw the best out of other people. In achieving this, personal friendliness will accomplish much more than prolonged and even successful argument. It was John R. Mott's counsel to "rule by the heart. When logic and argument and other forms of persuasion fail, fall back on the heart–genuine friendship."

In his biography of Robert A. Jaffray, who played a major part in opening Vietnam to the gospel, A. W. Tozer pointed out that in one respect all spiritual leaders have been alike. They have all had large hearts.

> Nothing can take the place of affection. Those who have it in generous measure have a magic power over men. Intellect will not do. Bible knowledge is not enough. Robert Jaffray loved people for their own sakes. He was happy in the presence of human beings, whatever their race and color.[14]

Few have exercised in their own generation the leadership in spiritual things wielded by Charles Haddon Spurgeon. It was his biographer's conviction that "he exercised an absolute authority, not because of sheer willfulness, though he was a willful man, but because of his acknowledged worth. Men bowed to his authority because it was authority backed by united wisdom and affection."

One greater than David or Paul also ruled His followers by friendship and affection. Of Him it was written, "Having loved his own which were in the world, he loved them unto the end" (John 13:1). It was the knowledge of this personal affection for him that at last broke Peter's heart and forced from him the confession: "Thou knowest all things; thou knowest that I love thee" (John 21:17).

Tact And Diplomacy

These are closely related. *Tact* is defined as "intuitive perception, especially a quick and fine perception of what is fit and proper or right; a ready appreciation of the proper thing to do or say, especially a fine sense of how to avoid giving offense." *Diplomacy* is dexterity and skill in managing affairs of any kind, but as a result of abuses practiced by some of those who engage in this art, the word has become somewhat debased. Combining these two words, the idea emerges of skill in reconciling opposing viewpoints without giving offense and without compromising principle. These are invaluable qualities in the spiritual leader. The ability to conduct delicate negotiations and matters concerning personnel in a way that recognized mutual rights and yet leads to a harmonious solution is an asset greatly to be coveted. It involves the ability to place oneself in the position of the persons involved and to accurately assess how they would feel and react.

The same thing can be said in a tactful and in an untactful manner. One shoe salesman said to his client, "I'm sorry, madam, but your foot is too large for this shoe." The other salesman said to his client who was in a similar situation, "I'm sorry, madam, but this shoe is too small for your foot.' Each used almost exactly the same words, but tact and diplomacy caused one to make a slightly different emphasis by a slight difference of phrasing, and secured a loyal and satisfied customer.

Joshua's division of the promised land among the Israelites affords an outstanding biblical example of the employment of these qualities. With a nation descended from scheming Jacob, such a delicate task in which human cupidity and greed were inevitably involved, held all the seeds of serious dissension and strife that could have rent the nation.

The tactful manner in which Joshua was able to handle the transaction was evidence not only of human sagacity but of his close walk with God. The diplomacy he displayed in resolving the potentially bitter and explosive misunderstanding created by the tribes of Reuben and Gad erecting another altar was further tribute not only to his native gift but to the wisdom he had learned in the school of God.

William Carey was unconsciously a diplomat. One of his fellow workers testified of him: "He has attained the happy art of ruling and overruling others without asserting his authority, or others feeling their subjection—and all is done without the least appearance of design on his part."[15] Tact and diplomacy are never more effective than when they are unconscious and unstudied.

Inspirational Power

The power of inspiring others to service and sacrifice will mark God's leader. His incandescence sets those around him alight. Charles Cowman not only achieved a prodigious amount of work himself but possessed the ability to inject the spirit of work into those with whom he was associated. His zeal and drive were infectious.[16]

Pastor Hsi was one of the truly great Christian leaders of his day in China. He, too, possessed this capacity to an extraordinary degree. One who was closely linked with him in the service of the Lord was asked, "Did you notice about him any special aptitude for leading and influencing others?" He replied, "His power in that direction was remarkable; without any effort, apparently, he seemed to sway everybody. Instinctively people followed and trusted him. Then, too, he possessed great power of initiative and an energy and enterprise that were extraordinary. One could not be with him without gaining a wholly new ideal of Christian life and service."[17]

Nehemiah also displayed this power in abundant measure. When he arrived in Jerusalem the people were utterly disheartened and dispirited. In no time he succeeded in welding them into an aggressive and effective working force. Such was his power to inspire that before long we read, "The people had a mind to work." It would be true to say that work on the walls would not have been commenced, much less completed, apart from the inspiration imparted by Nehemiah.

Executive Ability

One who lacks this quality to any considerable degree, however clearly he may see things spiritual, will be unable to translate his vision into action. It is true that subtle dangers lie in overmuch organization, for it can be a very unsatisfactory substitute for the presence and working of the Holy Spirit. But this is not necessarily so. Lack of method and organization has its dangers too, and has spelled failure for many a promising venture for God.

In his *Book of Isaiah,* Sir George Adam Smith calls attention to the word ambiguously translated "judgment" in the Authorized Version and reminds us that it means "method, order, system, law." So when Isaiah says, "the *Lord* is a God of judgment" (30:18), he means, among other things, that God is a God of method. His creation is superbly ordered. Because He is a God of order, He requires of those whom He entrusts with leadership "that all things be done decently and in order." "It is a great truth," Smith writes, "that the Almighty and All–merciful is the All–methodical too. No religion is completed in its creed, or healthy in its influence which does not insist equally on all these."[18]

It is for us to emulate the orderliness and method of God in our own work for Him. While it is true that men cannot be organized into the kingdom, this does not justify the absence of careful planning, in dependence on the Sprit's leading, and skillful execution of what has been planned for their salvation.

Lord Macaulay said that Wesley had a genius for government not inferior to that of Richelieu. The genius of his organization is still seen in the church which he founded. It is owing to his superb executive ability and powers of organization that the movement remained unshaken even when deprived of his presence and guidance.

His judgment of men, his skill in using them, his power to employ them to the best advantage and to attach them to himself in loyal submission to his authority amounted to genius and saved the movement from the most serious dangers.[19]

9

The Indispensable Requirement

Select men full of the Spirit.

And they chose Stephen, a man full of the Holy Spirit.

—*Acts 6:3, 5*

Spiritual leadership can be exercised only by Spirit–filled men. Other qualifications for spiritual leadership are desirable. This is indispensable.

The book of Acts, an inspired source–book for principles of leadership, is the story of the men who established the Christian church and led the missionary enterprise. It is of more than passing significance that the central qualification of those who were to occupy even subordinate positions of responsibility in the early church was that they be men "full of the Holy Spirit." They must be known by their integrity and sagacity, but preeminently for their spirituality. However brilliant a man may be intellectually, however capable an administrator, without this essential equipment he is incapable of giving truly spiritual leadership.

Behind the actions of the apostles, the executive activity of the Spirit is everywhere seen. As supreme Administrator of the church and chief Strategist of the missionary enterprise, He is everywhere prominent. It is abundantly evident in the record that the Holy Spirit is jealous of His prerogatives and will not delegate His power of authority to secular or carnal hands. Even men whose duties would be largely in the temporal affairs of the church must be men mastered and controlled by Him. Their selection must not be influenced by considerations of worldly wisdom, financial acumen or social acceptability, but primarily because of their genuine spirituality. When a church or other Christian organization departs from this pattern, it amounts to a virtual ousting of the Spirit from

His place of leadership. As a consequence He is grieved and quenched, with resulting spiritual dearth and death.

Choosing men for office in the church or any of its auxiliaries without reference to spiritual qualifications must of necessity result in an unspiritual administration. In illustrating such a situation, Dr. A. T. Pierson likened it to the course sometimes pursued in a large company when it desires to rid itself of its controlling head. Gradually, in the subordinate offices and in the Board of Trustees or Directors, men are introduced who are opposed to the presiding officer in method and spirit. They quietly antagonize his measures, obstruct his plans, thwart his policy. Instead of cooperation and support, he meets inertia and indifference, if not violent opposition, until at last, unable to conduct affairs, he resigns from sheer inability to carry out his policy of administration.[1] Appointment of men with a secular or materialistic outlook prevents the Holy Spirit from carrying out His program for the church in the world.

The Holy Spirit does not take control of any man or body of men against their will. When He sees men elected to positions of leadership who lack spiritual fitness to cooperate with Him He quietly withdraws and leaves them to implement their own policy according to their own standards, but without His aid. The inevitable issue is an unspiritual administration.

The church at Jerusalem was sensitive to the exhortation of the apostles and selected seven men possessing the requisite qualities. As a result of their Spirit–filled activity, the disaffection was quickly healed, the church was blessed, and the men selected to dispense earthly benefits were soon seen as the Spirit's agents in dispensing heavenly blessings. Stephen became the first martyr for Christ, and his death played no small part in the conversion of Saul. Philip became the first lay evangelist and was used by the Spirit to lead the great revival in Samaria. Faithfulness in the exercise of gifts of nature and grace prepares the way for elevation to greater planes of usefulness and, perhaps, the multiplication of those gifts.

It stands clear in the book of Acts that the leaders who significantly influence the Christian movement were men who were filled with the Holy Spirit. It is recorded of Him who commanded His disciples to tarry in Jerusalem until they were endued with power from on high that He was Himself "anointed with the Holy Spirit and with power" (10:38). The privileged one hundred and twenty in the upper room were all filled with the Spirit (2:4). Peter was filled with the Spirit when he addressed the Sanhedrin (4:8). Stephen, filled with the Spirit, was enabled to bear irresistible witness to Christ and to die as a radiant martyr (6:3, 5; 7:55). It was in the Spirit's fullness that Paul commenced and exercised his unique ministry (9:17; 13:9). His missionary companion, Barnabas, was filled with the Spirit (11:24). He would be strangely blind who did not discern in this fact the fundamental criterion and equipment for spiritual leadership.

These men were very sensitive to the overriding leading of the Holy Spirit. Because they had willingly submitted to His control, they were delighted to obey His promptings and leadings. Philip left the flourishing revival in Samaria without demur, at the Spirit's prompting, accepting instead designation to a desert! But what a fish he was to catch in the desert! (8:29). It was the Spirit who overcame Peter's reluctance and led him to Cornelius, with incalculable blessings resulting for the Gentile world (10:19; 11:12). The Spirit called and sent out Saul and Barnabas as the first missionaries (13:1–4). In his missionary travels, Paul was obedient to the restraints as well as the constraints of the Spirit (16:6–7; 19:21; 20:22). The recognized leaders of the church, meeting in council at Jerusalem, deferred to the leading of the Spirit. "It seemed good to the Holy Ghost and to us" was the way in which the findings of the council were promulgated. It should be noted that each of the interventions of the Holy Spirit had as its objective the bringing of the gospel to the Gentiles. His great preoccupation, then as now, was to make the church a missionary church. Should His preoccupation not be ours too?

One of the most encouraging features of missionary work in East Asia at the time of writing is the moving of the Spirit in some of the Asian churches, imparting to them a new missionary vision and passion. For instance, the Japanese churches have sent out no fewer than one hundred of their own number as foreign missionaries to countries as widely separated as Taiwan and Brazil. At a time when the missionary force from Western lands has become numerically static, the heavenly Strategist is awaking the Asian church to her missionary obligations. There are at this time no fewer than six hundred forty–three Asian Christians who, at the call of God, have become bona fide foreign missionaries.

Paul's counsel to the church leaders at Ephesus throws an illuminating sidelight on the way in which their office should be viewed. "Take heed therefore unto yourselves, and to all the flock, over the which the Holy Spirit hath made you overseers" (20:28). They did not hold their office by apostolic selection or popular election, but by divine appointment. They are answerable not to the church alone, but also to the Holy Spirit. What a sense of assurance and responsibility, what a spiritual authority this consciousness would impart to them!

The purposes of the Pentecostal filling were eminently practical. The apostles were faced with a superhuman task for which nothing less than supernatural power would avail. The fullness of the Spirit imparted the power they needed for the truceless warfare to which they were committed (Luke 24:29; Eph. 6:10–18).

Reduced to its simplest terms, to be filled with the Spirit means that, through voluntary surrender and in response to appropriating faith, the human personality is filled, mastered, controlled by the Holy Spirit. The very word *filled* supports this meaning. The idea is not that of something being poured into a passive empty receptacle. "That which takes possession of the mind is said to fill it," says Thayer, the great lexicographer. This usage of the word is found in Luke 5:26: "They were *filled* with fear," and in John 16:6: "Because I have said these things unto you, sorrow hath *filled* your heart." Their fear and sorrow possessed them to the exclusion of other emotions; they mastered and controlled them. This is what the Holy Spirit does when we invite Him to fill us.

To be filled with the Spirit, then, is to be controlled by the Spirit. Intellect and emotions and volition as well as physical powers all become available to Him for achieving the purposes of God. Under His control, natural gifts of leadership are sanctified and lifted to their highest power. The now ungrieved and unhindered Spirit is able to produce the fruit of the Spirit in the life of the leader, with added winsomeness and attractiveness in his service and with power in his witness to Christ. All real service is but the effluence of the Holy Spirit through yielded and filled lives (John 7:37–39).

A. W. Tozer had clear insight into the possibility of superficiality in seeking after this experience when he said:

> No one whose senses have been exercised to know good and evil can but grieve over the sight of zealous souls seeking to be filled with the Holy Spirit while they are living in a state of moral carelessness and borderline sin. Whoever would be indwelt by the Spirit must judge his life for any hidden iniquities. He must expel from his heart everything that is out of accord with the character of God as revealed by the Holy Scriptures.... There can be no tolerance of evil, no laughing off the things that God hates.[2]

The fullness of the Spirit is an essential and indispensable experience for spiritual leadership. And each of us is as full of the Spirit as we really want to be.

10

The Leader And His Praying

First of all, supplications, prayers, intercessions.

—I Timothy 2:1

In nothing should the leader be ahead of his followers more than in the realm of prayer. And yet the most advanced Christian is conscious of the possibility of endless development in his prayer life. Nor does he ever feel that he has "already attained." Dean C. J. Vaughan once said: "If I wished to humble anyone, I should question him about his prayers. I know nothing to compare with this topic for its sorrowful self–confessions."

Prayer is the most ancient, most universal, most intense expression of the religious instinct. It touches infinite extremes, for it is at once the simplest form of speech that infant lips can try and the sublimest strains that reach the Majesty on high. It is indeed the Christian's vital breath and native air.

But, strange paradox, most of us are plagued with a subtle aversion to praying. We do not naturally delight in drawing near to God. We pay lip service to the delight and potency and value of prayer. We assert that it is an indispensable adjunct of mature spiritual life. We know that it is constantly enjoined and exemplified in the Scriptures. But in spite of all, too often we fail to pray.

Let us take encouragement from the lives of men of like passions with ourselves who have conquered their natural reluctance and become mighty men of prayer.

The biographer of Samuel Chadwick wrote:

> He was essentially a man of prayer. Every morning he would be astir shortly after six o'clock, and he kept a little room which was his private

> sanctum for his quiet hour before breakfast. He was mighty in public prayer because he was constant in private devotion.... When he prayed he expected God to do something. "I wish I had prayed more," he wrote toward the end of his life, "even if I had worked less; and from the bottom of my heart I wish I had prayed better."[1]

"When I go to prayer," confessed an eminent Christian, "I find my heart so loath to go to God, and when it is with Him, so loath to stay." It is just at this point that self–discipline must be exercised. "When thou feelest most indisposed to pray, yield not to it," he counseled, "but strive and endeavor to pray, even when thou thinkest thou canst not pray."

Mastering the art of prayer, like any other art, will take time, and the amount of time we allocate to it will be the true measure of our conception of its importance. We always contrive to find time for that which we deem most important. To most, crowding duties are a reason for curtailing time spent in prayer. To busy Martin Luther, extra work was a compelling argument for spending more time in prayer. Hear his answer to an iniquity about his plans for the next day's work: "Work, work from early till late. In fact I have so much to do that I shall spend the first three hours in prayer." If our view of the importance of prayer in any degree approximates that of Luther and Luther's Lord, we will somehow make more time for it.

It is of course true that prayer poses intellectual problems. But those who are skeptical of its validity and efficacy are usually those who do not seriously put it to the test, or who fail to comply with the revealed conditions. There is no way to learn to pray except by praying. No reasoned philosophy by itself ever taught a soul to pray. But to the man who fulfills the conditions, the problems are met in the indisputable fact of answered prayer and the joy of conscious fellowship with God.

For the supreme example of a life of prayer, the leader will naturally turn to the life of the Lord Himself, since belief in the rationality and necessity of prayer is based not merely on logic but preeminently on His example and precept. If prayer could have been dispensed with in any life, surely it would have been in that of the sinless Son of man. If prayer was unnecessary or unreasonable, we would naturally expect it to be omitted from His life and teaching. On the contrary, it was the dominant feature of His life and a recurrent element in His teaching. An examination of its incidence reveals that prayer kept the vision of His moral duty sharp and clear. It was prayer that nerved Him to do and endure the perfect but costly will of His Father. Prayer paved the way for the transfiguration. To Him, prayer was not a reluctant addendum, but a joyous necessity.

D. M. McIntyre wrote:

> In Luke 5:16 we have a general statement which throws a vivid light on the daily practice of the Lord. "And He withdrew Himself in the deserts and prayed." It is not of one occasion but of many that the evangelist

> speaks in this place. It was our Lord's habit to seek retirement for prayer. When He withdrew Himself from men, He was accustomed to press far into the uninhabited country—He was *in the deserts.* The surprise of the onlookers lay in this, that one so mighty, so richly endowed with spiritual power, should find it necessary for Himself to repair to the source of strength, that there He might refresh His weary spirit. To us, the wonder is still greater, that He, the Prince of Life, the Eternal Word, the Only–begotten of the Father, should prostrate Himself in meekness before the throne of God, making entreaty for grace to help in time of need.[2]

Christ used to spend nights in prayer (Luke 6:12). He often rose a great while before day in order to have unbroken communion with His Father (Mark 1:35). The great crises of His life and ministry were preceded by special prayer (e.g., Luke 5:16), "He withdrew himself into the desert and prayed," a statement that indicated a regular habit. Both by word and example He impressed upon His disciples the importance of solitude in prayer (Mark 6:46; Luke 9:28). To the man on whom devolves the responsibility for selecting personnel for specific spiritual responsibilities, the example of the Lord in His choice of His disciples is luminous.

Both our Lord and His bondslave Paul made it clear that true prayer is not pleasant dreamy reverie. "All vital praying makes a drain on a man's vitality. True intercession is a sacrifice, a bleeding sacrifice," wrote J. H. Jowett. Jesus performed many mighty works without outward sign of strain, but of His praying it is recorded that "he offered up prayers and supplications with strong cryings and tears" (Heb. 5:7).

How pale a reflection of Paul's and Epaphras' strivings and wrestlings are our pallid and languid intercessions! "Epaphras is always wrestling for you in his prayers," wrote Paul to the believers at Colosse (4:12, Berkeley). And to the same group, "I would that ye knew how great conflict I have for you" (2:1, AV). The word for "wrestling," "conflict," is that from which our "agonize" is derived. It is used of a man toiling at his work until utterly weary (Col. 1:29); or competing in the arena for the coveted prize (I Cor. 9:25). It describes the soldier battling for his life (I Tim. 6:12); or a man struggling to deliver his friend from danger (John 18:36). From these and other considerations it is clear that true praying is a strenuous spiritual exercise which demands the utmost mental discipline and concentration.

It is encouraging to recall that Paul, probably the greatest human exponent and example of the exercise of prayer, confessed, "We do not even know how we ought to pray." But he hastened to add, "The Spirit comes to the aid of our weakness...but through our inarticulate groans the Spirit himself is pleading for us, and God who searches our inmost being knows what the Spirit means, because he pleads for god's own people in God's own way" (Rom. 8:26–28, NEB). The Spirit links Himself with us in our praying and pours His supplications into our own.

We may master the technique of prayer and understand its philosophy; we may have unlimited confidence in the veracity and the validity of the promises concerning prayer. We may plead them earnestly. But if we ignore the part played by the Holy Spirit, we have failed to use the master key.

Progressive teaching in the art of praying is needed, and the Holy Spirit is the master Teacher. His assistance in prayer is more frequently mentioned in Scripture than any of His other offices. All true praying stems from His activity in the soul. Both Paul and Jude teach the effective prayer is "praying in the Spirit." The phrase has been interpreted as praying along the same lines, about the same things, in the same name, as the Holy Spirit. True prayer rises in the spirit of the Christian from the Spirit who indwells him.

"Praying in the Spirit" may have a dual significance. It may mean praying *in the realm of the Spirit,* for the Holy Spirit is the sphere and atmosphere of the Christian's life. But in fact, many of our prayers are *psychical* rather than spiritual. They move in the realm of the mind alone, the product of our own thinking and not of the Spirit's teaching. But this is something deeper. The type of praying envisaged in this phrase "utilizes the body, demands the cooperation of the mind, but moves in the supernatural realm of the Spirit." This kind of prayer transacts its business in the heavenly realm.

But the phrase "praying in the Spirit" may also mean praying *in the power and energy of the Spirit.* "Give yourselves wholly to prayer and entreaty; pray on every occasion in the power of the Spirit," is the New English Bible rendering of Ephesians 6:18. For its superhuman task, prayer demands more than mere human power, and this is supplied by the Holy Spirit. He is the Spirit of power as well as the Spirit of prayer. Human energy of heart and mind and will can achieve only human results, but praying in the Holy Spirit releases supernatural resources.

It is the Spirit's delight to aid the man entrusted with spiritual leadership in his moral and physical weakness in this matter of prayer, for the praying soul labors under three handicaps. But in each of them he may count upon the Spirit's assistance. Sometimes he is kept from prayer by the conscious *iniquity of his heart.* As he trusts Him, the Holy Spirit will lead him to and enable him to appropriate the cleansing of that mighty solvent, the blood of Christ. Then the spiritual leader is hampered by the *ignorance of his mind.* The Spirit who knows the mind of God will share that knowledge with him as he receptively waits on Him. He does this by imparting a clear conviction that a petition is or is not according to the will of God. Again, the spiritual leader will often be earthbound through the benumbing *infirmity of his body,* and especially so if he lives in the enervating climate of the tropics. The Spirit will quicken his mortal body in response to his faith, and will enable him to rise above adverse physical and climatic conditions.

In addition to these personal handicaps, the praying man has to overcome the subtle opposition of Satan who will seek to oppress or depress, to create doubt or discouragement. In the Holy Spirit the praying man has been given a heavenly ally against a supernatural adversary.

The foregoing thoughts are doubtless not new ground to many who have read them, but is the mighty assistance, the power, of the Spirit in prayer a present and enjoyed experience? Have we slipped into an unintentional independence of the Spirit in prayer? Are we habitually "praying in the Spirit" and receiving the full answer to our prayers? It is very easy for our intellectual apprehension of spiritual truths to outrun our practical experience of their reality and power.

Prayer is frequently represented in Scripture under the figure of spiritual warfare. "We wrestle…against principalities, against powers, against the rules of the darkness of this age, against spiritual wickedness in high places" (Eph. 6:12) In this phase of the prayer life, three personalities are involved, not two. Between God on the one hand and the devil on the other, stands the praying man. Though weak in himself, he occupies a strategic role in the deathless struggle between the dragon and the Lamb. The power and authority he wields are not inherent but are delegated to him by the victorious Christ to whom he is united by faith. His faith is the reticulating system through which the victory gained on Calvary over Satan and his hosts reaches the captives and delivers them.

Throughout the gospels, the thoughtful reader will discern that Jesus was concerned not so much with the wicked men and the evil conditions He confronted as with the forces of evil at the back of them. Behind well–meaning and ever–vocal Peter, behind the traitorous Judas, Jesus saw the black hand of Satan. "Get thee behind me Satan," was the Lord's response to Peter's well–intentioned but presumptuous rebuke. We see men around us bound in sin, and in captivity to the devil, but our concern in prayer should be not only *to pray for them* but *to pray against Satan* who holds them captive. He must be compelled to relax his grip on them and this can be achieved only by Christ's victory on the cross. Jesus dealt with the cause rather than the effect, and the leader should adopt the same method in this aspect of his praying. And he must know how to lead those under him to victory in this spiritual warfare.

In a graphic illustration, Jesus likened Satan to a strong man, fully armed, who kept his palace and goods in peace. Before he could be dispossessed and his captives released, Jesus said he must first be bound, or rendered powerless. Only then could the rescue be effected (Matt. 12:28–29). What does it mean to "bind the strong man," if not to neutralize his power by drawing on the conquering power of Christ who was manifested "to destroy [nullify, render inoperative] the works of the devil"? And how can this be done but by the prayer of faith which lays hold on the victory of Calvary and believes for its repetition in the specific context of the prayer? We must not make the mistake of reversing our Lord's order, and expect to effect the rescue without first disarming the adversary. The divinely delegated authority placed in our hands may be confidently exercised, for did not our Lord say to His weak disciples, "Behold, *I have given you power over all the power of the enemy?"* (Luke 10:19, RV).

Since leadership is the ability to move and influence people, the spiritual leader will be alert to discover the most effective way of doing this. One of the most frequently quoted of Hudson Taylor's statements is his expression of conviction that "it is possible to move men, through God, *by prayer alone."* In the course of his missionary career he demonstrated its truth a thousand times. However, it is one thing to give mental assent to his motto, but quite another thing consistently to put it into practice. Men are difficult objects to move, and it is much easier to pray for temporal needs than for situations which involve the intricacies and stubbornness of the human heart. But it is in just such situations that the leader must prove his power to move human hearts in the direction in which he believes the will of God lies. And God has placed in his hands the key to this complicated lock.

It is the supreme dignity and glory of man that he can say "No" as well as "Yes" to the omnipotent God, for he has been endowed with the Godlike quality of freewill. This fact poses a genuine problem to the student of the subject of prayer. If by our prayers we can affect the conduct of a fellowman, does that not trespass upon his free will? Will God violate one person's free will in order to answer another person's prayer? And yet, if our prayers cannot so influence Him, what is the point in praying?

In considering the problem, the first thing to remember is that *God is always consistent with Himself in His actions.* He does not contradict Himself. If He promises to answer the prayer of faith, He will do so, but not in a manner that would be contrary to His divine nature. He will fulfill all His obligations, but in a way consistent with His own attributes and undertakings, for "he cannot deny himself." No word or action will contradict any other word or action.

Then there is the indisputable fact that *intercessory prayer is a divine ordinance.* Since God has ordained it, we can be confident that as we fulfill the revealed conditions, the answer will most surely be granted, despite any seeming problems that might be involved. God obviously sees no insuperable problem or contradiction between human free will and His answering prayer. When He commands us to pray "for kings and those that are in authority," there is implicit in the command the assurance that our prayers can move them and significantly influence the course of events. Else, why pray? Whether or not we find a final mental answer to our prayer problems, we are still under obligation to pray.

Further, *we can know the will of God* concerning the subject of the prayer we offer, and that fact constitutes the basis for our being able to pray the prayer of faith. God can speak to us very convincingly through the channel of our own faculties. We have the Word of God which presents the will of God on all matters of principle. We have the ministry of the Holy Spirit in our hearts, interceding for us according to the will of God (Rom. 8:26–27). As we patiently seek to discover God's will concerning our petition, the

Spirit will impress us whether or not it is the will of God. It is this God–given conviction that enables us to proceed beyond the prayer of hope to the prayer of faith.

The very fact that God lays a burden of prayer on our hearts and keeps us praying is prima facie evidence that He purposes to grant the answer. When asked if he really believed that two men for whose salvation he had prayed for over fifty years would be converted, George Mueller of Bristol replied, "Do you think God would have kept me praying all these years if He did not intend to save them?" Both men were converted, one shortly before, the other after, Mueller's death.

In prayer, we deal directly with God, and only in a secondary sense with men and women. The goal of prayer is the ear of God. Prayer influences men by influencing God to influence them. It is not the prayer that moves men, but the God to whom we pray.

Prayer moves the arm
That moves the world
To bring deliverance down.

To move men, the leader must be able to move God, for He has made it clear that He moves them through the prayers of the intercessor. If a scheming Jacob could be given "power with God and with men," then is it not possible for any leader who is willing to comply with the conditions to enjoy the same power? (Gen. 32:8).

Prevailing prayer of this kind is the outcome of a correct relationship with God. Reasons for unanswered prayer are stated with great clarity in Scripture, and they all center around the believer's relationship with God. He will not be party to petitions of mere self–interest, nor will He countenance impurity of motive. Sin clung to and cherished will effectively close His ear. Least of all will He tolerate unbelief, the mother of sins. "He that cometh to God *must believe.*" Everywhere in prayer there is the condition, either expressed or implied, that the paramount motive in praying is the glory of God.

The eminence of great leaders of the Bible is attributable to the fact that they were great in their praying.

They were not leaders because of brilliancy of thought, because they were exhaustless in resources, because of their magnificent culture or native endowment, but because, by the power of prayer, they could command the power of God.[3]

11

The Leader And His Time

Make the best of your time.

—Ephesians 5:16; Phillips

Time has been defined as a stretch of duration in which things happen. The quality of a man's leadership is revealed in what happens during that stretch of duration. The character and career of a young person are determined largely by how and with whom he spends his spare time. He cannot regulate school or office hours—these are determined for him—but he can say what he will do before and after. The manner in which he employs the surplus hours after provision has been made for work, meals and sleep will make him either a mediocrity or a man to be reckoned with. Habits are formed in youth which make or mar a life. Leisure hours constitute a glorious opportunity or a subtle danger. Each moment of the day is a gift from God, and should be husbanded with miserly care, for time is life measured out to us for work.

Minutes and hours can be transmuted into rich and abundant life. Michelangelo grasped this fact. On one occasion when he was executing a work which he had been pressured into doing, someone warned him, "It may cost your life." The great artist responded, "What else is life for?" Our hours and days will keep on being used up, but they can be used purposefully and productively. Philosopher William James affirmed that the great use of one's life is to spend it for something that will outlast it, for the value of life is computed not by its duration but by its donation. Not how long we live, but how fully and how well.

Yet, in spite of its preciousness and vast potentialities, there is nothing which we squander so thoughtlessly as time. Moses considered it so invaluable a commodity that he prayed to be taught to measure it by days, not years (Ps. 90:12). If we are meticulously careful in the use of the days, the years will take care of themselves.

A sentence which will seldom be heard on the lips of a leader is "I don't have the time." Very seldom is it strictly true. It is usually the refuge of the small and inefficient person. We have each been entrusted with sufficient time to do the whole will of God and to fill out His perfect plan for our lives. "I think one of the cant phrases of our day is the familiar one by which we express our permanent want of time," said Dr. J. H. Jowett. "We repeat it so often that by the very repetition we have deceived ourselves into believing it. It is never the supremely busy men who have no time. So compact and systematic is the regulation of their day that whenever you make a demand on them, they seem to find additional corners to offer for unselfish service. I confess as a minister, that the men to whom I most hopefully look for additional service are the busiest men."

The problem is not that of needing more time, but of making better use of the time we have. Let us face the fact squarely that each of us has as much time as anyone else in the world. The President of the United States of America has twenty–four hours to his day, and so have we. Others may have more ability, influence or money than we, but they have no more time.

As in the parable of the pounds (Luke 19:12–27), each servant was entrusted with the same amount of money, so we have each been granted the same amount of time. But few use it so wisely as to produce a tenfold return. It is true that not all have the same capacity; but that fact, too, is recognized in the parable. The servant who had less capacity but showed equal faithfulness received the same reward. While we cannot be held responsible for our capacity, we are responsible for the strategic employment of our time.

When Paul urged the Ephesian Christians to "redeem the time," he was indicating that in a sense time becomes ours by purchase. There is a price to be paid for its highest employment. We exchange time in the market of life for certain occupations and activities which may be either worthy or unworthy, productive or unproductive. Weymouth renders the sentence thus: "Buy up the opportunities," for time is opportunity, and herein lies the importance of a carefully planned life. "If we progress in the economy of time, we are learning to live. If we fail here, we fail everywhere."

Time can be lost, but it can never be retrieved It cannot be hoarded, it must be spent. Nor can it be postponed. If it is not used productively it is irretrievably lost, as these lines which were engraved on a sundial assert:

The shadow of my finger cast
Divides the future from the past;
Before it stands the unborn hour
In darkness and beyond thy power;
Behind its unreturning line
The vanished hour, no longer thine;
One hour alone is in thy hands,
The now on which the shadow stands.

In the face of this sobering fact, the leader must be meticulously careful in his selection or priorities. Comparative values of opportunities and responsibilities must be sedulously weighed. He cannot afford to squander time on that which is of only secondary importance while primary things are screaming our for attention. His day should therefore be carefully planned. If it is his ambition to excel, there must be selection and rejection, then concentration on the things of paramount importance. It is a salutary and revealing exercise to keep a faithful record of how each hour is spent in a normal week, and then to analyze it in the light of scriptural priorities. The result may well be startling, even shocking in terms of spiritual values. One undoubted result would be to convince the experimenter that he has much more time than he is productively using.

After making a generous allowance of eight hours a day for sleep and rest—and few really need more than that—three hours a day for meals and social intercourse, ten hours a day for work and travel on five days, there still remain no fewer than thirty–five hours unaccounted for in each week. What happens to them? How are the extra two days in the week invested? The whole of man's contribution to the kingdom of God might well turn upon how these crucial hours are employed. They will determine whether his life will be commonplace or extraordinary.

That intrepid missionary Mary Slessor, later to become known as "The White Queen of Okoyong," was the daughter of a drunkard. She commenced working in a factory in Dundee at the age of eleven, working from six in the morning until six at night. Yet this grueling program did not prevent her from educating herself for her notable career.

David Livingstone used to work in a cotton mill in his native Dumbarton from six in the morning until eight at night. He commenced work when he was ten. He could surely have been excused if he had pleaded that he had no time for study. But so purposefully did he utilize his "leisure" hours that he mastered Latin and could read Horace and Virgil with ease before he was sixteen. By the time he was twenty–seven, he had battled his way through a medical course, as well as a course in theology.[1]

In the light of these achievements, and with a host of similar examples before us, we have little basis for pleading insufficient time to achieve something worthwhile in life.

As in all else, our Lord sets the perfect example of the strategic use of time. He moved through life with measured tread, never in a hurry, though always thronged and often harassed by demanding crowds. To those who came to Him for help He gave the impression that He had no more important concern than their interests. The secret of His serenity lay in His assurance that He was working according to His Father's plan for His life—a plan that embraced every hour and made provision for every contingency. His calendar had been arranged, and through communion with His Father He received each day both the words He was to say and the works He was to do. "the words that I speak unto you I speak not of myself: but the Father that dwelleth in me, he doeth the works" (John 14:10).

Christ's overriding concern was to fulfill the work committed to Him within the allotted hours. He moved in the consciousness that there was a divine timing for the events of His life. (See John 7:6; 12:23, 27; 13:1; 17:1.) not even His loved mother was allowed to interfere with His divinely planned timetable. "Is that your concern, or mine?...My time has not come yet," were His salutary words (John 2:4, Phillips).

Even the strong drawings of His affection for Martha and Mary and the possibility of misunderstanding could not induce Him to advance His schedule by two days (John 11:6, 9). As He reviewed His life on earth at its close, with unself–conscious complacency He claimed: "I have finished the work thou gavest me to do" (John 17:4). And He finished that work without any part having been spoiled through undue haste or imperfectly completed through lack of time. He found the twenty–four hours of the day sufficient time to complete the whole will of God.

This is reflected in His corrective words to his disciples: "Are there not twelve hours in the day?" His question suggested His settled confidence in his Father's plan and His assurance of the ability to finish His work in the allotted span. Dr. J. Stuart Holden saw in our Lord's words the implications of the shortness of time, and yet the sufficiency of time. There were only twelve hours in the day, but there were fully twelve hours in the day.[2] Was it not this consciousness that accounted for the selective power of the Lord? He spent His time doing things that mattered. No time was wasted on things that were not vital. The strength of moral character is derived and conserved by the refusing of the unimportant.

We could, however, become panic–stricken if we forget the number of hours in the day. We have a full twelve hours in which to learn life's lessons and to fulfill life's duties. Our Lord assures us that that will be sufficient.

No trifling in this life of mine;
Not this the path the blessed Master trod;
But every hour and power employed
Always and all for God.

Viewed in the light of this overheated and overpressured age, it is a striking fact that in the Gospels there is no indication of interruptions disturbing the serenity of the Son of God. Few things are more apt to produce agitation and tension in a busy life than unexpected and unwelcome interruptions. To Him there were no such things as interruptions in His God–planned life. These had been foreseen in His Father's planning and He could therefore afford to be undisturbed by them. True, at times there was "no leisure so much as to eat," but there would always be time for Him to accomplish all God intended Him to do. Often the pressures which come upon the spiritual leader are the result of his having assumed responsibilities not assigned to him by God and therefore for which he cannot expect God to give the extra strength required.

One busy man told how he mastered the problem of interruptions. "Up to some years ago," he testified, "I was always annoyed by interruptions, which was really a form of selfishness on my part. People used to walk in and say, "Well, I just had two hours to kill here in between trains, and I thought I would come and see you.' That used to bother me. Then the Lord convinced me that God sends people our way. He sent Philip to the Ethiopian eunuch. He sent Barnabas to look up Saul of Tarsus. The same applies today; God sends people our way.

"So when someone comes in, I say, 'The Lord must have brought you here. Let us find out why He sent you. Let us have prayer about it.' Well, this does two things. It puts the interview on a different level because God is brought into it. Also it generally shortens the interview. If a person knows that you are looking for a reason why he is there, under God, if he doesn't have one, he soon leaves for greener pastures. So take interruptions from the Lord. Then they belong in your schedule, because God was simply rearranging your daily pattern to suit Him." To the alert Christian, interruptions are only divinely interjected opportunities.

This all fits into Paul's affirmation that God has a plan for every life, that we each have been created unto good works which God has before ordained that we should walk in them (Eph. 2:10). Through daily prayer and communion, the leader must discover the details of that plan and arrange his work accordingly. Each half hour should carry its own quota of usefulness.

Some large companies require young executives to submit their plans for the coming week to their superiors by Friday evening, so important do they conceive careful planning of time to be. John Wesley and F. B. Meyer, men who achieved an incredible amount of work and exercised vast influence throughout the world, used to divide their lives into periods of five minutes, and endeavored to make each period constructive.[3] Few of us could or would achieve this, but all could benefit greatly by some similar if less ambitious discipline. It is incredible how much reading can be crowded into the odd minutes which might otherwise be wasted. If this is questioned, let the reader experiment with the odd minutes of the coming week.

A concrete example of the way in which Dr. F. B. Meyer redeemed his time, bought up the opportunities, is recorded in his biography. "If he had a long railway journey before him, he would settle himself in his corner of the railway carriage, open his dispatch case which was fitted up as a sort of stationery cabinet, and set to work on some abstruse article, quite oblivious of his surroundings. Often at protracted conventions, and even in committee meetings, when the proceedings did not demand his undivided attention, he would unobtrusively open his case and proceed to answer letters." Another man who was a miser with time was Dr. W. E. Sangster. His son wrote of him:

> Time was never wasted. The difference between one minute and two was of considerable consequence to him. He would appear from his study. "My boy, you're not doing anything. I have exactly twenty–two minutes. We'll go for a walk. We can walk right round the common in that time." He then hurtled out of the house at tremendous speed and I normally had to run to catch him up. He would then discourse on current affairs (five minutes), Surrey's prospects in the country championship (two minutes), the necessity for revival (five minutes), the reality of the Loch Ness Monster (two minutes), and the sanctity of William Romaine (three minutes). By that time we would be home again.[4]

Few things tend to bring a conscientious leader into bondage more than the use of his time, and a balanced view of the matter must be arrived at. If he does not find a satisfactory answer, he will work under unnecessary strain. Even after he has done everything in his power to fulfill his obligations, there will still remain vast areas of unmet need. Every call for help is by no means necessarily a call from God, for every such call cannot be responded to. If he sincerely plans his day in the Lord's presence, and carries out that plan to the best of his ability, he can and must leave it there. His responsibility extends only to those matters which lie within his control. The rest he can trustfully commit to his loving and competent heavenly Father.

Procrastination, the thief of time, is one of the devil's most potent weapons in defrauding man of his eternal heritage. It is a habit that is absolutely fatal to effective spiritual leadership. Its subtlety and power lie in the fact that it corresponds so well to our natural inclinations and innate reluctance to make important decisions. Making decisions and carrying them through always involves considerable moral effort. But instead of making that effort easier, the passage of time has the reverse effect. The decision will be even more difficult to make tomorrow—and, indeed, circumstances may have so changed that it will be too late for advantageous decision. The nettle will never grow more easy to grasp than it is now.

Do it now is a principle of action which has led many a man to worldly success, and it is no less relevant in the realm of the spiritual. A most helpful method of overcoming a built–in tendency to procrastinate is to set deadlines for oneself for reading a book, writing a difficult letter or article, doing a task, and then steadfastly refusing to overrun them.

A lifelong reader, who was also busier than most, was constantly asked by his friends, "How do you get time for it?" He always replied, "I don't get time for it, I take it."[5]

12

The Leader And His Reading

Please bring with you...the books, especially the manuscripts.

—II Timothy 4:13, Phillips

Reading maketh a full man; speaking, a ready man; writing, an exact man.

—Bacon

Paul's counsel to Timothy, "Give heed to reading," doubtless had reference to the public reading of the Old Testament Scriptures. His injunction is nevertheless most appropriate for other areas of reading as well. The books which Paul desired Timothy to bring to him were most probably a few choice works—Jewish history books exegetical and explanatory of the Law and the Prophets, and perhaps some of the heathen poets from which he quoted in his sermons and letters. He wished to spend his last weeks or months to the highest profit in studying his precious books—a student to the end.

There is a parallel story told of William Tyndale during his imprisonment and shortly before his martyrdom in 1536. He wrote to the governor–in–chief asking that some of his goods might be sent:

> a warmer cap, a candle, a piece of cloth to patch my leggings.... But above all, I beseech and entreat your clemency to be urgent with the Procureur that he may kindly permit me to have my Hebrew Bible, Hebrew Grammar, and Hebrew Dictionary, that I may spend time with that in study.

Both Paul and Tyndale devoted the days before martyrdom to the study of the parchments.

In this chapter it is assumed that the main preoccupation and paramount interest of the spiritual leader will be through diligent study and the illumination of the Holy Spirit to attain a mastery of the Word of God. It is his supplementary reading, however, that is our present concern.

The man who desires to grow spiritually and intellectually will be constantly at his books. The lawyer who desires to succeed in his profession must keep abreast of important cases and changes in the law. The medical practitioner must follow the constantly changing discoveries in his field. Even so the spiritual leader must master God's Word and its principles, and know as well what is going on in the minds of those who look to him for guidance. To achieve these ends, he must, hand in hand with his personal contacts, engage in a course of selective reading. Today, the practice of reading solid and rewarding spiritual and classical literature is seriously on the wane. In an age in which people have more leisure than ever before in the history of the world, many claim that they have no time to read. This excuse is never valid with a spiritual leader.

John Wesley had a passion for reading and most of it was done on horseback. He rode sometimes ninety and often fifty miles in a day. He read deeply on a wide range of subjects. It was his habit to travel with a volume of science or history or medicine propped on the pommel of his saddle, and in that way he got through thousands of volumes. After his Greek New Testament, three great books took complete possession of Wesley's mind and heart during his Oxford days. "It was about this time that he began the earnest study of the *Imitation of Christ, Holy Living and Dying* and *The Serious Call.* These three books became very much his spiritual guides.[1] He told the younger ministers of the Wesleyan societies either to read or get out of the ministry!

The determination to spend a minimum of half an hour a day in reading worthwhile books which provide food for the soul and further mental and spiritual development will prove richly rewarding to those who have been inclined to limit their reading to predigested or superficial books.

In a very perceptive series of articles in *The Alliance Weekly* on the subject "The Use and Abuse of Books," Dr. A. W. Tozer had some arresting things to say:

> Why does today's Christian find the reading of great books always beyond him? Certainly intellectual powers do not wane from one generation to another. We are as smart as our fathers, and any thought they could entertain we can entertain if we are sufficiently interested to make the effort. The major cause of the decline in the quality of current Christian literature is not intellectual but spiritual. To enjoy a great religious book requires a degree of consecration to God and detachment from the world that few modern Christians have. The early Christian Fathers, the Mystics, the Puritans, are not hard to understand, but they inhabit the highlands where the air is crisp and rarefied, and none but

> the God–enamoured can come.... One reason why people are unable to understand great Christian classics is that they are trying to understand without any intention of obeying them.[2]

Why Read?

"Read to refill the wells of inspiration," was the advice of Harold J. Ockenga, who took a suitcase full of books on his honeymoon!3

Bacon's famous rule for reading was:

> Read, not to contradict or confute, not to believe and take for granted, nor to find talk and discourse, but to weigh and consider. Some books are to be tested, others to be swallowed, and some few to be chewed and digested.[4]

Another writer gave it as his opinion that if we read because we want to stock our minds like a warehouse or because we like feeling superior or being thought intellectual, then it is useless or worse than useless.

The spiritual leader should read for *spiritual quickening* and profit, and this will strongly influence his selection of books for reading. There are some authors whose writings challenge heart and conscience, and hold us to the highest. That reading which provides impulse and inspiration is to be cherished.

The spiritual leader should read with a view to *mental stimulation* and should have on hand, among others, some book that involves him in mental gymnastics—something that calls for his utmost mental powers and stimulates fresh thoughts and ideas.

He should read for *cultivation of style* in his preaching and teaching and writing. For this, nothing can equal the writing of those masters who enlarge our vocabularies, teach us to think, and instruct us in the art of incisive and compelling speech. In speaking for the masters, Dr. Tozer recommended "John Bunyan for simplicity, Joseph Addison for clarity and elegance, John Milton for nobility and consistent elevation of thought, Charles Dickens for sprightliness, and Francis Bacon for conciseness and dignity."[5] Bacon himself claimed that "histories make men wise; poets, witty; the mathematics, subtle; natural philosophy, deep; moral, grave; logic and rhetoric, able to contend." The leader should read, too, with a view to the *acquiring of information.* Never was there such a vast range of information within the reach of every reader as today. It is mainly through reading that information is assimilated. He should read, therefore, to keep abreast of his age, and should be reasonably well informed in his own field.

He should read in order to have *fellowship with great minds.* It is possible to hold communion with the greatest and godliest of men of all ages through the medium of their writings.

The power for good of even one book is impossible to estimate. In his *Curiosities of Literature* Benjamin Disraeli entitles one chapter "The Man of One Book," and gives a number of instances of the remarkable influence of a solitary work. In reading the biographies of a number of great Christians whom God used in a unique way in the past century, the author noticed time and again that the same book had induced a crisis in their lives and produced a revolution in their ministry. The book was *Lectures on Revivals of Religion* by Charles G. Finney.

On the other hand, who can measure the power for evil of a single book such as Hitler's *Mein Kampf?* Who can gauge the spiritual havoc wrought by Bishop Robinson's *Honest to God?*

What To Read

If it is true that a man is known by the company he keeps, it is no less true that his character is reflected in the books he reads, for they are the outward expression of his inner hungers and aspirations. The vast number of books both secular and religious that are pouring from the presses today makes discrimination in reading imperative. We can afford to read only the best, and what will be most helpful to us in the fulfillment of our mission. In other words, our reading should be regulated largely by what we are and what we do or intend to do.

An old writer who adopted the pseudonym Cladius Clear suggested that a booklover could divide his books as he would people. A few he would term "lovers," and they would be the books he would take with him if he were exiled. Others, and more than in the first class, he would call "friends." The majority he would designate "acquaintances," books with which he was on nodding terms and to which he occasionally referred.[6]

Matthew Arnold gave it as his opinion that the best of literature was to be found within the covers of five hundred books. Daniel Webster preferred to master a few books rather than to read indiscriminately. It was his contention that reading a few great writers who have built up the permanent literature of the English language, well mastered, was better than skimming a multitude of ephemeral works. He maintained it was to them we should turn for a real knowledge of the human heart, its aspirations and tragedies, hopes and disappointments. Hobbes the English philosopher once said, "If I had read as many books as other people, I would know as little."

Samuel Brengle had this to say about his preferences in poetry:

> I like the poets whose writings reveal great moral character and passion—such as Tennyson's and some of Browning's. The works of others have light, but I prefer flame to just light. Shakespeare? A mind as clear as a sunbeam—but passionless, light without heat. Shelley? Keats? There's a sense in which they were perfect poets. But they don't move

> me. Beautiful—but wordmongers. There's an infinite difference between the beauty of holiness and the holiness of beauty. One leads to the highest, loftiest, most Godlike character; the other often—too often—leads to an orgy of sensation.[7]

Sir W. Robertson Nicoll, for many years editor of *The British Weekly,* found biography the most attractive form of general reading because biography transmits personality. One cannot read the lives of great and consecrated men and women without having inspiration kindled and aspiration aroused. The "lives of great men still remind us that we may make our lives sublime." Who can gauge the inspiration to the cause of missions of great biographies like those of William Carey, Adoniram Judson, Hudson Taylor, Charles Studd or Albert Simpson?

Joseph W. Kemp, who exercised a wide preaching and teaching ministry, made a point of always keeping a good biography on hand. Ransome W. Cooper maintains that

> the reading of good biography forms an important part of a Christian's education. It provides him with numberless illustrations for use in his own service. He learns to assess the true worth of character, to glimpse a work goal for his own life, to decide how best to attain it, what self–denial is needed to curb unworthy aspirations; and all the time he learns how God breaks into the dedicated life to bring about His own purposes.

What satisfies those who follow him should not satisfy the leader in the matter of the books he reads. Nor should he be content to read only those books which can be easily read or books along the line of his own speciality.

Muriel Ormrod counseled:

> It is better that we should always tackle something a bit beyond us. "We should always aim to read something different—not only the writers with whom we agree, but those with whom we are ready to do battle. And let us not condemn them out of hand because they do not agree with us; their point of view challenges us to examine the truth and to test their views against Scripture. And let us not comment on nor criticize writers of whom we have heard only second–hand, or third–hand, without troubling to read their works for ourselves.... Don't be afraid of new ideas—and don't be carried away with them either.[8]

A little learning is a dangerous thing;
Drink deep, or taste not the Pierian Spring;
There shallow draughts intoxicate the brain,
And drinking largely sobers us again.
—Alexander Pope

The leader, then, should immerse himself in books which will further equip him for a higher quality of service and leadership in the kingdom of God.

How To Read

Reading, in one of its senses, is defined as learning from written or printed matter; and this involves not only scanning the reading symbols but meditating on the thoughts they express. "It is easy to read. It is much more difficult to secure effectually the fruit of reading in the mind. And yet, to what profit is our reading if it does not achieve this end?"

When Southey the poet was telling an old Quaker lady how he learned Portuguese grammar while he washed, and something else while he dressed, and how he gleaned in another field while he breakfasted, and so on, filling his day utterly, she said quietly, "And when does thee think?" It is possible to read without thinking, but we cannot profit from what we read unless we think. Charles H. Spurgeon counseled his students:

> Master those books you have. Read them thoroughly. Bathe in them until they saturate you. Read and reread them, masticate them and digest them. Let them go into your very self. Peruse a good book several times and make notes and analyses of it. A student will find that his mental constitution is more affected by one book thoroughly mastered than by twenty books he has merely skimmed. Little learning and much pride come of hasty reading. Some men are disabled from thinking by their putting meditation away for the sake of much reading. In reading let your motto be "much, not many."[9]

The following rules for reading have been found to make reading more meaningful and of more lasting benefit:

1. Read little that is to be immediately forgotten since that only helps to form the habit of forgetting. Exercise the same discrimination in choosing books as in choosing friends.
2. Read with pencil and notebook in hand. Unless the memory is unusually vigorous and retentive, much reading will be a waste of time. Develop a system of note–taking, and it will be astonishing to discover how greatly this practice aids the memory.
3. Have a "commonplace book," as it used to be called, a book in which to put what is striking, interesting, suggestive and worthy of permanent record. One's own comments and criticisms can be added. In this way an irreplaceable accumulation of material will be preserved and indexed for future use.

4. Verify as far as possible historical, scientific and other data, and let no word slip past until its meaning is understood.
5. Let reading be varied, because the mind so easily runs into ruts. Variety is as restful to the mind as to the body.
6. Reading should be correlated where possible—history with poetry, biography with historical novels; e.g., when reading the history of the American Civil War, read the biographies of Lincoln and Grant and the poems written by Walt Whitman on Abraham Lincoln.

Canon Yates gives advice on reading which would be most helpful to those able to follow it. To some, however, the pressures of the space age might make it seem a counsel of perfection.

He suggests that every solid book requires three readings. The first reading should be rapid and continuous. The subconscious mind will then go to work on it and link it up with what you already know on the subject. Then take time to think what contribution it has made to your knowledge. The second reading should be *careful, slow and detailed,* thinking out each new point and making notes for later use. After an interval, the third reading should be *fairly rapid and continuous, and a brief analysis should be written in the back of the book, with page references to subjects and illustrations.*

A minister in the little manse of Lumsden in Scotland, gathered around him no fewer than 17,000 volumes, among which he browsed with great delight. But of him and his books his son had this to say: "Though he spent much time and pains on his sermons, he did not cut a channel between them and his reading."[10]

Here is a danger of which the leader must be aware. Ideally a book is a channel through which ideas can flow from one mind to another. The Lumsden minister did not fail to cut a channel linking his reading and his own spiritual life, but his congregation did not derive the benefit it should have enjoyed as a result of his wide reading. It is for the leader to cut a channel between what he reads and what he says or writes, so that others may reap its benefits to the full.

A country minister in Australia who is known to the author is a great book lover. Early in his ministry he decided that he would aim at developing a biblically and theologically literate congregation. He succeeded in conveying to members of his church his own love of books, and introduced them gradually to spiritual works of increasing weight and depth. The result is that in that district a number of farmers have accumulated libraries that would be no disgrace to a minister of the gospel. If they aimed at it, many more ministers could communicate their appreciation of spiritual books to their congregations by guiding them in a course of selected reading.

13

The Cost Of Leadership

Can ye drink of the cup that I drink of? and be baptized with the baptism that I am baptized with?

—Mark 10:38

No one need aspire to leadership in the work of God who is not prepared to pay a price greater than his contemporaries and colleagues are willing to pay. True leadership always exacts a heavy toll on the whole man, and the more effective the leadership is, the higher the price to be paid.

Quinton Hogg, founder of the London Polytechnic Institute, devoted a great fortune to the enterprise. Asked how much it had cost to build up such a great institution, Hogg replied: "Not very much, simply one man's life blood."[1] That is the cost of every great achievement, and it is not paid in a lump sum. It is bought on the time–payment plan, a further installment each new day. Fresh drafts are constantly being made, and when the payment ceases the leadership wanes. This fact was taught by the Lord when He indicated that we could not save others and save ourselves at the same time.

Samuel Brengle wrote:

> Spiritual power is the outpouring of spiritual life, and like all life, from that of the moss and lichen on the wall to that of the archangel before the throne, is from God. Therefore those who aspire to leadership must pay the price, and seek it from God.[2]

Self–Sacrifice

This is part of the price which must be paid daily. A cross stands in the way of spiritual leadership, a cross upon which the leader must consent to be impaled. Heaven's demands are absolute. "He laid down his life for us: and we ought to lay down our lives for the brethren" (I John 3:16). The degree in which we allow the cross of Christ to work in us will be the measure in which the resurrection life of Christ can be manifested through us. "Death worketh in me, but life in you." To evade the cross is to forfeit leadership.

"Whoever wants to hold the first positions among you must be *everybody's slave.* For the Son of man did not come to be served but to serve, and *to give His life* a ransom" (Mark 10:44–45, C. B. Williams). Each of the heroes of faith immortalized in Hebrews 11 was called to sacrifice as well as to service. Willingness to renounce personal preferences, to sacrifice legitimate and natural desires for the sake of His kingdom, will characterize those marked out by God for positions of influence in His work. Bruce Barton quotes an apposite advertisement on a motor service station: "We will crawl under your car oftener, and get ourselves dirtier than any of our competitors." Is that not the service station you would patronize?

Dr. Samuel M. Zwemer recalls the striking fact that the only thing Jesus took pains to show after His resurrection was His scars.[3] His disciples recognized neither Him nor His message on the Emmaus road. Not until He broke the bread and they saw the scars were their sensibilities aroused. When He stood in the midst of His demoralized disciples in the upper room after the resurrection, "he showed them his hands and his side." Scars are the authentic marks of faithful discipleship and true spiritual leadership. It was said of one leader, "He belonged to that class of early martyrs whose passionate soul made an early holocaust of the physical man."[4] Nothing moves people more than the print of the nails and the mark of the spear. These are tests of sincerity which no one can challenge, as Paul well knew. "From henceforth let no man trouble me: for I bear in my body the marks of the Lord Jesus" (Gal. 6:17).

Hast thou no scar?
No hidden scar on foot, or side, or hand?
I hear thee sung as mighty in the land,
I hear them hail thy bright ascendant star:
Hast thou no scar?

Hast thou no wound?
Yet, I was wounded by the archers, spent,
Leaned me against the tree to die, and rent
By ravening beasts that compassed me, I swooned:
Hast thou no wound?

No wound? No scar?
Yes, as the master shall the servant be,
And pierced are the feet that follow Me;
But thine are whole. Can he have followed far
Who has no wound? No scar?
—Amy Carmichael

That Paul was willing to pay the price and carried the authentic scars incidental to leadership is attested by an autobiographical paragraph in one of his letters.

On every hand hard–pressed am I—yet not crushed!
In desperate plight am I—yet not in despair!
Close followed by pursuers—yet not abandoned by Him!
Beaten to earth—yet never destroyed!
Evermore bearing about in my body
The imminence of such a death as Jesus died,
So that the life, too, of Jesus might be shown forth
In this body of mine
Always, always while I yet live
Am I being handed over to death's doom
For Jesus' sake!
So that in this mortal flesh of mine, may be
Shown forth also
The very life of Jesus

—II Corinthians 4:8–11, Way

Loneliness

From its very nature, the lot of the leader must be a lonely one. He must always be ahead of his followers. Though he be the friendliest of men, there are areas of life in which he must be prepared to tread a lonely path. This fact dawned painfully on Dixon E. Hoste when Hudson Taylor laid down the direction of the China Inland Mission and appointed Hoste his successor. After the interview during which the appointment was made, the new leader, sensible of the weight of responsibility which now was his said, "And now I have no one, no one but God!" In his journey to the top he had left behind all his contemporaries and stood alone in the mount with his God.

Human nature craves company, and it is only natural to wish to share with others the heavy burdens of responsibility and care. It is often heartbreaking to have to make decisions of far–reaching importance which affect the lives of loved fellow workers—and to make them alone. This is one of the heaviest prices to pay, but it must be paid. Moses paid this price for his leadership—alone in the mount, and alone in the plain; the crushing loneliness of misunderstanding and criticism and impugning of motive. And times have not changed.

The prophets were the loneliest of men. Enoch walked alone in a decadent society as he proclaimed the impending judgment, but he was compensated by the presence of God. Who could have experienced the pangs of loneliness more than Jonah, as he proclaimed the message of an imminent judgment which could be averted only by immediate repentance, to a heathen city of a million souls? The loneliest preacher today is the man who has been entrusted with a prophetic message that is ahead of his times, a message that cuts across the prevailing temper of the age.

The gregarious Paul was a lonely man who experienced to the full the bitterness of being misunderstood by his contemporaries, misrepresentation by enemies and desertion by converts and friends. How poignant is his word to Timothy: "This thou knowest, that all they which are in Asia be turned away from me" (II Tim. 1:15).

"Most of the world's great would have been lonely," wrote A. W. Tozer. "Loneliness seems to be the price a saint must pay for his saintliness." The leader must be a man who, while welcoming the friendship and support of all who can offer it, has sufficient inner resources to stand alone, even in the face of fierce opposition, in the discharge of his responsibilities. He must be prepared to have "no one but God."

On without cheer of sister or of daughter,
Yes, without stay of father or of son,
Lone on the land, and homeless on the water,
Pass I in patience till my work be done.

—F. W.H Meyers

Fatigue

"The world is run by tired men." While this statement may be challenged, there is more than a grain of reality in the assertion. The ever increasing demands made on a leader drain the nervous resources and wear down the most robust physique. But he knows where to go for renewal. Paul was familiar with the secret. "This is the reason that we never collapse. The outward man does indeed suffer wear and tear, but *every day the inward man receives fresh strength*" (II Cor. 4:15–16, Phillips). The ministry of our Lord wearied Him, so He rested by the well (John 4:6). When the needy woman touched the hem of His garment in faith, Jesus was "aware that power had gone out of him" (Mark 5:30, NEB). No real lasting good can be done without the outgoing of power and the expenditure of nervous energy.

The man who has absorbed the spirit of the welfare state is not of the caliber required in a leader. If he is not willing to rise earlier and stay up later than others, to work harder and study more diligently than his contemporaries, he will not greatly impress his generation. If he is unwilling to pay the price of fatigue for his leadership, it will always be mediocre, unless he is a man of unusual physique and resilience. If he is wise, however, he will seize every legitimate opportunity for recuperation and recreation, or he will limit his own usefulness and ministry.

Writing to the Secretary of the Church Missionary Society, Douglas M. Thornton of Egypt said:

> But I am weary! I have only written because I am too weary to be working now, and too tired to sleep....I am getting prematurely old, they tell me, and doctors do not give me long to live unless the strain is eased a bit. My wife is wearier than I am. She needs complete rest a while....Oh, that the church at home but realized one half of the opportunities of today! Will no one hear the call? Please do your best to help us.[5]

Here were missionary leaders willing to pay the price of fatigue in order to grasp the swiftly passing opportunities of their day.

When Robert Murray McCheyne, the saintly young Scottish minister, lay dying at the age of twenty–nine, he turned to a friend who was sitting with him and said: "God gave me a message to deliver and a horse to ride. Alas, I have killed the horse and now I cannot deliver the message." There is no virtue in flogging the tired horse to death.

Criticism

No leader is exempt from criticism, and his humility will nowhere be seen more clearly than in the manner in which he accepts and reacts to it.

In a letter to a young minister, Fred Mitchell once wrote:

> I am glad to know that you are taking any blessing there is about the criticism brought against you by ______________ , in which case even his bitter attack will yield sweetness. A sentence which has been a great help to Mrs. Mitchell and myself is: "It does not matter what happens to us, but our reaction to what happens to us is of vital importance." I think you must expect more and more criticism, for with increasing responsibility this is inevitable. It causes one to walk humbly with God, and to take such action as He desires.[6]

Samuel Brengle, who was noted for his genuine holiness, had been subjected to caustic criticism. Instead of replying in kind or resorting to self–justification, he replied: "From my heart I thank you for your rebuke. I think I deserved it. Will you, my comrade, remember me in prayer?" On another occasion, a biting, censorious attack was made on his spiritual life. His answer was: "I thank you for your criticism of my life. It set me to self–examination and heart–searching and prayer, which always leads me into a deeper sense of my utter dependence on Jesus for holiness of heart, and into sweeter fellowship with Him."[7]

With such an attitude, criticism is turned from a curse into a blessing, from a liability into an asset.

Rejection

The leader who maintains high spiritual standards may sometimes find himself following his Master on the pathway of rejection, for "he came unto his own and his own received him not." This is not always the case, but it has been the experience of many.

Dr. J. Gregory Mantle tells of a ministerial friend whose congregation persistently refused to accept his message. He wanted to lead his flock into the green pastures and beside the still waters, but they were unwilling to be led. His choir, with their ungodly practices, brought things to a head.

The position became so untenable that he invited the choir to resign. The choir not only resigned but persuaded the congregation to desist from taking any part in the singing on the following Sunday. The result was that whatever singing was done, had to be done by the minister, while the choir and congregation enjoyed his discomfiture. This state of things continued for some time and the minister was greatly dejected and perplexed at the turn events had taken.

He was at his wits' end when God spoke to him. One day he was sitting on a seat in a park when he saw part of a torn newspaper before him on the ground. The torn piece bore a message for him which exactly suited his need. It was this:

No man is ever fully accepted until
he has, first of all, been utterly rejected.

He needed nothing more. He had been utterly rejected for Christ's sake, and his recognition of the fact was the beginning of a most fruitful ministry. Though utterly rejected by man, he had been fully accepted by God.

When in response to the clear call of God Dr. A. B. Simpson resigned his pastorate, he learned what it meant to be "destitute, despised, forsaken." He surrendered a salary of $5,000, a position as a leading pastor in the greatest American city, and all claim on his denomination for assistance in a yet untried work. He was in a great city with no following, no organization, no financial resources, with a large family dependent on him, and with his most intimate ministerial friends and former associates predicting failure. So completely was he misunderstood, even by those from whom he expected sympathy, that he once said he often looked down upon the paving stones in the street for the sympathy denied him elsewhere.

"The rugged path of utter rejection was trodden not only uncomplainingly, but with rejoicing. He knew that though he…was going through fire and water, it was the divinely appointed way to the wealthy place."[8]

And it was a wealthy place into which Dr. Simpson was brought. At his death he left behind five schools for the training of missionaries, hundreds of missionaries in sixteen lands, and a large number of congregations in the United States and Canada which exerted a spiritual influence far beyond their numerical strength.

"Often the crowd does not recognize a leader until he has gone, and then they build a monument for him with the stones they threw at him in life."[9]

Pressure And Perplexity

It might be thought by those who have not found themselves in a position of leadership that greater experience and a longer walk with God would result in much greater ease in discerning the will of God in perplexing situations. But the reverse is often the case. God treats the leader as a mature adult, leaving more and more to his spiritual discernment and giving fewer sensible and tangible evidences of His guidance than in earlier years. This perplexity adds to the inevitable pressures incidental to any responsible office.

In one of his few moments of self–revelation, D. E. Hoste said to a friend:

> The pressure! It goes on from stage to stage, pressed beyond measure.…It changes with every period of your life. The most killing years of my life were 1904 – 1906, terrible! I was half–killed! One has been able to make arrangements since then. But other things develop. He eases you at one end, brings you into new things at the other.
>
> I more and more see that as we go on in the Christian life, the Lord very often does not want to give us the sense of His presence, or the consciousness of His help. There again Mr. Hudson Taylor helped me very much. We were talking about guidance. He said how in his younger days, things used to come so clearly, so quickly to him. "But," he said, "now as I have gone on, and God has used me more and more, I seem often to be like a man going along in a fog. I do not know what to do."[10]

But when the time came to act, God always responded to His servant's trust.

Cost To Others

There is often a very real cost which has to be paid by others than the one entrusted with leadership. Indeed, it is they who sometimes pay the heavier price. When Fred Mitchell, a valued colleague of the author, was invited to become British Director of the China Inland Mission, he realized that there would be a price to pay, not only by himself but by those dearest to him.

He wrote:

> My hands were already full, and I had no desire for more work. I have lived long enough, and have already had sufficient responsibility to know that it is not to be sought, for it is usually carried at a heavy price.

To one of his children he later wrote:

> I have had many a sorrow of heart, and it still remains one of my chief regrets that I have not been able to give myself to mother and you children more. The harvest is great and the laborers few, which means that there have been many calls upon me. I do not justify my negligence…; but any sacrifice made by you for our dear Lord Jesus' sake has not been unrewarded.[11]

14

The Responsibilities Of Leadership

That which cometh upon me daily, the care of all the churches.

—II Corinthians 11:28

To serve was Jesus' definition of leadership, and this is true whether in the realm of the secular or of the sacred. Lord Montgomery said that his war experience led him to believe that the staff must be the servant of the troops, and that a good staff officer must serve his commander and troops, but must himself be anonymous.

In his *Training of the Twelve,* Dr. A. B. Bruce wrote: "In other kingdoms they rule, whose privilege it is to be ministered unto. In the Divine commonwealth, they rule who account it a privilege to minister." Dr. John A. MacKay of Princeton maintained that the servant image is the essential of the Christian religion. The Son of God became the servant of God in order to fulfill the mission of God. This same image provides a pattern and norm whereby individual Christians, missionary societies and Christian churches may learn how to fulfill their God–given mission.

The true leader regards the welfare of others rather than his own comfort and prestige as of primary concern. He manifests sympathy and concern for those under him in their problems, difficulties and cares, but it is a sympathy that fortifies and stimulates, not that softens and weakens. He will always direct their confidence to the Lord. He sees in each emergency a new opportunity for helpfulness. It is noteworthy that when God chose a leader to follow the great Moses, He chose Joshua, the man who had proved himself a faithful servant (Exodus 33:11).

In an address giving some of the secrets of Hudson Taylor's remarkably successful leadership, his successor, D. E. Hoste, had this to say: "Another secret of his influence among us lay in his great sympathy and thoughtful consideration for the welfare and comfort of those about him. The high standard of self–sacrifice and toil which he ever kept before himself, never made him lacking in tenderness and sympathy toward those who were not able to go as far as he did in these respects. He manifested great tenderness and patience toward the failures and shortcomings of his brethren, and was thus able in many cases to help them reach a higher plane of devotion."[1]

To discipline is another responsibility of the leader, a responsibility that is onerous and often unwelcome. In any church or religious society there is the necessity to maintain godly and loving discipline if divine standards are to be maintained, especially in matters of soundness in the faith, morals, and Christian conduct.

Paul stipulates the spirit required in those who exercise discipline. "Brethren, if a man be overtaken in a fault, *ye which are spiritual,* restore such an one in the spirit of meekness; considering thyself, lest thou also be tempted" (Gal. 6:1). The fundamental requirement in all disciplinary action is *love.* "Admonish him as a brother" (II Thess. 3:15). "I beseech you that ye would confirm your love toward him" (II Cor. 2:8). The person who has faced and honestly dealt with his own failures and shortcomings is best qualified to deal with the failures of others in a sympathetic and yet firm manner. The spirit of meekness will achieve far more than a critical and censorious spirit.

In approaching a matter that appears to require disciplinary action five points should be borne in mind. (1) Such action should be taken only after the most thorough and impartial inquiry. (2) It should be undertaken only when it would be for the overall good of the work and the individual. (3) It should always be in a spirit of genuine love, and conducted in the most considerate manner. (4) It should always be with the spiritual help and restoration of the offender in view. (5) It should be done only with much prayer.

To guide is a third responsibility. The spiritual leader must know where he is going and, like the Eastern shepherd, go ahead of his flock. This was the method of the chief Shepherd. "When he putteth forth his own sheep, he goeth before them, and the sheep follow him" (John 10:4). "The ideal leader," said A. W. Tozer, "is one who hears the voice of God, and beckons on as the voice calls him and them." Paul gave this challenge to the Corinthian Christians: "Be ye followers of me, even as I also am of Christ" (I Cor. 11:1). He knew who he was following and where he was going, and was therefore able to challenge them to follow him.

But it is not always a simple task to guide people who, though godly, have strong opinions of their own. The leader must not ruthlessly assert his will. D. E. Hoste emphasized this fact:

In a mission like ours, those guiding its affairs must be prepared to put up with waywardness and opposition, and be able to desist from courses of action which, though they may be intrinsically sound and beneficial are not approved by some of those affected. Hudson Taylor again and again was obliged either to greatly modify, or lay aside projects which were sound and helpful, but met with determined opposition, and so tended to create greater evils than those which might have been removed or mitigated by the changes in question. Later on, in answer to patient continuance in prayer, many of such projects were give effect to.[2]

To initiate is an important function of the office of a leader. Some have more gift for conserving gains than for initiating new ventures; more gift for achieving order than for generating ardor. The true leader must have venturesomeness as well as vision. He must be an initiator rather than a mere conserver. Most of us prefer to play safe, but Paul did not play safe. He constantly took carefully and prayerfully calculated risks.

Robert Louis Stevenson indicted the attitude of safety, security and prudence as "that dismal fungus."[3] Hudson Taylor did not play safe. The tremendous steps of faith which he took with monotonous regularity were denounced as wildcat schemes. But that did not deter him, and today history is on his side. The greatest achievements in the history of the church and of missions have been the outcome of some leader in touch with God taking courageous, carefully calculated risks.

A great deal more failure is the result of an excess of caution than of bold experimentation with new ideas. A friend who has filled with distinction an important post with global outreach in the Christian world recently remarked to the author that, in reviewing his life, he was surprised to discover that most of his failures were because he had not been sufficiently daring. "The frontiers of the kingdom of God were never advanced by men and women of caution," said Mrs. H. W. K. Mowll.[4]

A leader cannot afford to ignore the counsel of cautious men around him. They will often save him from unnecessary mistakes. But he must beware of allowing their excess of caution to curb his initiative, if he feels his vision is of God. Nor must he allow them to restrain him from taking daring steps of faith to which God is calling both him and them.

To undertake responsibility and to do it willingly is a necessary mark of a leader. If he is not prepared for this, he disqualifies himself for office. One who evades the more onerous and difficult involvements incidental to his position limits his influence to that extent.

Joshua demonstrated his leadership quality in accepting without hesitation the awesome responsibility of following in the steps of the great leader Moses. Joshua had far greater reason to plead his inadequacy than Moses, but he did not repeat the sin of his leader. Instead, he promptly accepted the responsibility and gave himself to the task.

When Elijah was translated, Elisha assumed without hesitation the responsibilities of the prophetic office vacated by his master. He accepted the authority conferred with the falling mantle and became a leader in his own right. In each case the determining factor was the assurance of a divine call. Granted that assurance, no one need hesitate to assume the responsibilities God allots.

It is always inspiring to be granted a glimpse into the inner life of great men and to know some of the elements that contributed to their spiritual effectiveness.

In the *Life of Robert E. Speer* are recorded the rules by which Archbishop Benson, a man carrying heavy responsibilities, conducted his life. They are both revealing and challenging. Although he belonged to a different age, many of his rules are of continuing relevance and merit our emulation.

Not to be dilatory in commencing the day's main work.

Not to murmur in the multitude of business or the shortness of time but to buy up the time all around.

Not to groan when letters are brought in; not even a murmur.

Not to magnify undertaken duties by seeming to suffer under them, but to treat all as liberties and gladness.

Not to call attention to crowded work or trivial experiences.

Before censuring anyone, obtain from God a real love for him. Be sure that you know and that you allow all allowances that can be made. Otherwise, how ineffective, how unintelligible or perhaps provocative your best–meant censure may be.

Oh, how well it doth make for peace to be silent about others, not to believe everything without discernment, and not to go on easily telling things.

Not to seek praise, gratitude, respect or regard from superiors or equals of age or past service.

Not to feel uneasiness when your advice or opinion is not asked, or is set aside.

Never to let yourself be placed in favorable contrast with another.

Not to hunger for conversation to turn on yourself.

To seek no favor, no compassion; to deserve, not to ask for, tenderness.

To bear blame rather than share or transmit it.

When credit for your own design or execution is given to another, not to be disturbed, but to give thanks.

15

Searching Tests To Leadership

And...God did tempt (test) Abraham.

—Genesis 22:1

Then was Jesus led up of the spirit into the wilderness to be tempted of the devil.

—Matthew 4:1

There are tests to leadership as well as tests of leadership. "And...God did...[test] Abraham" is history expressing an eternal principle. To everyone entrusted with spiritual authority, searching tests are bound to come.

Compromise

Compromise is the partial waiving of principle for the sake of reaching agreement. It is always a backward step when we consent to lower our standards, and all too often this is involved in arriving at a compromise. It nearly always involves a scaling down of standards.

The epic contest of Moses with Pharaoh affords a classic example of the progressive temptation to compromise. When Pharaoh discerned Moses' inflexible purpose to take Israel out of Egypt to worship Jehovah, he used all his wiles to frustrate him. "Worship God if you will," was the first suggestion, "but there is no need to leave Egypt to do it. Worship God where you are." The modern counterpart would be: "Don't neglect religion. But there is no need to be narrow and make a complete break with the world."

When this approach failed, Pharaoh's suggestion was: "If you must go out of Egypt to worship, there is no need to go very far away. Just go outside the borders." "Religion is good and necessary, but you are not called on to be fanatical about it. Stay as near to the world as you can."

His next proposal played upon natural affection. "Let the men go and worship, but there is no need for the women and children to accompany them." "Break with the world yourself, if you must, but don't be so extreme as to interfere with the worldly advancement of your family by making them conform to your Victorian standards."

His final attempt was an appeal to their covetousness and love of material things: "Go if you must, but let your flocks and herds remain in Egypt while you go to worship." "Don't allow your legitimate religious convictions to conflict with your business interests and activities."

With clear spiritual insight Moses saw through each specious suggestion, and his reply was clear–cut and decisive: "There shall not an hoof be left behind" (Exodus 8:25, 28; 10:11, 24, 26). So Moses passed with honors the first great test to his quality as a leader.

Ambition

Like all great leaders, Moses was sifted by the test of ambition. When, during his absence on Mount Sinai alone with God, Israel turned to idolatry, the holy anger of the Lord was kindled. "Now, therefore, let Me alone," He said in effect to Moses, "that My wrath may wax hot against them, that I may consume them; and I will make of thee a great nation" (Num. 14:12). Already Israel's chronic complaining and unbelief must have proved a great trial to Moses, and he might have been excused if he had seen in this divine proposal a lifting of his burdens and a wonderful opportunity for self–advancement.

Since it was God who initiated the suggestion, the test was the more searching. Never were Moses' selflessness and nobility of character more clearly seen than in his reaction to God's message. His concern was solely for God's glory and the people's welfare. Not for a moment did the thought of self–aggrandizement take root in his lofty mind. He held on to God audaciously and tenaciously; and through his intercession, judgment on the apostate nation was averted.

The Impossible Situation

"How does he face impossible situations?" was one of John R. Mott's tests for men of leadership caliber: It was his practice to encourage leaders to deal with impossible tasks rather than with easy ones, because that would draw out their powers, teach them their dependence on others, and drive them to God. "I long since ceased to occupy myself with minor things that can be done by others," he said. A true leader is at his best in baffling circumstances.

It would not be exaggeration to affirm that never in human history have leaders been confronted with such a concentration of unresolved crises and impossible situations as in our day. Consequently, if they are to survive, they must be able to thrive on difficulties and regard them as routine.

Moses faced the test of the impossible when Israel reached the Red Sea. On one side lay the impassable range of Baal Zephon, on the other side an impassable waste of sand. Before them lay the impassable Red Sea, behind them the invincible army of Pharaoh. He found himself shut up with a dismayed and complaining horde in a perfect cul–de–sac. In this unexpected and shattering experience the morale of the nation dropped below zero. "Because there were no graves in Egypt hast thou taken us away to die in the wilderness?" they moaned. But Moses the man of faith stayed himself on God. His order of the day sounded like sheer fantasy to the demoralized Israelites, but in point of fact it was a demonstration of superb leadership.

"Fear not!" he cried when there was every reason to fear.

"Stand still!" when Pharaoh was rapidly overtaking them, and to stand still meant death.

"See the salvation of the Lord," which seemed a very long distance away (Exodus 14:11–13).

In this sublime declaration of faith, Moses passed the test of the impossible situation with first–class honors, and he was gloriously vindicated by God. His sanguine prediction came true: "The Egyptians whom ye have seen today ye shall see no more for ever." They saw the salvation of God and the total destruction of their enemies. The bracing lesson is that God delights to shut people up to Himself and then, in response to their trust, display His power and grace in doing the impossible.

In the evangelization of inland China, Hudson Taylor often found himself face to face with such situations. As a result of his experience he used to say that there were three faces in most great tasks undertaken for God—impossible, *difficult,* DONE.

Have you come to the Red Sea place in your life,
Where in spite of all you can do,
There is no way out, there is no way back,
There is no other way but through?
Then wait on the Lord with a trust serene
Till the night of your feat is gone;
He will send the wind, He will heap the floods,
When He says to your soul "Go on."

And His hand will lead you through—clear through—
Ere the watery walls roll down,
No foe can reach you, no wave can touch,
No mightiest sea can drown;
The tossing billows may rear their crests,

Their foam at your feet may break,
But over their bed you shall walk dryshod
In the path that your Lord will make.

In the morning watch, 'neath the lifted cloud,
You shall see but the Lord alone,
When He leads you on from the place of the sea
To a land that you have not known;
And your fears shall pass as your foes have passed,
You shall no more be afraid;
You shall sing His praise in a better place,
A place that His hand has made.

—Annie Johnson Flint

Failure

If we could see into the inmost hearts of many men whom we think are riding on the crest of the wave, we should experience some great surprises. Alexander Maclaren, the peerless expositor, after delivering a wonderful address to a large gathering, went away overwhelmed with a sense of failure. "I must not speak on such an occasion again," he exclaimed, while the congregation went away blessed and inspired. Allowance must always be made for the reaction which comes from the rebound of the overstrung bow. Nor can we ignore the subtle attacks of our unsleeping adversary.

The manner in which a leader meets his own failure will have a significant effect on his future ministry. One would have been justified in concluding that Peter's failure in the judgment hall had forever slammed the door on leadership in Christ's kingdom. Instead, the depth of his repentance and the reality of his love for Christ reopened the door of opportunity to a yet wider sphere of service. "Where sin abounded, grace did much more abound."

A study of Bible characters reveals that most of those who made history were men who failed at some point, and some of them drastically, but who refused to continue lying in the dust. Their very failure and repentance secured for them a more ample conception of the grace of God. They learned to know Him as the God of the second chance to His children who had failed Him—and the third chance, too.

The historian Froude wrote: "The worth of a man must be measured by his life, not by his failure under a singular and peculiar trail. Peter the apostle, though forewarned, thrice denied his Master on the first alarm of danger; yet that Master, who knew his nature in its strength and in its infirmity, chose him to be the rock on which He would build His church."

The successful leader is a man who has learned that no failure need be final, and acts on that belief, whether the failure is his own or that of another.

Jealousy

It is to be expected that at times leadership will be challenged by ambitious or jealous rivals. As his influence grew in its sweep, even the mighty Moses met with this experience. Disaffection is a common weapon of the adversary.

The first challenge to Moses' leadership came, tragically enough, from his loved sister and brother. They did not remember that but for his self–abnegating response to the divine call they would still have been smarting under the taskmaster's lash.

Miriam was by this time an elderly woman, whose experience of God should have taught her the evil and ugliness of jealousy. Apparently she had instigated a whispering campaign against Moses, using his marriage to an Ethiopian woman as an excuse to challenge his authority. Race hatred is no modern phenomenon! She resented being supplanted by a foreigner, and drew the weak Aaron into the rebellion.

It is clear that Miriam and Aaron were not content to take second place to Moses, and at the instigation of Satan they attempted to oust him from his influential position. Their jealousy was piously cloaked in a simulated zeal for God. "Hath the Lord spoken only by Moses? Hath He not also spoken by us?" They refused to concede Moses' sole right to speak for God to the people.

Moses' reaction was exemplary. Though deeply wounded, he said nothing in vindication of himself, for his main concern was for the glory of God, not his own prestige. It was in this very connection that testimony was borne to his unique meekness. "The man Moses was very meek above all the men that were upon the face of the earth" (Num. 12:3). But although he maintained a dignified silence, God would not allow such a challenge to the authority of His servant to pass.

Because it was a public offense, it must be publicly judged and punished. "Behold, Miriam was leprous, as white as snow," the record runs. This drastic punishment from God indicated His estimate of the gravity of the sin of touching the Lord's anointed, frail and fallible man though he be. Once again Moses' greatness shines out. His only response was to intercede for his sister—intercession to which God graciously responded.

The lesson for the leader is plain. The man who is in the place of God's appointment need not attempt to vindicate himself when challenged by jealous rivals. That he is safe in the hands of his heavenly Protector, the Lord's rebuke to Miriam gives abundant confirmation. "Wherefore were ye not afraid to speak against my servant Moses?"

The second challenge came from Korah and his associates who entertained an unreasoning jealousy of Moses and Aaron. Why should they alone enjoy the privileges of high office? Were there not others equally deserving and qualified, themselves included? Were

Moses and Aaron the only ones fitted to mediate the message of God? "You have gone too far," they charged, "for all the congregation of God are holy, every one of them, and the Lord is among them; why then do you exalt yourselves above the assembly of the Lord?" (Num. 16:4).

Although Moses once again refused to vindicate himself, God intervened and just judgment was meted out to the jealous dissidents. Fear fell on the people, and the prestige of Moses stood higher than ever.

God is jealous for the leaders who He has called and appointed. He honors them, protects and vindicates them, and relieves them of any necessity to stand up for their rights.

16

The Art Of Delegation

And Moses chose able men out of Israel and made them heads over the people.

—Exodus 18:25

One definition of leadership is the ability to recognize the special abilities and limitations of others, combined with the capacity to fit each one into the job where he will do his best. He who is successful in getting things done through others is exercising the highest type of leadership. That shrewd judge of men, Dwight L. Moody, once said that he would rather put a thousand men to work than do the work of a thousand men. The ability to choose men to whom he can safely delgate authority, and then actually to delegate it, is that of the true leader. When General Director of the China Inland Mission, Dixon E. Hoste said:

> The capacity to appreciate the gifts of widely varying kinds of workers, and then to help them along the lines of their own personalities and workings, is the main quality for oversight in a mission such as ours.[1]
>
> This capacity will save the leader the frustrating experience of trying to fit square pegs into round holes.

Delegation of responsibility together with commensurate authority to enable that responsibility to be discharged is not always relished by one who enjoys exercising the authority himself. He is glad to devolve the responsibility, but reluctant to let the reins of power slip from his own hands. This is unfair to his subordinate, and is unlikely to prove satisfactory or effective. Such an attitude would tend to be interpreted as indicating a lack of confidence, and this does not induce the best cooperation. Nor will it draw out the highest powers of the one being trained for leadership. It is very possible that he may not do the task as well as his superior, but experience proves that this is by no means necessarily the case. Given the chance, the younger man may do it better because he is better able to feel the pulse of contemporary life. But in any case, how is he to gain experience unless both responsibility and authority are delegated to him?

The man in a place of leadership who fails to delegate is constantly enmeshed in a morass of secondary detail that not only overburdens him but deflects him from his primary responsibilities. He also fails to release the leadership potential of those under him. To insist on doing things oneself because it will be done better is not only a short–sighted policy but may be evidence of an unwarranted conceit. The leader who is meticulous in observing priorities adds immeasurably to his own effectiveness.

Once delgation has been effected, he should manifest the utmost confidence in his colleagues. It was said of Dr. A. B. Simpson, founder of the Christian and Missionary Alliance, that he trusted those in charge of the different institutions, and then left them free to exercise their own gifts.[2]

If they did not succeed, then he felt it was a reflection on his own leadership, for it was he who selected them for that position. Subordinates should be utterly sure of their leader's support in any action they feel called upon to take, no matter what the result, so long as they have acted within their terms of reference. This presupposes that areas of responsibility have been clearly defined and committed to writing so that no misunderstanding can occur. Many unhappy situations have arisen through failure to do this.

Writing of his association with Dr. John R. Mott, Paul Super said:

> One of my greatest resources these ten years in Poland is the sense of backing. My greatest pride is his belief in me. Surely one of my greatest motives is to be worthy of his support and to measure up to his expectations of me.[3]

The outstanding biblical illustration of this important principle of delegation of responsibility and authority is that of Jethro's advice to his son–in–law Moses, as recorded in Exodus 18:1–27.

Israel had emerged from Egypt, an unorganized horde of slaves. By this time a new national spirit was developing, and they were becoming an organized nation. The intolerable administrative burdens which this development imposed on Moses sparked Jethro's sound advice. From morn till night he saw Moses hearing and adjudicating on the endless problems which arose from these new conditions. Moses was saddled with both legislative and judicial functions, and his decisions were accepted by the people as the oracles of God.

Jethro saw that Moses could not endure this strain indefinitely and advanced two strong reasons in favor of delegation of some of his responsiblities. First, "Thou wilt surely wear away…this thing is too heavy for thee, thou art not able to perform it thyself alone" (v. 18). There are limits to the expenditure of physical and nervous force beyond which it is not safe to go. Second, the present method was too slow and the people were getting dissatisfied because they were not receiving the attention they desired. Sharing responsibility would speed up legal decisions and the people would go away satisfied (v. 23).

Jethro then proposed a twofold course of action. Moses should continue to act as God's representative, teaching spiritual principles and exercising his legislative functions. It would be for him to bring the hard cases to God (vv. 16, 19–20). He should delegate the judicial functions which he had hitherto exercised to competent legal officers who could thus lighten his intolerable burden. This was wise advice, for had Moses succumbed to the strain of his office, he would have left behind him no one experienced and trained in the exercise of authority and the bearing of responsibility. Failure to make such provision has spelled ruin to many a promising work of God.

Several benefits accrued to Moses through following Jethro's advice. He was able to concentrate on the higher aspects and responsibilities of his office. The latent and unsuspected talents of many of his subordinates were discovered. These gifted men, who might have become his critics had he continued to keep things in his own hands, were developed by the burden of their office and became his staunch allies. Incipient disaffection was stifled by the speeding up of legal processes. He also made provision for the effective leadership of the nation after his death.

Jethro encouraged his son–in–law by stating a spiritual principle of timeless relevance. "If thou shalt do this thing, and God command thee so, then thou shalt be able to endure" (Exodus 18:23). He submitted his advice to the ultimate direction of God. The principle is that God assumes full responsibility for enabling His man to fulfill every task to which He has appointed him. There are some self–imposed tasks which others can do better than we can, and we should relinquish them. But even should they do them worse, we should still relinquish them—a severe test for the perfectionist! Moses could doubtless have done the task better than the seventy men whom he selected, but had he persisted in doing so, he would soon have been only a memory.

Jethro's suggested standards of selection of helpers for Moses evidenced true spiritual discernment. They must be men of *ability,* for theirs would be an exacting task; men of *piety* who feared God and respected their fellowmen; men of *honor* who hated covetousness, and would not be susceptible to bribery.

Among other lessons for leaders in this incident are these: It is a mistake to assume more duties than we can adquately and satisfactorily discharge. There is no virtue in doing more than our fair share of the work. It is good to be able to recognize and accept our own limitations. Our Jethros can often discern, more clearly than we, the cost at which our leadership is being exercised, and we would be wise to heed their admonitions. If we break natural law, even in the service of God, we are not exempted from its penalties. It is easy to assume responsibilities under pressure from men rather than by direction from God. For such extracurricular activities God accepts no responsibility.

One of the acid tests of missionary leadership is willingness to delegate responsibility to emerging national leaders the moment they evidence sufficient spiritual maturity, and then to stand by, ready to help, while they gain experience in the same way as the missionary did, by trial and error. This devolving of responsibility fulfills the important function of discovering, training and using the latent talent of national colleagues. In the earlier stages, a wise watchfulness will be necessary, but a resort to interference should be made only if the need becomes acute. The sense of being watched destroys confidence.

When Dr. W. E. Sangster was appointed General Secretary of the Home Mission Department of the Methodist Church of Britain, he arranged the division of labor between all the members of his department, and assigned to each responsibilities over which he gave up all supervision. Trusting his colleagues absolutely, he delegated his powers and never regretted it. It was said of him: "Perhaps his greatest grasp of leadership was knowing the importance of delegation and of choosing assistants with care. He was always a master of that art."[4]

Writing of the leader of a large missionary society, a member of his staff commented: "He had a great gift of leadership in that he never interfered with those who worked under him. Everyone was left to do his own work." Another member wrote, "He knew what people could do, and saw that they did it, leaving them to make the best of their opportunities, and investigating only if things went wrong."[5]

17

The Replacement Of Leaders

Moses my servant is dead; now therefore arise, go over this Jordan, thou, and all this people....As I was with Moses, so I will be with thee.

—Joshua 1:2, 5

When a movement develops around a dominant personality, the real test of the quality of his leadership is the manner in which that work survives the crisis of his removal. This fact was tacitly recognized by Gamaliel when he counseled his fellow Pharisees: "Refrain from these men, and let them alone: for if this counsel or this work be of men, it will come to nought: But if it be of God, ye cannot overthrow it" (Acts 5:38–39). A work originated by God and conducted on spiritual principles will surmount the shock of a change of leadership and indeed will probably thrive better as a result.

It is possible to entertain an unholy solicitude for God and His work. The death of one of His workman does not take Him by surpirse and cause Him to take emergency action. Even though we may be taken unawares and shattered by the removal, we need not tremble for the ark of God. We must bear in mind that there are factors in Christian leadership which are absent from that of the world. In the ultimate it is God and not man who prepares and selects those who are to assume positions of leadership in His kingdom (Mark 10:40). No work which He has initiated will be left unprovided for until His purpose through it has been achieved.

It has been asserted that every great movement is thrown into crisis on the death of its founder. While this may be true, the crisis is by no means always fatal. When the first secretary of the American Board of Missions died, Lyman Beecher said he inclined to despair of the future of the work of their foreign missions. But another took up the work so admirably that his death brought the same temptation. At last, when the third secretary proved himself the equal of his predecessors, Dr. Beecher began to think that God's resources were quite equal to taking care of the board and its affairs. When he himself was laid aside, some mourned it as an irreplacable loss to temperance, to orthodoxy and to foreign missions. But all these causes found new leaders in God's time and way.[1] The fact is that no man, however gifted and devoted, is indispensable to the work of the kingdom.

God is always at work, unperceived by men, preparing those of his choice for leadership. When the crisis arises, He dexterously fits His appointee into the place He has ordained for him. It is often true that the replacement for a certain position is not immediately obvious to those concerned, but time will reveal him.

Not the promised land, but men like Moses and David and Isaiah were God's greatest gifts to Israel, for His greatest gifts are always men. His greatest endowment to His church was the gift of twelve men whom He had trained for leadership.

It is not difficult to picture the dismay and even despair that gripped the nation when the time drew near for the firm, capable hand of Moses to be withdrawn from the helm. For four decades their whole national life had revolved around him. It was to him they had looked for the solution of their problems and the settlement of their disputes. It was he who had interpreted the will of God to them. They could be forgiven for feeling that he was irreplaceable. True, there were the seventy elders who served under him, but there was not another Moses on the horizon. The fact that his death occurred at the very moment they were about to enter Canaan imparted added acuteness to the crisis. They found it hard to believe that God had in reserve the very man to meet the emergency. But God had long been preparing Joshua. It only took the crisis to bring him to the fore.

This situation constantly recurs in history, and each generation has to learn the same lesson for itself. The loss of an outstanding leader always awakens the same doubts and fears. "What will happen to Methodism when John Wesley dies?" "What will happen to the Salvation Army when William Booth dies?" "What will happen when our pastor moves?"

The paths of glory ever lead but to the grave, but a new glory will be revealed. The greatest leader must inevitably be removed by death or some other cause, and the sense of loss will vary with the caliber of his leadership. But in retrospect it will usually be seen that the seeming tragedy has actually turned out to be in the best interests of the work.

Only after his removal are the character and achievements of a leader fully revealed. It was not until after Moses' death that Israel saw his greatness in its true perspective. "The emphasis of death makes perfect the lessons of the life."

On the other hand, the removal of a leader cuts him down to size in relation to the work of God. However great his achievements, he is not irreplaceable. The time comes when his special contribution is not the need of the hour. The most gifted leader has limitations that become apparent only after the complementary gifts of his successor cause the work to develop along lines for which the former leader was unfitted. It frequently emerges that a smaller man with different gifts can develop a work more effectively than his predecessor who initiated it. Moses may well have been unable to achieve the conquest and division of Canaan as ably and acceptably as Joshua.

The removal of a strong and dominating leader makes for the emergence and development of new leadership. It is often discovered that one who has been in a subordinate position develops totally unsuspected qualities when the weight of responsibility is thrown upon him. Latent powers and capacities which others have never suspected are awakened. Joshua would never have been the outstanding leader he subsequently proved to be had he remained "Moses' minister."

A shift of leadership also provides opportunity for the display of the versatility of God in adapting the means to the end in view. His resources in any work He initiates are inexhaustible. If a man possessing great gifts will not place them at the disposal of God, He is not defeated. He will take a man of lesser gifts which are fully available to Him, and will supplement them with His own mighty power. This thought is implicit in Paul's intriguing statement to the brilliant Corinthians: "For ye see your calling, brethren, how that not many wise men after the flesh, not many mighty, not many noble, are called: but God hath chosen the foolish things of the world to confound the wise; and God hath chosen the weak things of the world to confound the things which are mighty; and base things of the world, and things which are despised, hath God chosen, yea, and things which are not, to bring to nought things that are: that no flesh should glory in his presence" (I Cor. 1:26–29).

It is not that God does not desire to use the powers of the nobly gifted, but that few of them are as willing as was Paul to place those gifts without reservation at God's disposal. When such men renounce reliance on their own power and wisdom and depend on God's, there is no limit to the way in which He will use them for His glory.

Toward the end of the life of the greatly gifted Dr. A. B. Simpson, founder of the Christian and Missionary Alliance, a prominent New York minister suggested at one of Dr. Simpson's great conventions that, as there was no one similarly qualified to continue leadership of the organization, a large endowment fund should be raised to ensure the perpetuation of the work. Dr. Simpson said nothing and did nothing. He rightly believed that if the work was of God, nothing could overthow it, and if it were not of God, no good purpose would be served by perpetuating it.[2]

How he rejoiced during the last months of his life, when he had no part in the leadership of the Alliance, to receive reports of largely increased missionary offerings and marvelous progress on the foreign fields. The year after his death proved to be the most prosperous in the history of the society. No greater tribute could be paid to the quality of his leadership.

There is one Leader who holds office in perpetuity, for whom no replacement is needed. It is a striking fact that His disciples made no move to appoint one of their number to take His place after His ascension, tacit evidence that they were gloriously conscious that He was still their living Leader. The church at times has lost the vivid sense of His presence, but there has never been the panic cry of a leaderless army. He has always demonstrated that the distresses and perils of His church lie deeply on His heart.

"We tell our Lord plainly," says Martin Luther, "that if He will have His church then He must look to and maintain and defend it, for we can neither uphold nor protect it; and if we could, then we should become the proudest asses under heaven."

Since we have a Leader who conducts His work in the power of an endless life, the same yesterday, and today and forever, changes in human leadership need not shake or dismay us.

18

The Reproduction Of Leaders

The things you learned from me before many witnesses you must commit to trustworthy men who will be competent to teach others too.

—II Timothy 2:2, C. B. Williams

In these words Paul presses home the responsibility of the spiritual leader to reproduce and multiply himself. If he is to discharge his trust fully he will devote time to training younger men to succeed, and perhaps even supersede him. The spiritual stature of Barnabas is seen in his entire freedom from jealousy when his brilliant protégé, Paul, outstripped him and became the dominant member of the team. It follows that the leader must give his subordinates adequate scope for the exercise and development of their powers.

At a recent conference of missionaries, a national leader was invited to express frankly, from an Asian standpoint, what he considered to be the role of the missionary in the world of today. Among other things he said: "The missionary of today in the Orient should cease to be so much a performer, and become more a trainer." While this is, of course, not true in every missionary situation, it does highlight one of the great needs in current missionary strategy.

The task of training prospective leaders is a delicate one, requiring considerable finesse. The wise leader will not advertise the end he has in view. Out of his wide experience, Bishop Stephen Neill pinpointed some of the dangers of a wrong approach to this vital aspect of Christian work: "If we set out to produce a race of leaders, what we shall succeed in doing is probably to produce a race of restless, ambitious and discontented intellectuals. To tell a man he is called to be a leader is the best way of ensuring his spiritual ruin, since in the Christian world ambition is more deadly than any other sin, and, if yielded to, makes a man unprofitable in the ministry. The most important thing today is the spiritual, rather than the intellectual, quality of those indigenous Christians who are called to bear responsibility in the younger churches."

Bishop Leslie Newbigin even goes so far as to question how far the conception of leadership is one which we really ought to encourage. It is so difficult to use it without being misled by its non–Christian counterpart. The need is not so much for leaders as for saints and servants, and unless this fact is held steadily in the foreground, the whole idea of leadership training becomes dangerous. The pattern of training in Christian leadership must still be that given by our Lord in His training of the twelve.[1]

Perhaps the most strategic and fruitful work of the missionary in the contemporary world is to aid the leaders of tomorrow in developing their spiritual potential. It is a task which requires careful thought, wise planning, endless patience and genuine Christian love. It should not be left haphazard. Our Lord devoted the greater part of His three years of ministry to molding the characters and disciplining the spirits of His disciples. Time was no object in this essential work. Paul trod in the steps of his Lord in training such promising young men as Timothy and Titus.

His method of preparing Timothy for the responsibility of ministering to the well–taught Ephesian church is deeply instructive. Timothy would have been about twenty years of age when his tutelage began. He had been brought up in a feminine atmosphere, and a tendency to effeminacy was probably accentuated by his own indifferent health. His innate timidity, too, required correction. The record indicates that he needed more iron in his makeup. There was a tendency to be desultory about his work, and to be overtolerant and partial with important people. He could be petulant and irritable with opponents. He was apt to rely on an old spiritual experience instead of rekindling its dying flame. But Paul had very high and exacting aspirations for him, and did not spare him experiences or shelter him from hardships that would toughen his fiber and impart virility. He did not hesitate to assign to him tasks beyond his powers. How else could a young man develop greater capacity than by tackling tasks which extended him to the utmost?[2]

Traveling with Paul would bring Timothy into contact with men of all kinds, men of stature, whose personalities and achievements would kindle in him a wholesome ambition. From his tutor he learned how to meet triumphantly the crises which seemed routine in Paul's life and ministry. He was accorded the privilege of sharing the preaching. He was entrusted with the responsibility of establishing the group of Christians at Thessalonica, and confirming them in the faith. Nor did he fail to justify this expression of confidence. Paul's exacting standards, high expectations and heavy demands served to bring out the best in Timothy and probably saved him from mediocrity.

Altogether apart from the merits of his movement, Frank Buchman, founder of Moral Rearmament, displayed a real flair for leadership. It was his claim that if he did not train others to do what he had been doing better than he did it, he would have failed. For many years he worked to make himself dispensable, and it was in this that he differed from many other leaders.[3]

On the mission fields no work is more important and rewarding than this, for on the spiritual caliber and training of the national Christians will depend the development of the church. Once the initial pioneer stage in any field has been passed, this phase of the work should have high priority. The multiplying of himself in the lives of the promising young people among whom he works should rank as one of the main goals of the missionary.

In the training of younger missionaries for leadership, room should be left for flexibility in the case of the exceptional or unusual missionary. God has His "irregulars," and many of them have made an outstanding contribution to the evangelization of the world. Who could have poured Charles T. Studd into any one mold? Such men and women cannot be measured by ordinary standards or made to conform to any fixed pattern.

One such missionary was Douglas Thornton, who made an indelible mark in his work among Muslims in the Near East. He was a man of rare gifts, and even as a raw recruit he did not hesitate to express views that to his seniors seemed radical and impracticable.

His biographer writes:

> It is hardly surprising to learn that he felt constrained to write to his society a memorandum setting forth his views on the past, present and future of the work in Egypt. It is not a precedent that young missionaries after three and a half months on the field should be invited to follow, and on this occasion, too, heads were shaken. But Thornton was an exceptional man, and time has proved that his views and even his effusions were worthy of being studied. It was never safe to neglect them. Most juniors had best reserve their observations for a more mature season. But when the exceptional man arrives, two things have to be observed—the man has to learn to make his observations in the right way, so as to carry his seniors with him; the seniors have to learn how to learn from one who is possibly able, in spite of his want of local knowledge, to benefit them enormously by his fresh and spontaneous ideas. Each is a difficult lesson.[4]

It remains to be said that the training of leaders cannot be done by employing the techniques of mass production. It will require patient and careful instruction and prayerful and personal guidance of the individual over a considerable period. "Disciples are not manufactured wholesale. They are produced one by one, because someone has taken the pains to discipline, to instruct and enlighten, to nurture and train one that is younger."

When a man is really marked out by God for leadership, He will see to it that he receives the necessary disciplines to make him effective.

When God wants to drill a man
And thrill a man
And skill a man,
When God wants to mold a man
To play the noblest part;
When He yearns with all His heart
To create so great and bold a man
That all the world shall be amazed,
Watch His methods, watch His ways!
How He ruthlessly perfects
Whom He royally elects!
How He hammers him and hurts him,
And with mighty blows converts him
Into trial shapes of clay which
Only God understands;
While his tortured heart is crying
And he lifts beseeching hands!
How He bends but never breaks
When his good He undertakes;
How He uses whom He chooses
And with every purpose fuses him;
By every act induces him
To try His splendor out—
God knows what He's about!

19

The Peculiar Perils Of Leadership

Lest, when I have preached to others, I myself should be disapproved.

I Corinthians 9:27

While there are occupational hazards in all callings, the perils of the spiritual leader are especially subtle. Although he is by no means immune to the temptations of the flesh, the dangers most to be guarded against lie in the realm of the spirit. He must remember that "sabbathless Satan," his relentless enemy, will take advantage of every inch of ground he concedes in any area of his life.

Pride

The very fact that a man has risen to a position of leadership with its attendant prominence tends to engender a secret self–congratulation and pride which, if not checked, will unfit him for further advancement in the service of the kingdom, for "everyone that is proud in heart is an abomination to the Lord" (Prov. 16:5). Strong and searching words, these! Nothing is more distateful to God than self–conceit. This first and fundamental sin in essence aims at enthroning self at the expense of God. This was the sin that changed the anointed cherub, guardian of the throne of God, into the foul fiend of hell, and caused his expulsion from heaven.

Of the myriad forms which this sin assumes, none is more abhorrent than spiritual pride. To be proud of spiritual gifts which God has bestowed, or of the position to which His love and grace have elevated us, is to forget that grace is a gift, and that all we have has been received.

Pride is a sin of whose presence its victim is least conscious. There are, however, three tests by means of which it can soon be discovered whether or not we have succumbed to its blandishments.

The test of precedence. How do we react when another is selected for the assignment we expected, or for the office we coveted? When another is promoted and we are overlooked? When another outshines us in gifts and accomplishments?

The test of sincerity. In our moments of honest self–criticism we will say many things about ourselves, and really mean them. But how do we feel when others, especially our rivals, say exactly the same things about us?

The test of criticism. Does criticism arouse hostility and resentment in our hearts, and cause us to fly to immediate self–justification? Do we hasten to criticize the critic?

If we are honest, when we measure ourselves by the life of our Lord who humbled Himself even to death on a cross, we cannot but be overwhelmed with the tawdriness and shabbiness, and even the vileness, of our hearts. As we see our pride in its true colors, our cry will be:

Boasting excluded, pride I abase;
I'm only a sinner, saved by grace.

Egotism

Egotism is one of the repulsive manifestations of pride. It is the practice of thinking and speaking much of oneself, the habit of magnifying one's attainments or importance. It leads one to consider everything in its relation to himself rather than in relation to God and the welfare of His people. The leader who has for long been admired and deferred to by his followers is in great danger of succumbing to this peril.

When Robert Louis Stevenson arrived in Samoa, he was invited by the head of the Malua Institute for training native pastors to address the students. He willingly consented. His address was based on the Muhammadan story of the veiled prophet. This prophet, a burning and shining light among the teachers of his people, wore a veil over his face because, he said, the glory of his countenance was so great that no one could bear the sight.

But at last the veil grew old and fell into decay. Then the people discovered that he was only an ugly old man trying to hide his own ugliness. Stevenson went on to enforce the need of sincerity on the ground that, however high the truths the preacher taught, and however skillfully he might excuse blemishes of character, the time comes when the veil falls away, and a man is seen by people as he really is. It is seen whether beneath the veil is the ugly face of unmortified egotism or the transfigured glory of Christlike character.

> It is a good test to the rise and fall of egotism to notice how you listen to the praises of other men of your own standing. Until you can listen to the praises of a rival without any desire to indulge in detraction, or

> any attempt to belittle his work, you may be sure there is an unmortified prairie of egotistic impulse in your nature yet to be brought under the grace of God.[1]

Jealousy

Jealousy is a near relative of pride. The jealous person is apprehensive and suspicious of rivals. This temptation came to Moses through the touching loyalty of his own colleagues. "Eldad and Medad do prophesy in the camp," said the outraged Joshua to his master. "My lord Moses, forbid them" (Num. 11:28). These two from among the men whom Moses had appointed to assist him had broken into prophecy, and his loyal followers were jealous on his behalf at the usurping of his prophetic prerogatives and challenge to his prestige. But envy and jealousy found no culture bed in the generous nature of the man who used to speak with God face to face. Such matters could safely be left with the God who had called him.

"Art thou jealous for my sake?" was his untroubled rejoinder. "Would God all the people were prophets." The leader who is jealous for God's glory need have no concern for his own prestige and prerogatives. They are safe in His hands.

Popularity

The cult of the personality is not confined to Communism. In Paul's day it reared its head in Corinth, and it is with us today. There will always be those unwise souls who accord an undue deference to their spiritual leaders and advisers, and who tend to exalt one above another.

This practice was prevalent in Corinth and caused Paul to write: "When one says, 'I am Paul's man,' and another, 'I am for Apollos,' are you not all too human? After all, what is Apollos? What is Paul? We are simply God's agents in bringing you to the faith. Each of us performed the task…allotted to him: I planted the seed, and Apollos watered it; but God made it grow.…We are God's fellow–workers" (I Cor. 3:4–6, 9, NEB).

An exaggerated deference to leaders in the church is a mark of spiritual immaturity and carnality. And an acceptance of such fawning deference by the leader is an evidence of the very same weaknesses. Paul was shocked by it and vigorously repudiated it. It is not wrong to be greatly loved by those whom one has endeavored to serve, but there is always the danger that devotion may be deflected from the Master to the servant. Spiritual leaders are to be "esteemed very highly in love for their work's sake," but this esteem should not degenerate into adulation.

That leader is most successful who attaches the affection of his followers more to Christ than to himself. He can rightly draw encouragement from the fact that his service has been fruitful and appreciated, but he must sedulously refuse to be idolized.

What leader or preacher does not desire to be popular with his constituency? Certainly there is no virtue in unpopularity, but popularity can be purchased at too high a price. Jesus made this crystal–clear when He said, "Woe unto you when all men speak well of you." And He expressed the complementary truth when He said, "Blessed are ye when men revile you and persecute you, and utter all kinds of evil against you falsely for my sake."

Bishop Stephen Neill said this in an address to theological students:

> Popularity is the most dangerous spiritual state imaginable, since it leads on so easily to the spiritual pride which drowns men in perdition. It is a symptom to be watched with anxiety since so often it has been purchased at the too heavy price of compromise with the world.[2]

The dangers of popularity and success were constantly before Spurgeon in his unique ministry:

> Success exposes a man to the pressure of people and thus tempts him to hold on to his gains by means of fleshly methods and practices, and to let himself be ruled wholly by the dictatorial demands of incessant expansion. Success can go to my head, and will unless I remember that it is God who accomplishes the work, that He can continue to do so without my help, and that He will be able to make out with other means whenever He cuts me down to size.[3]

Wherever he went, the popularity of George Whitefield was immense. However, he lived to grow tired of his popularity, and often envied the man who could enter a restaurant and take his choice of food with no one to think of his presence. But he had not always felt that way. In the early days of his career he said that to him it was death to think of being laughed at. "But I have seen enough of popularity to be sick of it," he declared.

To one who warned him to beware of the evils of popularity he replied:

> I thank you heartily. May God reward you for watching over my soul; and as to what my enemies say against me, I know worse things of myself than they say about me.[4]

Infallibility

Spirituality does not equate infallibility. The fact that a person is indwelt by the Spirit and seeks to be led by the Spirit will doubtless mean that he is less liable to make mistakes than those who do not; but since he is still in the flesh, he is not infallible. Even the divinely called and Spirit–filled apostles made mistakes which required divine overruling.

The leader who knows God, and probably knows Him better than his colleagues, is in danger of falling unconsciously into this subtle peril. Because his judgment has usually proved more accurate than theirs, because he has prayed and thought and wrestled with the problem more earnestly than they, it is difficult for him to concede the possibility of mistake and to yield to the judgment of his brethren. He must be a man of conviction and be prepared to stand for what he believes, but that is different from assuming virtual infallibility. Willingness to concede the possibility of an error of judgment and to defer to the judgment of one's brethren enhances rather than diminishes influence. Infallibility results in loss of confidence. It is strange but true that such an attitude can coexist with a genuine humility in other areas of life.

Indispensability

Many who have wielded great influence fall before the temptation to think that they are irreplaceable and that in the best interests of the work they should not relinquish office. They cling to authority long after it should have been passed on to younger men. In no sphere is this disastrous tendency more prevalent than in Christian work. Advance is held up for years by well–meaning but aging men who refuse to vacate office and insist on holding the reins in their failing hands. The author met a fine Christian of nearly ninety years of age who was still superintendent of the Sunday school of a city church. And it was not because there were no younger men available. Apparently no officials in the church were courageous enough to handle the situation realistically. Unfortunately there are well–intentioned people who encourage such men in the myth of their indispensability, and as we get older we become progressively less able to assess our own contribution objectively.

The missionary who has made himself indispensable to the church he has helped into being, has done it a grave disservice. From earliest days it should have been his studied aim to remain in the background, to cultivate in its members a real dependence on the Lord, and to train spiritual men who, as soon as practicable, could assume complete responsibility for the work.

Elation And Depression

In every work for God there are inevitably times of discouragement and frustration as well as days of uplift and achievement. The leader is in peril of being unduly depressed by the one and unduly elated by the other. Nor is it always easy to discover the mean between the two.

The seventy disciples returned from their mission, highly elated with their success. Jesus quickly checked this natural but soulish reaction. "Do not rejoice that demons are subject to you," He admonished them, "but rejoice that your names are written in heaven" (Luke 10:20). He directed their attention to the fate of the exalted being who let high privilege go to his head. "I beheld Satan fall as lightning from heaven."

After the drama on Carmel, Elijah experienced such acute depression that he wished to die. The Lord corrected his morbid, self–pitying reactions in a very prosaic manner. He did not approach his overwrought prophet with a spiritual probe or scalpel. Instead, He made him take two long sleeps and eat two square meals. Only then did He begin to deal with the deeper spiritual problem—a lesson of abiding value. He was then able to show Elijah that no real basis for his discouragement existed. There were still seven thousand of his compatriots who had never bowed the knee to Baal. By fleeing, he had deprived the nation of the leadership of which it was in desperate need.

It is realistic to face the fact that not all our ideals for God's work will be realized. Cherished idols prove to have feet of clay. People on whom we lean will prove broken reeds. Even leadership which has been deeply sacrificial will sometimes be challenged. But the spiritually mature leader will know how to discern the true origin of depression and discouragement, and will deal with it accordingly.

> Most people who knew Dr. F. B. Meyer would have no hesitation in writing him down as a convinced optimist, ever seeing the bright side of things, ever hopeful, ever vigorous, ever confident of the ultimate triumph of good over evil. And they would have been right. He was delightfully hopeful and inspiring. But he was far too keen and thoughtful a man, too great a student of humanity, and in himself he was unmeasurably human not to be overcome now and again by the pessimistic view of life. He occasionally went down into the very depths of human despair. He had seen to often and too clearly the seamy side of life not to be sad and pessimistic now and then.[5]
>
> He was a man of like passions, but he never stayed long in the depths.

There can be depression of another kind as C. H. Spurgeon testified in his lecture on "The Minister's Fainting Fits":

> Before any great achievement, some measure of depression is very usual.…Such was my experience when I first became a pastor in London. My success appalled me, and the thought of the career which seemed to open up, so far from elating me, cast me into the lowest depth, out of which I uttered my *miserere* and found no room for a *Gloria in excelsis.* Who was I that I should continue to lead so great a multitude? I would betake me to my village obscurity, or emigrate to America and find a solitary nest in the backwoods where I might be sufficient for the things that were demanded of me. It was just then the curtain was rising on my lifework, and I dreaded what it might reveal. I

> hope I was not faithless, but I was timorous and filled with a sense of my own unfitness.…This depression comes over me whenever the Lord is preparing a larger blessing for my ministry.[6]

There are seasons when everything goes well. Goals are reached, planned endeavors are crowned with success, the Spirit moves, souls are saved and saints blessed. In these times the mature leader knows on whose brow to place the crown of achievement. When Robert Murray McCheyne experienced times of blessing in his ministry, on returning home from the service, he would kneel down and symbolically place the crown of success on the brow of the Lord to whom he knew it rightly belonged. This practice helped to save him from the peril of arrogating to himself the glory which belonged to God alone.

Samuel Chadwick summed up the wise attitude to this peril in these cryptic words: If successful, don't crow; if defeated, don't croak.[7]

Prophet Or Leader?

Sometimes there is a conflict between two ministries for each of which a man is fitted. For example, a preacher who possesses marked gifts of leadership may reach a place in his church or organization which compels him to choose whether his role is to be one of popular leader or unpopular prophet.

Such a dilemma was pictured by Dr. A. C. Dixon, who was pastor of the Moody Church in Chicago, and later of Spurgeon's Tabernacle in London:

> Every preacher ought to be primarily a prophet of God who preaches as God bids him, without regard to results. When he becomes conscious of the fact that he is a leader in his own church or denomination, he has reached a crisis in his ministry. He must now choose one of two courses, that of prophet of God or a leader of men. If he seeks to be a prophet and a leader, he is apt to make a failure of both. If he decides to be a prophet only insofar as he can do without losing his leadership, he becomes a diplomat and ceases to be a prophet at all. If he decides to maintain leadership at all costs, he may easily fall to the level of a politician who pulls the wires in order to gain or hold a position.[8]

Of course there is not such a clear–cut dichotomy between the two roles as Dr. Dixon suggests, and the one does not necessarily exclude the other. But a situation can very easily develop when one has to choose between a spiritual ministry and a leadership which would prevent its highest exercise. Herein lies the peril.

Dr. Reuben A. Torrey, whom God used at the turn of the century to bring revival to half the world, was faced with such a choice. Dr. Dixon wrote of him:

> The thousands who have heard Dr. Torrey know the man and his message. He loves the Bible, and believing it to be the infallible Word of God, preaches it with the fervour of red–hot conviction. He never compromises. *He has chosen to be a prophet of God rather than a mere leader of men,* and that is the secret of his power with God and men.[9]

Disqualification

Even his glowing record of sacrifice and boundless success in the service of Christ could not quiet in Paul's heart a wholesome fear that after having preached to others, he might himself be disqualified (I Cor. 9:27). To him it was an ever present challenge and warning, as it should be to all entrusted with spiritual responsibilities. High attainment and vast experience did not engender in Paul a smug complacency, nor did he consider himself immune to such a dire anticlimax to his life of sacrificial service.

The word translated "castaway" or "disapproved" is used of metals, and has reference to that which, having been tested, fails to survive the test. It suggests something which has been rejected after testing because it has failed to reach the required standard. From the context it is clear that Paul has in view being rejected for the coveted prize, not being disqualified from entering the race. He will fail to win it if he fails to comply with all the rules of the contest.

Paul appears to view himself in a dual role. He is both competitor and herald of the lists. It was the herald's function to announce the rules of the game and to call out the competitors. The word *preached* is derived from the verb "to herald." It was Paul's fear that after having acted as a herald who bids others enter the contest, he himself should fail when tested by the same standards. In such case, his exalted position as a herald would only serve to aggravate the possible disgrace.

It should be noted that the failure he has in view stems from the body, and to guard against it he practiced rigorous self–discipline. Charles Hodge affirms that in Scripture the body as "the seat and organ of sin, is used of our whole sinful nature. It was not merely his sensual nature Paul endeavored to bring into subjection, but all the evil propensities of his heart."

The panacea for this ever present peril Paul conceived to lie not merely in the realm of doctrine or ethics but in the physical realm. The word *temperate* signifies self–mastered moderation—neither asceticism on the one hand nor self–indulgence on the other. He was not prepared to allow his body to become master whether through appetite or lax indulgence. The clause "I bring it into subjection" pictures the victorious general leading home in his triumphal march those whom he has vanquished in battle and are now his slaves. A. S. Way appropriately renders this passage: "I browbeat my own animal nature, and treat it not as my master but my slave."

20

An Exemplary Leader, Nehemiah

One of the most striking biblical examples of inspiring and authoritative leadership is seen in the life of Nehemiah. At times his methods seemed somewhat vigorous, but he was used by God to achieve spectacular reforms in the life of his nation in an amazingly short time. An analysis of his personality and methods discloses that the methods he adopted were effective only because of the quality of his own character.

His Character

The first impression gained from reading his artless story is of a man of *prayer.* His first reaction on hearing of the pitiable plight of Jerusalem was to turn to God in prayer, evidence that he was no stranger at the throne of grace. Throughout, the record is liberally sprinkled with ejaculatory prayers. To him prayer was not merely an exercise for set seasons but an integral part of ordinary living and working (1:4, 6; 2:4; 4:4, 9; 5:19; 6:14; 13:14, 22, 29).

He displayed *courage* in the face of great danger. "Should such a man as I flee? And who is there, that, being as I am, would go into the temple to save his life? I will not go in" (6:11). This display of firmness and fearlessness would do much to increase the morale of a discouraged people.

He manifested *genuine concern* for the welfare of the people, a concern so obvious that even his adversaries commented on it. "It grieved them exceedingly that there was come a man to seek the welfare of the children of Israel" (2:10). His concern found expression in fasting and prayers and tears (1:4–6). Nehemiah identified himself with his people, not only in their sorrows but also in their sins: "The sins of the children of Israel, which *we* have sinned against thee: both I and my father's house have sinned" (1:6).

He exhibited keen *foresight.* Having secured the favorable attention of the king, he asked for letters to the governors through whose territories he was to travel. But his thoughts ranged further to the task awaiting him in Jerusalem, and he requested also letters to the keeper of the king's forests, so that he might obtain the timber necessary "to make beams for the gates of the palace...and for the wall of the city" (2:8). He thought things through carefully.

There was a strain of wholesome *caution* running through Nehemiah's venturesome activities. On reaching Jerusalem, he did not precipitately embark upon his work. "So I came to Jerusalem, and was there three days" (2:11). Only after this lapse of time, during which he had been carefully appraising the situation, did he act. And even then his innate caution caused him to maintain silence as to the purpose of his coming. Even his reconnaissance was done under cover of night.

Nehemiah was essentially a man of *clear decision.* He did not defer when he should decide. Procrastination found no place in his energetic nature.

He possessed the quality of *empathy* to an unusual degree. He was willing to lend an understanding and sympathetic ear to the problems and grievances of the people, and took remedial action (4:10–12; 5:1–5). (A leader remarked concerning one of his subordinates, "I was not going to have him weeping on my shoulder!" But that is what the leader's shoulder is for!)

Nehemiah's decisions and actions were characterized by *strict impartiality.* He manifested no respect of persons. The nobles and rulers received his censure when they deserved it just as freely as did the common people. "I rebuked the nobles, and the rulers....And I set a great assembly against them" (5:7).

His spiritual approach to problems did not exclude a *healthy realism.* "We made our prayer...and set a watch...day and night" (4:9).

In *accepting responsibility,* he did not evade its more onerous implications, but was prepared to carry his assignment, with all its attendant difficulties, right through to a successful conclusion.

Nehemiah emerges as a man who was vigorous in administration, calm in crisis, fearless in danger, courageous in decision, thorough in organization, disinterested in leadership, persevering before opposition, resolute in the face of threats, vigilant against intrigue—a leader who won and held the full confidence of his followers.

His Methods

He raised the morale of his colleagues. This is an important function of the responsible leader. He achieved this end by stimulating their faith and directing their thoughts away from the magnitude of their immediate problems to the greatness and trustworthiness of God. Scattered throughout the record are such assurances as these:

"The God of heaven…will prosper us" (2:20).

"Be not afraid…: remember the Lord…great and terrible" (4:14).

"Our God shall fight for us" (4:20).

"The joy of the Lord is your strength" (8:10).

Faith begets faith. Pessimism begets unbelief. It is a primary responsibility of the spiritual leader to feed faith to his colleagues.

He was generous in appreciation and encouragement. Nehemiah came to a discouraged and demoralized people. His first aim was to kindle hope and then to secure their cooperation. This he did in part by recounting the good hand of God which had been on him and sharing with them his vision and utter confidence in God. "Then I told them of the hand of my God which was good upon me; as also the king's words that he had spoken unto me. And they said, Let us rise and build. So they strengthened their hands for this good work" (2:18).

Faults and failings must be faithfully corrected, but it is the manner in which this is done which is important. Nehemiah appeared to be able to do it in such a way as to inspire the people to do better. More than this, his faithful and firm discipline won him continued confidence and further established his authority.

He dealt promptly with potential causes of weakness. Two typical cases are recorded.

The people were *discouraged through weariness and obstruction* (4:10–16). They were utterly tired; accumulated rubbish impeded their progress; their adversaries were intimidating them. What tactics did Nehemiah employ? He directed their thoughts to God. He saw to it that they were properly armed. He regrouped them and stationed them at strategic points. He harnessed the strengths of the family unit. He ordered half of them to work while the other half defended and rested. Courage returned to the people when they saw that their leader appreciated and was grappling with their problems.

In the second case the people were *disillusioned through greed and heartlessness* on the part of their rich brethren (5:1–5). Their lands were mortgaged; some of their children had been sold into slavery. "Neither is it in our power to redeem them; for other men have our lands and vineyards." Nothing lowers the morale of people more than when the welfare of their children is adversely affected.

Again the tactics employed by Nehemiah are full of instruction. He listened attentively to their complaints and sympathized with them in their dilemma. He rebuked and shamed the nobles for their heartlessness in exacting harsh usury from their kinsmen (5:7). He contrasted their actions with his own altruism (5:14). He appealed for immediate restitution (5:11). So great was his spiritual ascendancy that they replied: "We will restore them, and will require nothing of them; so will we do as thou sayest" (5:12).

Nehemiah restored the authority of the Word of God (8:1–8). The reforms which he instituted would have been short–lived or even impossible apart from this. He vigorously enforced the standards of the Word of God, and this imparted spiritual authority to his actions.

He ordered the restoration of the Feast of Tabernacles which had not been observed since Joshua's day (8:14). How the work–weary people would welcome this week's holiday and festivities! The reading of the Scriptures induced repentance and confession of sin on the part of both people and priests (9:3–5). They cleansed the temple of Tobiah's sacrilegious furniture (13:4–9). The holy vessels were restored (13:9) and the tithes were once again brought to the treasury (13:5). The sabbath rest was again enforced (13:15), intermarriage with the surrounding nations forbidden (13:23–25), and separation from them effected (13:30).

He was skillful in organization. Before making detailed plans he conducted a careful survey and made an objective appraisal of the situation (2:11–16). He made a detailed assessment of the personnel available. He did not neglect unglamorous paper work. Each group was entrusted with a specific and clearly defined area of responsibility. He gave adequate recognition to subordinate leaders, mentioning them by name, and the place where each worked. They were given a sense that they were more than mere cogs in a machine. He practiced a wise delegation of responsibility. "I gave my brother Hanani, and Hananiah the ruler of the palace, charge over Jerusalem" (7:2). He was thus giving other able men the opportunity to develop their leadership potential. He had high standards for the subordinates whom he chose (7:2)—faithfulness, "he was a faithful man," and unusual piety, "he feared God above many."

His leadership was demonstrated in *his attitude to organized opposition* which took varied forms—insult, innuendo, infiltration, intimidation and intrigue. It required wise and resolute guidance to steer a steady course amid these swirling currents.

Again his first recourse was to prayer. "We made our prayer unto our God" (4:9). When it was safe to do so, he simply ignored the adversaries. He steadfastly refused to allow them to deflect from his central task, but at the same time he took all necessary precautionary measures (4:16). Most important of all, he never deviated from an attitude of unwavering faith in God (4:20).

The test of spiritual leadership is whether it results in the successful achievement of its objective. In the case of Nehemiah, this is not left in doubt. The record stands: "So the wall was finished" (6:15).

Endnotes

Chapter 1: An Honorable Ambition

[1] *The Record*, March 28, 1947, p. 161.
[2] *Samuel Logan Brengle*, by C. W. Hall, p. 274.

Chapter 2: The Search For Leaders

[1] *Doctor Sangster*, by Paul E. Sangster, p. 109.
[2] *The Soul–Winner's Secret*, by S.L. Brengle, p. 22.

Chapter 3: Natural And Spiritual Leadership

[1] *Memoirs of Field–Marshall Montgomery*, Bernard L. Montgomery, p. 70.
[2] *Charles E. Cowman*, by L. B. Cowman, p. 251.
[3] *Montgomery, op. cit.*
[4] *D. E. Hoste*, by P. Thompson, p. 122.
[5] *The Reaper*, February, 1962, p. 459.
[6] *Doctor Sangster*, by Paul Sangster, p. 109.
[7] *Revivals, Their Laws and Leaders*, by James Burns, p. 95.
[8] Montgomery.
[9] *John R. Mott*, by B. Mathews, p. 346.
[10] *Ibid.* p. 353.

Chapter 4: Criteria Of Leadership Potential

[1] *World Vision*, February, 1966, p. 4.

Chapter 5: Pauline Sidelights On Leadership

[1] *Letters to Timothy, Titus and Philemon* by William Barclay, p. 92.
[2] *Samuel Logan Brengle*, p. 112.
[3] *I & II Timothy and Titus*, by William Hendriksen.
[4] Barclay, p. 86.

Chapter 6: Petrine Sidelights On Leadership

[1] *The Letters of Peter and Jude*, by Wm. Barclay, p. 156.
[2] *Triumphant in Trouble*, by P.S. Rees, p. 126.
[3] *The Epistles of Peter*, by J.H. Jowett, p. 188.
[4] *On the Ministry*, by Stephen Neill, pp. 107–8.

Chapter 7: Qualities Essential To Leadership, I

[1] *Revivals, Their Laws and Leaders*, James Burns, p. 182.
[2] *Climbing on Track*, by Phyllis Thompson, p. 116.
[3] *Samuel Chadwick*, by N.G. Dunning, p. 15.
[4] *George Whitefield*, by J. R. Andrews, pp. 410–11.
[5] *World Vision*, January, 1966, p. 5.
[6] *Geroge W. Truett*, by P. James, p. 266.
[7] *Charles E. Cowman*, by L.B. Cowman, p. 259.
[8] *Douglas M. Thornton*, by W.H.T. Gairdner, p. 80.
[9] *Ibid.*, p. 43.
[10] *Archbishop Mowll*, by M. Loane, p. 202.

[11] *Dunning,* p. 20.
[12] *John R. Mott,* p. 355.
[13] *D. E. Hoste,* p. 155.
[14] Burns, pp. 181–82.
[15] *Ibid.,* pp. 167–68.
[16] *Samuel Logan Brengle,* p. 275.

Chapter 8: Qualities Essential To Spiritual Leadership, II

[1] *Samuel L. Brengle,* p. 278.
[2] *Encounter with Spurgeon,* by H. Thielecke, p. 26.
[3] *Christian Leadership,* by A. E. Norrish, p. 28.
[4] *D. M. Thornton,* p. 84.
[5] *Latin America Evangelist,* May–June, 1965.
[6] *Christ and Life,* by R. E. Speer, p. 103.
[7] *Op. cit.* p. 104.
[8] *Letter of Peter and Jude,* by W. Barclay, p. 258.
[9] *Hudson Taylor and Maria,* by J. C. Pollock, p. 35.
[10] *A. J. Gordon,* by E. Gordon, p. 191.
[11] *D. E. Hoste,* p. 158.
[12] *A. B. Simpson,* by A. E. Thompson, p. 204.
[13] *St. Paul's Friends,* by H. C. Lees, p. 11.
[14] *Let My People Go,* by A. W. Tozer, p. 36.
[15] *William Carey,* by S. P. Carey, p. 256.
[16] *Charles E. Cowman,* p. 269.
[17] *Pastor Hsi,* by Mrs. H. Taylor, pp. 164, 167.
[18] *The Book of Isaiah,* by G. A. Smith, p. 229.
[19] *Revivals, Their Laws and Leaders,* p. 311.

Chapter 9: The Indispensable Requirement

[1] *The Acts of the Holy Spirit,* by A. T. Pierson.
[2] *A. W. Tozer,* by D. J. Fant, pp. 73, 83.

Chapter 10: The Leader And His Praying

[1] *Samuel Chadwick,* p. 19.
[2] *The Prayer–life of our Lord,* by D. M. McIntyre, pp. 30–31.
[3] *Prayer and Praying Men,* by E. M. Bounds.

Chapter 11: The Leader And His Time

[1] *The Christian,* April 29, 1966, p. 10.
[2] *The Gospel of the Second Chance,* by J. S. Holden, p. 188.
[3] *F. B. Meyer,* by W. Y. Fullerton, p. 70.
[4] *Doctor Sangster,* Paul Sangster, p. 314.
[5] *The Sunday School Times,* November 22, 1913, p. 713.

Chapter 12: The Leader And His Reading

[1] *Thirteen Appreciations,* by Alexander Whyte, p. 364.
[2] *The Alliance Weekly,* February 22, 1956, p. 2.
[3] *Christianity Today,* March 4, 1966, p. 36.
[4] *The Alliance Weekly,* March 14, 1956, p. 2.
[5] *The Sunday School Times,* November 22, 1913, p. 713.
[6] *Life of Faith,* November 26, 1913, p. 1443.
[7] *Samuel Logan Brengle,* p. 269.

[8] *The Reaper,* August, 1965, p. 229.
[9] *Encounter with Spurgeon,* by H. Thielecke, p. 197.
[10] *The Sunday School Times,* November 22, 1913, p. 715.

Chapter 13: The Cost Of Leadership

[1] *Marks of a Man,* by R. E. Speer, p. 109.
[2] *The Soul–Winner's Secret,* p. 23.
[3] *It is Hard to Be a Christian,* by Samuel M. Zwemer, p. 139.
[4] *Charles E. Cowman,* L. B. Cowman, p. 260.
[5] *D. M. Thornton,* p. 225.
[6] *Climbing on Track,* Phyllis Thompson, p. 116.
[7] *Samuel Logan Brengle,* p. 272.
[8] *Beyond Humiliation,* by J. Gregory Mantle, pp. 140–41.
[9] *Cowman,* p. 258.
[10] *D. E. Hoste,* pp. 130–31.
[11] *Thompson,* p. 115.

Chapter 14: The Responsibilities Of Leadership

[1] *D. E. Hoste,* p. 217.
[2] *Ibid.,* p. 158.
[3] *The Reaper,* May 1961, p. 89.
[4] *Archbishop Mowll,* p. 249.

Chapter 16: The Art Of Delegation

[1] *D. E. Hoste,* p. 156.
[2] *Life of A. B. Simpson,* p. 208.
[3] *John R. Mott,* p. 364.
[4] *Doctor Sangster,* pp. 88, 221.
[5] *Climbing on Track,* p. 99.

Chapter 17: The Replacement Of Leaders

[1] *Sunday School Times,* November 8, 1913, p. 682.
[2] *Life of A. B. Simpson,* p. 208.

Chapter 18: The Reproduction Of Leaders

[1] *International Review of Missions,* April, 1950.
[2] *St. Paul's Friends,* by H. C. Lees, pp. 135–41.
[3] *Frank Buchman,* by P. Howard, p. 111.
[4] *Douglas M. Thornton,* p. 121.

Chapter 19: The Peculiar Perils Of Leadership

[1] *The Reaper,* July, 1942, p. 96.
[2] *The Record,* March 28, 1947, p. 161.
[3] *Encounter with Spurgeon,*by H. Thielecke.
[4] *George Whitfield,* by J. R. Andrews, p. 412.
[5] *F. B. Meyer,* p. 172.
[6] *Thielecke,* p. 219.
[7] *Samuel Chadwick,* p. 206.
[8] *A. C. Dixon,* by H. C. A. Dixon, p. 277.
[9] *Op cit.,* p. 158.

Recommended Reading List

Adams, Jay. *The Biblical View of Self-Esteem, Self-Love, & Self-Image.* Eugene, OR: Harvest House Publishers, 1986.

Aycock, David W. *Getting the Best of Yourself.* Wheaton, Ill.: Victor Books, 1989.

Bounds, E. M. *Power through Prayer.* Springdale, Pa.: Whitaker House, 1982.

Briscoe, Stuart. *The Sermon on the Mount: Daring to Be Different.* Wheaton, Ill.: Harold Shaw Publishers, 1995.

Byrd, Dennis. *Rise & Walk.* New York: HarperCollins Publishers, Inc., 1993.

Corley, Felix, and John Eibner. *In the Eye of the Romanian Storm.* Old Tappan, N. J.: Fleming H. Revell Co., 1990.

Dobbins, Gaines S. *Learning to Lead.* Nashville: Broadman Press, 1968.

Dravecky, Dave. *Comeback.* Grand Rapids: Zondervan Publishing House, 1990.

__________. *When You Can't Come Back.* Grand Rapids: Zondervan Publishing House, 1992.

Eastman, Dale. *No Easy Road: Inspirational Thoughts on Prayer.* Grand Rapids: Baker Book House, 1971.

Engstrom, Ted W., and R. Alec Mackenzie. *Managing Your Time.* Grand Rapids: Zondervan, 1967.

Erickson, Kenneth A. *Christian Time Management: Investing God's Gift Wisely.* St. Louis: Concordia Publishing House, 1985.

Foxe, John. *Foxe's Book of Martyrs.* Old Tappan, N.J.: Fleming H. Revell Co., 1968.

Ganz, Richard L. *The Secret of Self-Control.* Wheaton, Ill.: Crossway Books, 1998.

Havergal, Frances Ridley. *Kept for the Master's Use.* Chicago: Moody Press, 1999.

Hendricks, Howard G. *Don't Fake It...Say It With Love: The Art And Joy Of Telling The Good News.* Wheaton, IL: Victor Books, 1972.

Hybels, Bill. *Too Busy Not to Pray.* Downers Grove, Ill.: InterVarsity Press, 1988.

Kinkaid, Ron. *The Secrets of Deciding Wisely.* Downers Grove, Ill.: InterVarsity Press, 1994.

Larson, Knute. *Run Steady, Run Straight.* Wheaton, Ill.: Victor Books, 1987.

Lawrence, Brother. *The Practice of the Presence of God.* Springdale, Pa.: Whitaker House, 1982.

Littleton, Mark R. *Delighted by Discipline.* Wheaton, Ill.: Victor Books, 1990.

Mayhew, Richard. *Spiritual Intimacy.* Wheaton, Ill.: Victor Books, 1990

McCarthy, Kevin W. *The On-Purpose Person.* Colorado Springs, Colo.: NavPress, 1992.

Miller, Basil. *George Washington Carver: God's Ebony Scientist.* Grand Rapids: Zondervan, 1943.

Morgan, G. Campbell. *The Best of G. Campbell Morgan.* Grand Rapids: Baker Book House, 1972.

Müller, George. *The Autobiography of George Müller.* Springdale, Pa.: Whitaker House, 1984.

Murray, Andrew. *With Christ in the School of Prayer.* Old Tappan, N.J.: Fleming H. Revell, 1953.

Nee, Watchman. *Changed into His Likeness.* Fort Washington, Pa.: Christian Literature Crusade, 1967.

Nelson, Marion H. *How to Know God's Will.* Chicago: Moody Press, 1963.

O'Connor, Michael. *Sermon on the Mound.* Minneapolis: Bethany House, 2001.

Palmer, Earl. *The 24-Hour Christian.* Downers Grove, Ill.: InterVarsity Press, 1987.

Palms, Roger C. *Let God Help You Choose.* Minneapolis: Augsburg Fortress, 1989.

Petty, James C. *Step by Step: Divine Guidance for Ordinary Christians.* Phillipsburg, N. J.: P&R Publishing, 1999.

Pickering, Ernest. *Biblical Separation: The Struggle for a Pure Church.* Schaumburg, Ill.: Regular Baptist Press, 1979.

Pierson, Arthur T. *George Müller of Bristol.* Old Tappan, N. J.: Fleming H. Revell, n. d.

Ritter, Tim. *A Passionate Pursuit of God.* Downers Grove, Ill.: InterVarsity Press, 1990.

Robertson, James I. *Stonewall Jackson: The Man, the Soldier, the Legend.* New York: Macmillan Publishing USA, 1997.

Roecker, Ann. *A Workshop on Time Management.* Grand Rapids: Lamplighter Books, 1988.

Rogers, Henry C. "The Benefits of Failure," chapter ten in *Roger's Rules for Success* (pp. 227–245). New York: St. Martin's/Marek, 1984.

Sherman, Doug, and William Hendricks. *How to Balance Competing Time Demands.* Colorado Springs, Colo.: NavPress, 1989.

Simpson, A. B. *The Life of Prayer.* Camp Hill, Pa.: Christian Publications, 1989.

Smith, Fred, Sr. *Leading with Integrity.* Minneapolis: Bethany House, 1999.

Smith, Hannah Whitall. *The Christian's Secret of a Happy Life.* Old Tappan, N. J.: Fleming H. Revell Co., 1942.

Steer, Roger. *J. Hudson Taylor: A Man in Christ.* Wheaton, Ill.: Harold Shaw Publishers, 1993.

Stone, W. Clement. "The Amazing Power of a Bibliography," chapter twenty-two in *Success through a Positive Mental Attitude* (pp. 237–245). Englewood Cliffs, N. J.: Prentice-Hall, Inc., 1960.

Stott, John R. W. *The Message of the Sermon on the Mount (Matthew 5-7: Christian Counter-Culture).* Downers Grove, IL: Inter-Varsity Press, 1973.

Stowell, Joseph M. *Perilous Pursuits.* Chicago: Moody Press, 1994.

Sullivan, George. *Work Smart, not Hard.* New York: Facts on File, 1987.

Thomas, Dave. *Well Done!* Grand Rapids: Zondervan, 1994.

Torrey, R. A. *How to Pray.* Chicago: Moody Press, n. d.

__________. *How to Succeed in the Christian Life.* Chicago: Moody Press, n. d.

__________. "The Person and Work of the Holy Spirit," in *Power-Filled Living* (pp. 75ff). New Kensington, Pa.: Whitaker House, 1998.

Tozer, A. W. *The Pursuit of God.* Harrisburg, Pa.: Christian Publications, Inc., 1948.

Varner, Will. *The Chariot of Israel.* West Collingswood, N. J.: The Friends of Israel, 1984.

Vins, Georgi. *Testament from Prison.* Elgin, Ill.: David C. Cook Publishing Co., 1975.

Virkler, Henry A. *Speaking Your Mind without Stepping on Toes.* Wheaton, Ill.: Victor Books, 1991.

Watson, Thomas. *The Beatitudes.* Carlisle, Pa.: The Banner of Truth Trust, 1971.

Welch, Bob. *More to Life than Having It All.* Eugene, Ore.: Harvest House, 1992.

White, Jerry. *The Power of Commitment.* Colorado Springs, Colo.: NavPress, 1985.

Williams, Pat and Jill. *Twelve-Part Harmony.* Old Tappan, N. J.: Fleming H. Revell Co., 1990.

Wurmbrand, Richard. *In God's Underground.* Greenwich, Conn.: Fawcett Publications, 1968.

__________. *Tortured for Christ.* Tulsa, Okla.: Crossing Publishing, 1967.